Contents

A High Calling

— OR —

WHERE DO YOU GET YOUR

IDEAS FROM?

Navigating poetry with

JOHN GREENING

RENARD PRESS

RENARD PRESS LTD

124 City Road
London EC1V 2NX
United Kingdom
info@renardpress.com
020 8050 2928

www.renardpress.com

A High Calling first published by Renard Press Ltd in 2025

Cover design by Will Dady
Editorial support from Imogen Allen

Printed and bound in the UK on carbon-balanced papers by CMP Books

ISBN: 978-1-80447-149-4

9 8 7 6 5 4 3 2 1

EU Authorised Representative: Easy Access System Europe – Mustamäe tee 50, 10621 Tallinn, Estonia, gpsr.requests@easproject.com.

A HIGH CALLING

OR

WHERE DO YOU GET YOUR

IDEAS FROM?

For Edith
All in good time

…picturing the isolation in which a poet discerns that he is a poet, the delight and difficulty of the high calling to which he finds himself born

EDMUND BLUNDEN

Tear him for his bad verses

WILLIAM SHAKESPEARE

Why?

The subtitle of this book should perhaps have been the title, but familiar as it will be to most writers, it's what my old BBC boss Hans Keller would have called 'a subordinate question'.

All people really want to ask a poet is *why*. Why do you even bother looking for ideas if you're going to waste them on poetry? Why have you devoted so much of your life to something few of us care about and fewer still would regard as a high calling? 'Poetry? It's a hobby.'* Even today the speaker of Basil Bunting's 'What the Chairman Told Tom' would be heard with sympathy in certain quarters: 'My ten year old/can do it *and* rhyme.' It is a very odd pursuit, after all, this shuffling of words into different combinations. And for what? Not for money, on the evidence of the poets I know. For Posterity, then? That is hardly likely to oblige, as a glance at the names in Dr Johnson's *Lives of the Poets* will show. But more of Posterity anon – and Anon is, of course, Posterity's favourite poet.

A small part of me thinks that if you have to ask yourself why you write, you probably shouldn't be doing it. In my experience, the best poems – and poems are what I know best – are those that take both author and reader by surprise. What looked as though it was going to be a poem about tomatoes turns out to be a portrait of your grandfather. One glib reply would be to say that if I were capable of stopping, then I'd stop. Another, more oblique, might quote the Australian poet Les Murray's 'The Instrument',* which begins 'Who reads poetry?' and moves on to 'Why write poetry?', offering a string of reasons why you might, ranging from 'the weird unemployment' to 'working always beyond/your own intelligence' to what he calls 'a non-devouring fame'.

T.S. Eliot called poetry a 'superior amusement', and his example might prompt me to say that I write simply to amuse myself, to pass the time, as have so many parsons and schoolteachers, newspaper balladeers and local doggerel-walkers throughout history. There's always the chance that others might be equally diverted, intrigued, even moved or uplifted, although today that invariably comes down to the number of 'likes' on social media.

There are grander explanations available, however, embracing psychology and sociology and no doubt critical theory too, the kind that might have occurred to me had I ever been a Professor of Creative Writing. But the best response comes from the eighteenth century and Alexander Pope, who was forever asking himself the same thing:

> Why did I write? What sin to me unknown
> Dipp'd me in ink – my parents', or my own?
> As yet a child, nor yet a fool to fame,
> I lisp'd in numbers, for the numbers came.
> I left no calling for this idle trade,
> No duty broke, no father disobey'd.
> The Muse but serv'd to ease some friend, not wife,
> To help me through this long disease, my life...*

This is not really an answer, and nor was the question serious. Rather, Pope's lines are part of an exasperated verse tirade against all those scribblers who regularly besieged his grotto in Twickenham asking where he got his ideas from and whether he might cast an eye over their latest epic.

We happen to remember those lines by Alexander Pope, but how many other lines, how many other *poets* from his era can we name? The list will not, I think, include any of Samuel Johnson's choices: Yalden, Broome, Sprat, Garth, Stepney, nor even Hughes and Fenton.

There's a poem by the contemporary American, Richard Wilbur, that I find very affecting. 'To the Etruscan Poets'* is extremely short, but those six lines are enough to make any poet give up. If you are allergic to close reading of poems, rest assured that there isn't a huge amount of it in this book, and by all means skip this next paragraph – but consider returning to it later, and do seek out the poem. Wilbur's opening packs surprises into its first four words: 'Dream fluently, still brothers,' – we are not expecting such an adverb, and listen to the way that possibly ambiguous adjective slows us down, braked further by a pair of commas, before proceeding: 'who when young/Took with your mothers' milk the mother tongue'. A metrical inversion ('Took with'), alliteration ('mothers' milk') and a playful repetition, catching neatly the rhyme of the couplet, then: 'In which pure matrix, joining world and mind,/ You strove to leave some line of verse behind'.

The sentence is not over, but how cunningly that thought is placed right in the centre of the poem and the very sound of 'leave' brushes against 'strove'. How many poets could get away with such an archaism, which conjures Walter Landor's late miniature, 'I strove with none…'? The third and final couplet, carrying straight on from the last, is brilliantly poignant, its pauses and emphases consummately placed: 'Like a fresh track across a field of snow,/Not reckoning that all could melt and go.' The Etruscan language is long extinct, so Wilbur's point is that its poetry can never be read, a state of affairs that will come to the literature of all cultures in the end. It's a sobering thought, captured in just forty-nine words.

But assuming the Etruscan example doesn't make too many poets become taxi drivers instead, there are considerable advantages to writing in such an adaptable and internationally known language as English, though very few these days to actually being an English poet. In fact, it could be argued that Derek Walcott, Judith Wright, Les Murray had an easier time of it, as they had the opportunity to break fresh ground. No tired old skylarks and daffodils for them: the rain tanks of New South Wales and the sea grapes of St Lucia were waiting to be immortalised. And they didn't have to look back at the competition, though they were naturally aware of it.

Where I live, local parish churches have been presided over by John Donne and George Herbert; William Cowper was based in the next town and John Dryden was born up the road. Just as George Seferis, Yiannis Ritsos and Odysseus Elytis always felt the ancient Greek poets breathing down their necks, so English poets can't escape their own poetic heritage.* Wherever their place of birth, anyone writing poetry in English was born into an archive, and it's guarded by names that barely need naming, though there is a curse on the tomb of at least one of them, warning people not to disturb his bones. I don't think any decent poet considers posterity when writing, though it's occasionally worth asking yourself how soon your words are going to sound dated. The critic Geoffrey Grigson complained about Robert Lowell's once widely celebrated work that it was full of terminology which would soon be incomprehensible. It's undoubtedly true of films and TV that a shot of a computer or a phone can suddenly make you realise how old the show is – as future audiences may come to distinguish between footage that is pre- and post-Covid.

The poet Edmund Blunden maybe had the right idea when he decided on his own kind of mask and adopted a pastoral style forged in the eighteenth century. Imagine a modern film that excluded technology or a soap opera where the pandemic didn't happen, as in 2020's editions of *Neighbours*. It solves a certain problem – and all might have been well for Blunden had he not found himself on the Western Front of the First World War, which obliged him to write about very un-Augustan events, and the 'shepherd in a soldier's coat' quickly found a vocabulary of trench and bomb, itself now quaintly archaic.

I suspect that a good few of us writing today, not only the young, will find that our attempts to incorporate the latest pandemic jargon will come to nought. As my friend, the poet Stuart Henson, said: Zoom, for him, will always be an ice lolly. A poem, of course, may be about an ice lolly or digital communication; and a piece of writing called 'Zoom' may take the idea and run with it metaphorically – as Simon Armitage did in the remarkable title poem of his debut volume.* But that doesn't answer the question of why he might want to do that, and an elephant remains in the room.

There are authors – Stephen Romer is one – who will confess to being Muse poets in the line of W.B. Yeats and Robert Graves, who allege they have no choice but to write as they are bidden. This is all well and good unless you're a woman. The late Eavan Boland wrote an entire book on what it was like being a young female Irish poet in a world of older male Irish poets who courted the Muse.* There is a case to be made for some unsettling force which can precede the arrival of a poem, but pragmatically speaking I am less likely to be inspired to write by a mythical female than invited to write by a middle-aged male editor, sometimes even with the promise of very modest payment. That's true of other kinds of writing as well. Often it's a pleasant surprise to be asked and the effect of that can be to send one straight to the keyboard. Nothing gets the writer working more swiftly than the feeling that someone actually likes your work and wants more of it. That little sizzle in the sound of 'surprise' mustn't be allowed to cool. Get to work. No recipe book. Just use what's in the cupboard. It may be risky, but it's fun. Nor is it quite true that the editors these days are all ageing white men, though that was the case when I first started publishing in magazines: Emma Tennant and Hilary Davies were exceptional in every sense. But in the past decade there has been something of a revolution in the publishing houses and literary journals.

When Carol Ann Duffy sent out an invitation during the 2020 lockdown to contribute to her online anthology, *Write Where We Are Now*, there was no question of why I was writing. Suddenly there was purpose amid the general aimlessness of the pandemic. But being asked to write anything at any time is good – even book reviews. It's oddly enjoyable, in fact, to be pressured into producing 500 words by Friday on, say, a book about seven poets eating a peacock.* With reviews of new poetry, whether a pamphlet of haiku, or a blank-verse epic on the life of Nietzsche, there is an accompanying sense of good citizenship, of giving something back. This is the 100-metre sprinter taking a morning run to deliver the papers. It's not quite the main event. It's the warm-up. I don't have a great deal in common with Eliot, but we are both great believers in the need for poets to write prose.

But why do poets need to write poems? I have written plays, and that's self-evidently glamorous. The closest my poems have come to glamour is a reading at King's Place or a corner in the Christmas edition of *The Spectator*. No, that's unfair: there have been some glitzy occasions which do get a mention in this book, but most of them did not involve payment. Poetry makes no money in the known sense of the word. If you happen to write a poem that the reading world takes to its heart, such as Jenny Joseph's 'Warning', about growing old and wearing purple, the chances are that it will be attributed to someone else or to Anon, or even to the person who posts it on Instagram. As for fame, most readers – dare I suggest most writers? – will be hard pressed to name half a dozen contemporary poets. None is a household name. Not Simon Armitage, not Brian Bilston, not even Rupi Kaur (for all her online celebrity) are quite yet household names. When Louise Glück won the Nobel Prize, I imagine there was a great deal of scurrying around in UK newsrooms for contributors who might have heard of her or even read her.

Yet the word 'poet' does trail a few wisps of glory. W.H. Auden claimed it was the quickest way to clear a room (he preferred to say he was a medieval historian), but it can prompt a kind of mystified respect – and mystery is certainly part of the art's attraction to me, the way it helps us see – as Wordsworth learnt to – 'into the life of things'.

At its most basic, poetry is a way of 'getting something right in language' – a phrase of Howard Nemerov's that I keep coming back to.* It suggests a craftsmanlike satisfaction in seeing the job done, of solving the puzzle. Archibald MacLeish told Robert Frost that in writing his own poetry he loaded himself with chains and tried to get out of them. Frost's response was to ask if the younger poet had any readers at all, but we can see what MacLeish meant. So much of the pleasure lies in Yeats's 'click like a closing box'.* And there *must* be pleasure, as George Herbert noted when he wrote:

> I once more smell the dew and rain
> And relish versing*

If *you* don't relish your versing, your reader is unlikely to.

'The Word-House'

Why do I write poetry? It's not exactly for survival, although it has been that for some poets. Nor is it self-expression – that's the last thing it is.

I write, I would say, because I am driven to discover what's next: the next image, the next word, line, stanza. But what's coming in life, too. There is often something weirdly prophetic in poetry; it can feel like surfing a wave of occult knowledge, alongside W.B. Yeats, Edwin Muir, Kathleen Raine, Peter Redgrove, James Merrill…

Perhaps in the end I write because I have read.

'May your shelves always overflow with books' –
the framed poster, ghost of a Christmas present, looks
at home there among those three thousand backs

turned on me tonight as I sit writing. *Aren't
there enough of us?* they seem to ask. A faint
disturbance at the end of the field, look. Traffic can't

get through – our winterbourne has usurped the road:
we walk around and find a homeowner stood
cheerfully telling stories about the water, the flood

that always comes when you least expect it, like poetry,
how everyone rushes to seal their vulnerability
and keep it out. He has electricity

and his only book is safe. Lights flash, the cars
continue their plunge, carried away: one steers
hopelessly, stalls, gets stuck on this stretch of verse.

from From the East:
Sixty Huntingdonshire Codices

Reading

'Where do you get your ideas from?'

It's the sort of thing that might be asked by a well-meaning relative or a young member of the audience at the end of a reading, and at least suggests that something of poetry's bewildering richness and hyperconnectedness has reached the questioner.

The simple answer would be: from reading other poets – and that probably began earlier than I like to admit, with anonymous jingles like 'What a clamour, what a fuss/Getting on and off the bus', 'Whether the weather be fine or whether the weather be not...' and some often surreal nursery rhymes my mother played at the piano – baffling, unsettling things full of weird imagery: 'If all the world were paper and all the sea were ink', 'stepped in a puddle right up to his middle', 'cut off their tails with a carving knife'. I would doubtless have enjoyed the 'ear-candy' of *The Jumblies*, and one of my primary school teachers, Mr Angel, liked to recite 'Little Billee' for us, carefully enunciating the full name of its author – William Makepeace Thackeray – a kind of poetry in its own right. The *Rupert* books must have been an influence, since I was too lazy to read the prose narrative and preferred the brief verse couplets (what an interesting idea, though, to offer the reader a choice). I can also remember an aunt presenting me with Hilaire Belloc's *Cautionary Tales*, a lovely pale, squarish hardback, with slightly unnerving line drawings of Matilda telling dreadful lies or Henry King chewing bits of string. It came a few years before I received from the same aunt a copy of *Verse and Worse*, which I remember delighted me even though I didn't have any idea what was being parodied.

In much the same vein, when I was a little older, I couldn't get enough (and still can't) of Michael Flanders's witty and metrically ingenious lyrics for *At the Drop of a Hat*, the cabaret show he presented with pianist Donald Swann. Seeing Flanders and Swann live on stage in their second show, *At the Drop of Another Hat*, was one of the highlights of my childhood – especially when they sang 'Pee Po Belly Bum Drawers'. And as cardboard cut-outs they were even granted a command performance of 'A Song of Reproduction' at my Christmas model theatre variety performance, to which most of our neighbours were invited. The song, I hasten to add, is all about the Joy of Hi-fi.

There must have been hymns that appealed too.* 'There is a green hill far away/Without a city wall' continually raised the question: why would a hill have a wall anyway…? And 'From Greenland's Icy Mountains' struck a chord, since my sister Valerie and I liked to play a game called 'Going to Greenland'.

But as to what stirred me to write…?

Those Jumblies were surely behind a rollicking ballad I produced about 'Jehoshaphat Jim and Jehoshaphat Joe' when I was at primary school, and which must be one of my very earliest poems. I received my first ever review when the headmistress invited me into her study to congratulate me. Goodness knows where I found the word Jehoshaphat, but I clearly liked the noise it made, which is where poetry begins. I suspect that the instinct to make language sing is in all of us at some level, though not everyone becomes as obsessed with it as poets do.

The first proper poem I wrote would actually be about the Pyramids, composed when I was a teenager. This was long before I had any inkling that I would live two years in Upper Egypt, that my first collection would be entirely Egyptian in theme, and that in 2017 I would still be 'threading the dream' in a verse and prose memoir.* I felt early on that poetry was something I could do, that it was the closest I could come to composing music. I would like to have been granted that gift – music is so important to me, and it remains a beautiful,

Ozymandias's foot (the Ramesseum) with JG's mother.

dangerous distraction. Perhaps it was my very musical mother who introduced me to serious poetry. She certainly helped me choose a poem when I had to learn one for a school competition: 'Ozymandias' – yes, Egypt again. I've no idea whether I won or not, but I can still recite it by heart, and it may even mark the beginning of my love affair with the sonnet, although it's a very unconventional one, rhyming in a way unique to Percy Bysshe Shelley. It must have been a lesson in 'negative capability' too, since there are obscurities in 'Ozymandias' until you learn that by 'mock'd' he simply meant 'made', although there is mockery enough implied in the Pharaoh's demeanour. I attempted a response in my 'Ozymandias Revisited'* after visiting the fallen statue which was said to have inspired him. This photo shows my mother sitting on Ozymandias's foot.

My mother was also very fond of Matthew Arnold's 'The Scholar-Gipsy', William Wordsworth's 'Tintern Abbey' and other oddments, such as 'What is this life if full of care…?' by that diarist super-tramp W.H. Davies. My father was a more regular consumer of poetry: being a 9–5 Metropolitan Line man, he adored John Betjeman, and was never happier than with an anthology – usually Palgrave's *Golden Treasury* or *Other Men's Flowers*, edited by ex-army officer Arthur Wavell. He would quote certain lines on a regular basis, the odd expurgated rhyme from his war years and things remembered from school, like Leigh Hunt's 'Write me as one that loves his fellow men' – although I'm not sure Chas Greening did love his fellow men all that much.

Teachers played their part in forming my own taste too. One very old-fashioned and somewhat brutal master taught us *Paradise Lost* by reading it aloud, and the sound of that blank verse bowled me over. I coveted a glorious old edition of the poem in the school library, with its Doré illustrations, and 'Ben', as we called Mr Francis for some reason, very nearly agreed to let me have it. He put before us a great deal of Louis MacNeice, a poet I still return to. It was at school I also came to know the First World War Poets who would be so important to me later on. Ben was surprisingly enlightened in presenting us with newish poems, so I got to read Ted Hughes, for example.

One of the first poems that really affected me I discovered for myself. We were set the task of finding one we liked, and then we were to tell the class about it. I must have bought a copy of Michael Roberts's *Faber Book of Modern Verse* to browse in, and I can't have been much more than thirteen since the edition I used, revised by Donald Hall, was published in 1966. I found a poem called 'Brainstorm' by the American formalist Howard Nemerov, and I still have the text of the short talk I gave to my class, in which I admit that the poem 'gets rather complicated at points'. It's not a bad critique, and I had evidently bothered to look up some of the unfamiliar words.

When in 1990 I attended the Geraldine Dodge Poetry Festival in Waterloo, USA, I actually heard and met Nemerov – just a few months before his death – and was able to tell him this, standing beside the marquee in a weird blue floodlight. He thought it rather a grim poem to have made such an impression on a boy. We shook hands, then he was off, a tired old man, keen to escape. I am still drawn to Nemerov, finding in him an appealing mixture of the sardonic and the mysteriously lyrical. The poem of his that impressed me on that particular evening, however, was his brand-new elegy for Philip Larkin, in which he observes 'the face of truth,/Mortality knowing itself as told to do.'*

Larkin I came to know aurally, since I only had access to a reel-to-reel tape recording of him reading *High Windows* when I was a postgraduate student in Mannheim. When I eventually got to see the text of the poems I was astonished at how much rhyme and metre he deployed. That was a lesson in the art that conceals art. Those poems from the 1970s are firmly lodged in my brain, although I made no effort to learn them. I subsequently worked my way backwards through Larkin's collections, at last reaching *The North Ship* – as disappointing a debut finale as one can imagine.

Before I went to Germany with a reading list of chiefly non-German books, I had been largely ignorant of contemporary writers. I wanted to write but had barely read any of the key texts. My first poems were influenced by the dead white males who had been put before me in the English department of Swansea University, so a good deal of John Donne and W.B. Yeats crept into my writing. Dylan Thomas was there none, still less that other Swansea poet whom I would come to admire, Vernon Watkins, or that much-loved voice of the Welsh people, Harri Webb. I had somehow discovered odd individual poets such as Cumbria's Norman Nicholson, the West Indian Edward (later Kamau) Brathwaite, and the highly mystical Kathleen Raine, but generally I had minimal awareness of recent work. That was not necessarily a bad thing. After all, Auden recommended that young poets should write parodies of the masters, and it used to be the custom that a Collected edition of a poet's works would begin with youthful 'imitations'. It hardly even occurred to me as I began to scribble seriously that other people were writing verse out there. My first encounter with a Living Poet was when I was twenty, and John Montague came to read at Swansea.

I hadn't heard of Montague, nor had I ever been to a poetry reading, but the evening proved fortuitous because I was sitting next to a girl called Jane whom I had admired from a distance. Montague was one of the great love poets, and though I most vividly recall his 'mythical stammer' – the audience willing him on to the next word – I'll never forget that halting, mesmerising performance of 'Godoi, godoi, godoi!/Our city burns & so did Troy,/Finic, Finic, marshbirds cry...' from *The Cave of Night*. That pamphlet had only just appeared, selling

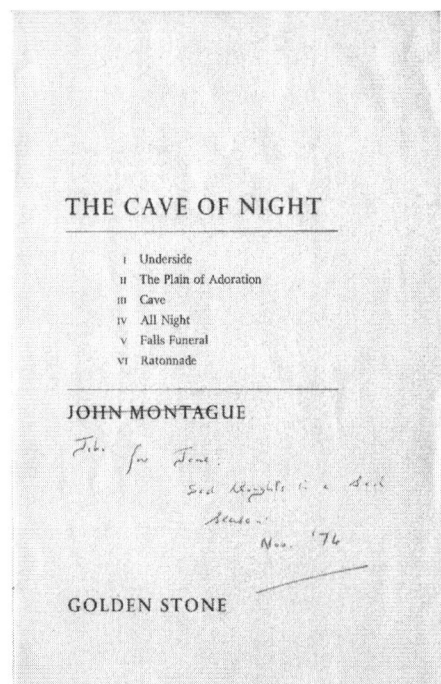

THE CAVE OF NIGHT

JOHN MONTAGUE

GOLDEN STONE

John Montague's inscription in The Cave of Night.

for 50p, and presumably this was a launch. We still have the copy Jane asked him to sign: 'John for Jane: sad thoughts in a sad season. Nov. '74'.

I wonder if it was hearing 'Raton-nade' that made me realise for the first time just how close to music poetry could be. Music was then the most important force in my life, and I spent far too many hours listening to Jean Sibelius or Anton Bruckner, filling in the spaces when I couldn't write and couldn't be bothered to read. During this 'sad season' I made a conscious decision to dedicate myself to poetry. I even have half a memory of saying as much to Jane, although at the time I wouldn't have made any connection with the Montague reading. I showed no particular interest in his work or in any other contemporary poetry. But some months later when we were boy- and girlfriend, I bought us each a remaindered hardback copy of *A Chosen Light*.* The erotic charge of those lyrics from the mid-sixties is still strong, even in lines about guddling a trout: 'As the curve of my hands/Swung under his body/He surged, with visible pleasure.'*

From then on, I read all the Montague I could find, and was always on the lookout for those beautiful Dolmen Press editions of the earlier volumes. I learnt a great deal from his work and used him as a model on several occasions. 'Under the Flight Path',* for example, I wrote while we were living in the USA, where he was born, in fact, and its sequence of remembered childhood figures owes much to his frequently anthologised 'Like Dolmens Round My Childhood, the Old People'. There was a satisfying sense of completeness when the poem appeared in a book of mine from John F. Deane's Irish press, Dedalus, in 1996.* I never heard Montague read again – although I almost did, just missing him by a day in Dublin in the 1990s; and at London's Troubadour Café just a few months before his death, where he was scheduled to perform but couldn't make it. Instead, we all read something by him or talked informally about him. It was a terrific evening. Then I had the sad honour of writing the great man's obituary for the *Guardian*.*

By the time I had left Swansea and was studying in Germany, I knew what I intended to do with my life, even though I also knew by then that T.S. Eliot had advised against wanting to 'be a poet' – just concentrate on the poetry was his advice. And that meant acquainting oneself with what had been done before. Poetry is, after all, a conversation with the past. It was in fact Jane who introduced me to Eliot's poetry, which I had somehow avoided until my third year at university. Quite crazily, I memorised much of *The Waste Land* in order to impress her; and a year or two later, I tried to do the same with *Four Quartets*, simply to come closer to the sounds of that work. Before we married, when I was trying to make a living as a children's conjuror (of which more in a later chapter), I used the whole of 'Macavity' as patter for one of my tricks. Eliot is in many ways the foundation for everything I have done, and I would choose any or all of his 'quartets' to take to my Desert Island, along with the late Beethoven that inspired them.

The truth is, I don't have a particularly good memory for poems, and I wince in envy when I hear those who have such a gift. What a marvellous thing to have been able to perform like James Fenton, Sarah Howe, Michael Donaghy, Alice Oswald or Benjamin Zephaniah without any text. But why don't we? It's assumed that classical soloists will have memorised their much more complex musical pieces. Those skills have been handed over to the rap artists and the slam participants, but it seems wrong to put up with second-rate readings. I rely on the text myself, but I don't script my introductory remarks, which is a sure way to kill any atmosphere. What I do find frustrating is not being able to roll off lines from favourite poems more spontaneously. I remember Dana Gioia standing in our little kitchen in Cambridgeshire and talking about Louis MacNeice. When I enthused about 'Meeting Point', Dana asked me if I would recite it for him. Of course, I couldn't, yet now it's one I can generally rely on remaining in my head, if not as assuredly as MacNeice's 'Sunlight on the Garden', an excellent antidote to the dentist's drill, I have found. Memorising poems has become unfashionable, although there have been some attempts to introduce competitive recitations again in schools. There can be no better recommendation for the internalisation of poems than Terry Waite's experience in Beirut. He was in solitary confinement for five years in tight spaces – for some of that time he was kept in an old fridge – and it was his mental library of verse that helped him survive.

After my return from Germany, Ted Hughes was the poet I was most aware of, partly because my accommodation in Exeter was a farm worker's cottage beside the River Exe, only a stone's throw from his farm in North Tawton. I sent him some of my poems and verse plays, and astonishingly he wrote back saying that he thought they were 'the real thing' and he liked the 'hold-all' quality to some of the verse. He was always very encouraging and seemed curiously impressed that I was making a go of it as a conjuror.* Whatever Hughes's failings as a human being, one cannot lightly dismiss the kindness he showed to young writers. It's true that I went on to ignore much of what he recommended, such as avoiding 'closed situation' teaching jobs, but that endorsement was of huge importance to me, although what I was writing was still immature, lacking some objective correlative. I was also determined to make it as a verse dramatist, a foolhardy quest if ever there was one, and much of my creative energy went on that doomed enterprise. But Hughes's ideas about poetry and the intensity of his vision, these stayed with me. I sat up one night as the Exe rose beside our cottage and read through the whole of *Crow* – as dark an experience as one can imagine. When *Gaudete* appeared I was off to the bookshop in Pinner near my parents' house on the day of publication. Hughes is one of those poets whose every new book had to be bought. There have not been many of those.

So it happened that I was caught between the poles of Larkin and Hughes, and it was from them that my enthusiasm took its charge. I began to discover others of the same period – Peter Redgrove and Penelope Shuttle, Patricia Beer, D.J. Enright. Eventually I got to Seamus Heaney, whose *Field Work* was a powerful influence. And the Americans – Robert Lowell was everywhere in those days, before he was overtaken by Elizabeth Bishop, but it was *For the Union Dead* that hooked me rather than the more celebrated *Life Studies*. In the late 1970s I read and read, trying to gauge the extent of the canon and come to terms with it. It was the Imagists who offered a way forward for my own poetry, especially the little Penguin anthology, which I took with me to Egypt when Jane

and I were sent as volunteers to Aswan for two years. I also had some William Carlos Williams in the edition prepared by Charles Tomlinson, who would later become much more important to me than Williams. That style of short-lined, intense, 'instamatic' verse was just what I needed initially to capture the excitement and exoticism of Egyptian life.

Towards the end of our tour, when we were in Alexandria for Mrs Sadat to award me the Alexandria Poetry Prize medal for some of those imagist

Medal presented by Jehan Sadat at Alexandria Poetry Prize ceremony.

25

scribblings, I picked up an ex-British Council Library edition of Ezra Pound's Confucius. I have it before me now, a dusty, dog-eared Faber paperback with its smudgy CANCELLED stamps. *The Classic Anthology defined by Confucius* had been borrowed a remarkable ten times between April 1975 and November 1977. Pound's economy of language fascinated me and immediately offered another way of coolly capturing the local exotica: something more substantial and expansive than his own imagism and an alternative to the alluring steamy densities of those Egyptophiles, Lawrence Durrell and Terence Tiller. By then, I was discovering too the rigorous emotional clarity of Constantine Cavafy and the lyrical enigma of George Seferis. So it was that my first book, *Westerners*,* emerged... and inevitably the reviewer in the *TLS* thought it reminded him of early Pound.

I read plenty of living poets, not only because I review books and judge competitions, but through choice and a desire to hear the tribal voice. But there is no substitute for the masters. If there is a period I return to more than most then it is the sixteenth and early seventeenth centuries. Much as I need Wordsworth and Cowper and Pope, I feel that if we are going to be thinking about sources, then that is where the purest refreshment is to be found. One book I especially enjoyed writ-

Hawthornden Castle, international writers' retreat in West Lothian.

ing contains verse letters to and from Elizabethan poets. It tells the story of how in the summer of 1618, the forty-six-year-old poet and playwright, Ben Jonson, travelled from London to Scotland on foot. He spent a month with the bibliophile and minor poet William Drummond at Hawthornden Castle in West Lothian (pictured here), before walking back home again. The conversations this literary celebrity enjoyed with his long-suffering friend, Drummond of Hawthornden, are well known and provide a good deal of the inside information we have about poets of the age, particularly Shakespeare.

My collection *Knot* was written during a stay of similar length in 2010 at Drummond's old home at Hawthornden, which is now a well-established 'international retreat for writers'. In the prose sections of my sequence, Jonson's journey is allegorised and set beside my own notes on life in a modern writers' retreat, then interwoven with sonnets and verse letters. The sonnets are in the imagined voices of various eminent poets of Jonson's time, and the verse letters are addressed to Philip Sidney, George Gascoigne, Walter Raleigh and Shakespeare himself on topics that we know interested these

Knot garden design from The Expert Gardener *(William Hunt, London, 1654).*

writers: art, war, travel, love. All this I planned, despite my above-mentioned belief that too much planning can be bad for poetry. The idea of calling the sequence *Knot* was an obvious and irresistible one, and I used an image from a mid-seventeenth-century gardening book of my father's for the cover.

But *Knot*'s second section came as a surprise after I thought I had finished the project. I suppose it was a kind of exercise to keep myself out of mischief, but also for the entertainment of the six resident fellows at Hawthornden, where there was no Internet and where a monastic silence was expected during the day. What I wrote was a masque, a form in which Jonson excelled, but one which has quite disappeared – unsurprisingly, since masques were expensive amateur dramatic indulgences for the nobility, much loved by the Stuarts and their courtiers, who would take all the leading roles. The budgets for Inigo Jones's designs and the extravagant costumes make them comparable with modern-day Hollywood – or even more with opening ceremonies for big sporting occasions. When Queen Elizabeth II made an appearance for the 2012 London Olympics, apparently being parachuted from a helicopter, this was very much in the masque tradition. There is something of that glamour and craving for fantasy in the entertainments whose texts have survived.

To write a modern masque without it becoming a parody was quite a challenge, but since there were six fellows at Hawthornden there was a resident 'court' willing to do the acting. Indeed, we had already 'performed' *Macbeth* while the crows made wing to the rooky woods around the castle. We had three men and three women, which was ideal: the cast would consist of three from the far side of the Atlantic (Ian Colford, Alfred Corn, Beena Kamlani) and three from this (Sophie Mayer, Fiona Shaw – the novelist – and me).

The convention of the masque is that all stage directions are in the past tense: this text is a record of something that happened, a one-off event, like a concert. Since the clock had stopped for us in our Internetless castle, and since this was in the spirit of the Elizabethan poets, time was the natural choice of subject. The title is also a quiet homage to Michael Tippett, whose late choral work I admire – although Joan Forman's book, *The Mask of Time*, about the paranormal* must have been at the back of my mind, too. So 'The Masque of Time' was in some respects a formal indulgence, a pastiche, a very contingent piece of artifice with references to specific details of William Drummond's home, but I hoped that its serious undertone, the satirical edge and some of my attempts at Jonsonian wit would bring pleasure to those who know nothing of seventeenth-century masques or William Drummond's castle.

I've never felt hobbled by my elders. I'm of a generation that tends to look up to them and assume they have things to teach us, which could explain why in the four decades or so since my first collection appeared I've spent so much time writing about and editing other poets. Some of those poets have themselves helped to restore reputations. Edmund Blunden, whose *Undertones of War* I edited in 2015, was responsible for the first selections of Wilfred Owen, Ivor Gurney, not to mention John Clare, whose forgotten manuscripts he salvaged from a cupboard in Peterborough Museum. I have also brought out an edition of verse by Geoffrey Grigson, a man whose thumbs up or thumbs down could make or break a career. More often than not it was a thumbs down. Nevertheless, although Grigson could be a difficult man, he was an interesting poet and doesn't deserve to be forgotten just because he was mean to those who didn't impress him. Personally, I feel it's important to encourage young writers, which is why for over a decade I was a judge of the Eric Gregory Award for poets under thirty: and one of the ways of encouraging them is to say: 'Go and read as many other poets as you can. You will be influenced, and that's unavoidable. Nor are you likely to find many readers for your work. But there will be some, like you, who understand what you are doing, who probably also write – so read their books in return.' As Grigson liked to point out, poems are made by 'members of a long narrow community through time', not admired or even known by the 'lateral many' in a poet's lifetime, but by the remainder, as he put it, 'stretching from the past into the future in a long thin line'.*

But a poet's reading shouldn't consist solely of poetry, and I've frequently found creative possibilities in non-fiction. Apsley Cherry-Garrard's *The Worst Journey in the World* is one example – a book I would recommend to anyone to help them through a pandemic or a long hibernation. As my wife likes to say, there are always others worse off.

Jane and I had returned from Egypt, and in 1982 were living in a council flat in Arbroath, north-east Scotland, teaching Vietnamese refugees. It was a ferociously cold winter, with temperatures of -27°C (apparently the lowest temperature ever recorded in the UK) in Braemar, and it was also the time of the Falklands War. 45 Commando Group were based just outside the town, and by some mysterious process this meant that the public library had a rich selection of Polar literature. We were also very near Kirriemuir, home of J.M. Barrie, Captain Scott's good friend. All these things combined when I found a copy of the classic Apsley Cherry-Garrard account of the pre-First World War Scott expedition and came to the chapter called 'The Winter Journey'. It told the story of a midwinter trek through pitch dark to retrieve specimens of an emperor penguin's egg, and the episode instantly gripped me. For one thing, it seemed to offer me the ideal way to teach myself to write sonnets – a way of teaching myself how to write them while telling a story. But also, with the winter temperatures we were experiencing and the task force heading for the South Atlantic... there was something deeply allegorical about this 1911 march to seek a mere egg. And an emperor's egg, no less.

I knew I had to write it, and decided to compose one sonnet a day for thirty-six days (the length of the original journey), trying a different sonnet type on each occasion. It became one of my best sequences, and has been reprinted several times.* Extracts have also been set to music by Cecilia McDowall for baritone Roderick Williams as an accompaniment to the Schubert song cycle *Winterreise* – to which my sequence continually alludes. I even got to see one of the eggs brought back by Wilson, Bowers and Cherry-Garrard, because I became friendly with the curator of birds' eggs in the British Museum collection at Tring in Hertfordshire.

Since then there have been other books to have suddenly struck a light. It happened with John Harvey's *The Plantagenets*, a battered copy of which I found in a long-vanished second-hand bookshop in Hampton Hill. I remember reading it in my father-in-law's house and being enthralled by the individual stories. There was nothing too complicated, just enough to get the juices stirring. That reading led to a sequence about those monarchs, which was part of my Bloodaxe collection, *The Tutankhamun Variations*. The title sequence of that book had itself emerged from Thomas Hoving's *Tutankhamun: The Untold Story*. The whole business of Tutankhamun had been too immense to fit into *Westerners*, and it was another five years before I managed to tackle it. I was at the time writing plays and something of that impulse drove me on: there were many monologues, drawing on information from the Hoving.

Later in the 1980s, Rowland Parker's *The Common Stream* was one of the spurs to my first set of Huntingdonshire poems, the *Huntingdonshire Eclogues* – although an essay by Seamus Heaney, 'Englands of the Mind', was also responsible. There was no narrative in either case, but both the Parker and the Heaney reminded me to look more closely at the landscape in which I was living. The importance of looking is hard to overstate, and I will be considering it in a later chapter. But looking without knowing what you are looking at is not much use. That's why so many of my favourite reference books offer help in that regard: a history of traditional crafts in Britain, a Victorian handbook on trees – and yes, those Geoffrey Grigson Shell Country Guides, all of them bought second-hand. I have measured out my life in used books, and while I will travel a long way to visit a second-hand bookshop and literally dream about them as described in the poem at the end of this chapter, I have never regarded myself as a collector. We don't have room at home for that, although my 'study', which is a wooden shed at the back of our mid-terrace cottage, has proved invaluable and must contain several thousand volumes.

When we were first married and living in Barnes, our landlady – who used to have the *Morning Star* delivered hidden inside the *Daily Telegraph* – was very concerned about the quantity of books I had carried to our upstairs flat. 'More than's good for it,' she would mutter. And that was long before the Internet made finding obscure volumes so much easier, although there's nothing like browsing the physical shelves. The habit started young. I used to go to the local Red Cross Fete and come back with wonderful things, several of which are beside me as I type now – notably

Fate and Fortune, Phrase and Fable.

that mixed-doubles match between *Dictionary of Phrase and Fable* and the *Book of Fate and Fortune* (I've made great play with fete and fate in my poems over the years). There were some lovely volumes of Dickens and a 1936 *Oxford Companion to English Literature* at that park fete too, still consulted regularly. My friend Stephen Hanvey and I used to and still do occasionally take ourselves off to the Charing Cross Road to browse, centring ourselves on Cecil Court, near Leicester Square Tube station, where the mystical bookshop, Watkins, is based.

There also used to be an excellent classical LP record exchange in the Court. But the odd thing is that one of my forebears, Arthur Collins, had his publishing house in Cecil Court. It was called Greening & Co., after his mother's maiden name because there was already a Collins publisher. He was quite a character, a friend of Oscar Wilde, something of a playboy, and had the good fortune to publish the bestseller of his day, *The Scarlet Pimpernel*, editions of which can still be found bearing the Greening & Co insignia... probably somewhere in the Charing Cross Road.

The Scarlet Pimpernel *in the edition published by Greening & Co.*

I am essentially a browser, happy to surf the waves of serendipity. Just as the best way to write a poem is to let yourself be led, so it's also the best way to find the right book, the one your unconscious has been trying to draw your attention to. This is not the time to go into that curious phenomenon I have noticed when the writing of a poem reaches a certain pitch of intensity, except to record the following: in that semi-trance state, I have found that I can reach out almost blindly to the bookshelves and find precisely the right book, then open it on to exactly the required page without flicking through. Much faster than any Internet search. It's inexplicable, but something similar must be going on when a poet enters a bookshop. It's those volumes we didn't realise would interest us that often prove the most useful creatively, the ones that were sitting there unloved for 30p. A few years ago, I found a hardback in Cambridge Market about chalk giants,* and instinctively felt that if I bought it, the book would lead to some poems.*

31

Ideas have frequently come from such chance encounters and, dull though it may seem, non-fiction is one of the richest sources of inspiration. I suspect this has been true for many poets – even Shakespeare had his Plutarch, after all – though they may not all have wished to dispel the romantic aura. It suited Samuel Taylor Coleridge to tell the story of the person from Porlock intruding on his mystical inspiration, but John Livingston Lowes has shown in *The Road to Xanadu* that there was an immense amount of reading as well as opium behind *The Rime of the Ancient Mariner*. A.E. Housman was a poet for the people, his lyrics heartfelt and apparently simple, adored by the 'Tommy' on the Western Front; yet the poet was one of the leading classical scholars of his age, his learning quietly underpinning those simple quatrains. Where too would Yeats's songs and ballads be without his esoteric studies, that Platonist labouring late in the tower? The same thing might be asked about Kathleen Raine's love lyrics. Occult researches may not be mentioned in Raine or Yeats, but reveal themselves in choice of diction, in unexpected connections.

Other Modernist poets have been less shy of wearing their reading lists on their sleeves, but beyond *The Golden Bough* and *The Waste Land* there are all kinds of little-known prose sources to well-known poems. Some of them are not even sources, but mere prompts. Nor is it exclusively non-fiction. When John Berryman sat down and read Saul Bellow's *The Adventures of Augie March** it moved him to take up the poem he had left unfinished five years previously, and thus his masterpiece 'Homage to Mistress Bradstreet' was born. And who knows how many now forgotten poems were the result of an obsession with a particular book or author – take the case of American Ronald Johnson, for instance, whose

The Book of the Green Man was apparently the result of reading all Geoffrey Grigson's prose (and that is a lot of reading).

Glasses at rest on a first edition of Edward Thomas's poems.

Arcadian

Shops that only pop up in your dreams
are not unlike the ones you visit
awake, except that what you buy then
vanishes in the blink of an eye.

In my case, it's never anything
Practical, but always some obscure
edition of verse or a record
salvaged from the Soviet archives,

and much of the delight's in finding
the shop itself, a shop that appears
to be managed by sleep, yet exists
along an everyday labyrinth –

part-shopping mall, part walk-in monkish
illumination. It feels somewhere
I'd like to be in the afterlife –
an old, darkly panelled, cigarette-

haunted, quiet centre of browsing,
whose stairs twist out of sight above shelves
laden with poetry, some of which
I feel sure I must have bought before.

Dreaming

The most level-headed and open-minded study of dreaming is *Private Myths* by the psychiatrist Anthony Stevens,* who takes his title from a remark of Joseph Campbell's that 'a myth is a public dream, a dream is a private myth'.* Stevens explores every possible explanation, going well beyond the obvious, but what emerges is the importance of making a place in one's life for dream, and it seems to me that this is particularly crucial for poets. One might even argue, as Les Murray does in his poem 'Poetry and Religion',* that true poetry has to retain at least some connection to the dream world, that the poems without any dream are really only verse. Most poets already have a healthy respect for dream, so are prepared to cope with the popular preconceptions and the language's inbuilt, long-established prejudice – just as 'myth' has come to mean something untrue, so to call someone a 'dreamer' is as dismissive now as it was when Julius Caesar brushed off the Soothsayer. But not all poets can handle what they dream.

I have long been drawn to the work of Swedish Nobel Prize winner Tomas Tranströmer, who is especially at home in that world, perhaps because of his professional life as a psychologist. (I would recommend the translations of Robin Fulton for Bloodaxe, briefly quoted here,* although those by Robert Bly (Penguin) and Robin Robertson (Enitharmon) have a great deal to offer too, and Patty Crane's recent gathering of the complete works for Copper Canyon Press comes with the original Swedish.) What first attracted me to Tranströmer may have been his interest in music – the way he would play Haydn on the piano 'after a black day', hoisting 'the Haydnflag' in the name of peace. In 'Balakirev's Dream' – surely the first poem about this underrated composer – he gives us a straight narrative of a dream. Mily Balakirev, dozing off during a piano recital in 1905, finds himself in the Tsar's droshky gliding out over the ice and boarding a battleship, where he is informed by the crew that he won't die if he can play a 'curious instrument' they give him, which the dreamer knows is what drives 'the man-o-war'.

But it is Tranströmer's more oblique dream-work that intrigues, where he tries to inhabit the hypnagogic state between waking and sleeping, or evokes it as he does in 'Tracks', where during the moonlit small hours a train 'has stopped/out in the middle of the plain'. As the lights from a distant town flicker 'coldly at the horizon', he feels it is as if someone were entering 'a dream so deep/he'll never remember having been there'. There are a lot of trains in his poetry, and I suspect he dreamt of them as I often do, the contrast between straight parallel lines and weird dark forest neatly conjuring the world of reason and imagination. 'The Station' features another stopped train, with hazy glimpses of 'a crowd/of shut-in figures, stirring to and fro', while a man walks along the coaches hammering the wheels. In Swedish, the lines have a marvellous onomatopoeic music ('en domkyrkoklockklang'), but the mood of half-dream is at least translatable. He likes to imagine people asleep in nearby villages while he drives through forest. 'Nocturne', for example, ends: 'Into the slit between wakefulness and dream/a large letter tries to push itself in vain.' When not on a train, the poet is often driving in his poetry, and one of his most anthologised poems tells of a near fatal accident when his car skidded. As he pulled at the wheel, a kind of dreamtime kicked in through 'a transparent terror' which he describes as floating like egg-white: 'The seconds grew – there was space in them – /they grew as big as hospital buildings.' Tranströmer has the rare gift of being able to capture those moments at which dream reality meets waking reality. Unsurprisingly he titled this poem 'Alone'.

Dream can be a dangerously alluring source of material for the poet, however, and some of the American 'deep image' poets have tended to get lost in the apparent profundity of their night adventures – a case in point being Tranströmer's Norwegian-American friend and translator, the sometime 'Iron Man', Robert Bly. Others have managed to find a convincing way through the hypnagogic zone, as is the case with another American, Louise Glück, whose work began to attract me thirty years before she received the Nobel Prize. Reading her, one has that same sensation of being in a lucid dream, inhabiting a landscape or in the company of people at once familiar and unfamiliar. Writing about George Oppen in one of her many engrossing essays, she has stressed the importance of the space between words and this strikes me as revealing.* Glück values 'the power to seem, simultaneously, whole and not final', which is just how dreams feel, never neatly resolving anything. It could be said that they are the fruitful spaces in our lives; they are timeless and yet somehow keep expanding, like that moment when Tranströmer's wheels hit the ice.

A rather more typically English way of handling dream is to relate what happened extensively but coolly, as Ruth Pitter does in her 'Six Dreams and a Vision', or Jenny Joseph – who did write poems other than the purple patch of 'Warning' – in 'Reported Missing': 'I had a strange dream the other night after I left you/And it seemed that we were going on a journey…' Sometimes there is a quiet bafflement and scepticism mixed with fascination, as in a sonnet which that most rational of poets, Anne Stevenson, sent me as a Christmas poem with a note explaining that it was a real dream.* 'The Inn' is dedicated to her husband: it imagines 'an inn for actors' and a room occupied by panting lovers. She knows that if she looks too closely they will turn to dust, 'As I would, dreaming, if I couldn't reach you,/Solid, asleep in this inn we've carefully built/ Of seasoned faith and uncorrupted trust.' There might be a mildly detached amusement of the kind Charles Tomlinson expresses in 'A Dream' (subtitled 'or the worst of both worlds').* In this early poem, 'Yevtushenko, Voznesensky and I/are playing to a full house' and while they 'ride in triumph' the bewildered English poet comes on 'sorting my pages, searching for the one/I've failed to write'. Tomlinson was always wary of excess, and perhaps success, generally refusing to be lured by the psyche's siren call. But there are those who take it rather further, and find themselves drawn in.

Ted Hughes, for example, had a famously influential dream in which a scorched fox on its hind legs warned him to give up studying English at Cambridge because all those essays were 'destroying us' (he also believed that the extensive prose he wrote for *Shakespeare and the Goddess of Complete Being* destroyed his immune system). But Hughes's actual poems have the quality of dream to them too. This is a poet who takes dreams very seriously – from the early 'A Dream of Horses' to Laureate offerings such as 'The Dream of the Lion' and the late 'Dreamers' from *Birthday Letters*. This last poem describes a nightmare from which 'None of us could wake up', one known all too well by those familiar with the Hughes-Plath-Wevill history. Alice Oswald, in many ways heir to Hughes, notably in her love affair with Devon, wrote in 2004 that 'poems, like dreams, have a visible subject and an invisible one. The invisible one is the one you can't choose, the one that writes itself.'*

Inevitably, poetry since 1900 and *The Interpretation of Dreams* has been dominated by Sigmund Freud, and later by C.G. Jung. Suddenly it wasn't possible to write a Robert Browning monologue and profess innocence as to what might lie behind all those murderous misogynistic male narrators, just as no latter-day Christina Rossetti could hope to deny the sexuality in her 'Goblin Market'. Some have persisted, and still do – Anthony Thwaite's *Victorian Voices*, for instance, or the American Richard Howard's monologues – but although Anthony Hecht made the form work for the 1980s in his *Venetian Vespers*, shifting attitudes and contemporary knowingness demand something a little more in the mould of Carol Ann Duffy. It's often the humour in British writers that makes their dream-work readable, although the seriously wild imaginings of, say, Peter Redgrove can be successful in another way. Neil Roberts's excellent biography of Redgrove was called *The Lucid Dreamer* and some of his poems follow the narrative of specific dreams – 'Davy Jones' Lioness' is one.

In medieval times there was something called the Dream Poem. Often an allegory, it would involve the narrator going out on a May morning and having some kind of vision, as Geoffrey Chaucer's does in *Legend of Good Women*, or like William Langland's in *Piers Plowman* who 'biful for to slepe' and saw 'a fair feld ful of folk' – the latter is a poem known to specialists, but hasn't really entered the popular imagination. *Pearl* is another matter: it has received much attention in the last decade, with new versions in recent years by Simon Armitage, Jane Draycott and John F. Deane, to name but three. There have been various attempts at the genre since the fourteenth century. Shakespeare draws on it repeatedly – not only for *A Midsummer Night's Dream*, but in the many visions that thread his plays, and climactically in *The Tempest*, which is more a play of dreaming than waking. There is no lack of examples among the Romantics, but it would be a mistake to think that the Age of Reason was not also an Age of Dream. Where else did Pope's sylphs come from? The Victorians were fascinated and terrified by dream, but the poem that makes boldest use of it does not often receive its due nowadays. In 2019 Cardinal Newman was canonised, and the media ran all kinds of items about his achievements, but his once celebrated verse narrative was barely mentioned.

The Dream of Gerontius was made popular by Sir Edward Elgar's setting, and the oratorio has preoccupied me since the days when my father loved to play (loudly) the classic Barbirolli recording. I would be up in my bedroom trying not to listen, trying not to think of him being embarrassingly overcome once again by the extraordinary summons of Janet Baker's Angel. These days I am regularly embarrassingly overcome by it myself. I cannot help thinking of Dad in his radio hut in wartime Iceland when I hear Richard Lewis singing 'And there in hope the lone night-watches keep'. I used the line as epigraph to my book about his wartime experience, *Iceland Spar*.

Since *The Dream of Gerontius* was published in 1866, there have been plenty more poets tinkering with the idea of the Dream Poem, often guided by Dante, who somewhere in the twentieth century overtook Milton as an influence on

Night watch in Iceland from JG's father's 1942 album.

poets. Yeats was steeped in dream, but Yeats's bête noire, Wilfred Owen, might be an unexpected candidate for his 'Strange Meeting', which at least takes its bearings from the medieval model. Others are Hope Mirrlees's *Paris* or H.D. [Hilda Doolittle]'s *Helen in Egypt*. More recently, the title sequence at the heart of Seamus Heaney's 1984 collection *Station Island* is cast in that mould. But less well-known examples include John Gurney's extraordinary epic poem, *War*, and Anne Stevenson's amusing parade of ghosts, 'A Lament for the Makers' (from *Stone Milk*, 2007). I would add also, from the mid-twentieth century, Andrew Young's *Out of the World and Back*. Young is remembered, if at all, as a lyric miniaturist, a nature poet; but the two poems in this book from the 1950s, 'Into Hades' and its sequel, 'A Traveller in Time', are of an entirely different breed and deserve to be better known. It's interesting that Young begins on a platform of the Paris Metro, where he might almost have met Ezra Pound on his way to *Imagisme* with his 'petals on a wet black bough'. The narrator suddenly has a vision of his own funeral and then, 'like waking in a strange room', listening 'For night's stealthy noises' in the silence: 'I had no fear, thinking of nothing more / Than the strange novelty of being dead.'

The novelist and poet Lindsay Clarke has all kinds of interesting things to say about dream in his 'reflections on imagination, myth and memory', *Green Man Dreaming*.* He reveals, for example, that it was 'a powerful and disturbing dream of Yeats which first summoned me out of the relative security of full-time teaching and demanded that I respond to the call of the writing life'. I have myself had some curiously prescient dreams, usually involving other poets. More than once I have dreamt of a particular writer only to wake up and learn that they have died. This happened on the occasion of my father's death, too – I saw a kind of coffin being raised by luminous figures – and he wasn't even ill.

Quite what use one can make of such prophetic insights, I'm not sure, but it can be fruitful for the poet to draw on residual dream, which is why some have made a point of writing first thing in the morning. I remember my old friend William Scammell talking about this in an interview with Hunter Davies,* how he would write the moment he got up, without even washing or eating: 'I avoid the radio, read no newspapers and speak to no one before I start work. I want to be in touch with my night-time life and have a clear, fresh mind.' That border between the day mind and the dreaming mind so memorably described by Edward Thomas in 'Lights Out' is precisely where poetry can be found patrolling. I have had dreams in which I read or write entire poems, and just occasionally a line will make it on to a piece of paper beside the bed. More often than not they are valueless when read in the cold light of day, but there was one – 'the forest believes in you' – which seemed important when I was in the process of writing my long Sibelius poem, 'The Silence', discussed in the chapter 'Flitting'. Although that poem underwent major reconstruction and was cut by almost half, those words stayed put. Dreams and forests do have much in common.

The occasion when I most drew on dream material was during my stay at Heinrich Böll's Cottage on Achill Island in 2018, where there are no forests, but the resident artist is exposed to all that the Atlantic can muster. This cottage is where the Nobel Laureate used

Plaque on the gate to the Heinrich Böll cottage, Achill Island.

to come to escape the controversies he stirred up back in Germany. It's about as far west as you can get in Ireland, but only an hour or so from Yeats country. One enters such a demesne prepared for anything from dancing fairies on Ben Bulben, to visions of the Sidhe over Sligo Bay, with possibly some low-flying ectoplasm from Drumcliffe Churchyard. I had reread Yeats before going to Achill, and brought with me a new copy of his *Collected*.

On my first night, as I was trying to sleep, I had a very curious sensation as of being prodded in the back by someone, although what dream narrative prompted the prodding I can't recall. It certainly prodded me into creativity

Achill Island landscape.

and the incident features in the first of my twenty-four Achill sonnets.* Only half playfully I mentioned in the sonnet that it might have been the ghost of Heinrich Böll. The strangest thing of all: that same first day when I eventually found a pub that had Wi-Fi, I discovered an email from my old German teacher, Jack Stevenson, who hadn't been in contact for a quarter of a century. He was an Irishman, and the one who had first introduced me to the work of Böll. Other weird dreams followed during that fortnight and fed into the poems in a way I have not known before. The fact that I was writing sonnets gave me the feeling that the form was containing and controlling the weirdness.

I think rhyme in particular can sometimes encourage the spread of oddity, as it does in John Berryman's *Dream Songs* and the later sonnets. All those random connections that happen in dreams are not unlike the connections that happen when words sound alike. In my final check through the proofs of *Achill Island Tagebuch*, incidentally, I noticed that one of the sonnets only had thirteen lines. How that is even possible I do not know. It's not easy to re-enter the dream zone that produced a poem, but in that case I was obliged to. Yeats may have said 'in dreams begins responsibility', but responsibility for proofreading they evidently leave to the waking brain.

Simple Gifts

A man brings stuff from Amazon. My phone
chimes to itself. The hard drive yawns and loads
beside your iPad. We're doing cards, each one
containing a handwritten note, damp words
pressed into space. It is a hard-won skill
we hardly need today. If there weren't exams,
the ballpoint would be lying with the goose quill.
When do we even have to sign our names?
That monk, who spent a life stooped at his desk
transcribing the only copy of some book
now digitised and free to click, might ask
quite why he bothered. But he'll add a joke
in Latin, sketch another snail, keep writing.
When Gutenberg arrived, they knew his type,
and scraped the vellum harder. Clients waiting
would understand the gifts required to shape
such nameless glories. Just a few more years...
The doorbell goes again. This time a drone:
your 3D printer's here, some GM flowers
and tickets for our round trip to the moon.

A Happy Medium

There was a time in the 1970s when Marshall McLuhan was so well known that Woody Allen could pluck him in person from a cinema queue to support an argument in *Annie Hall* and know that audiences would laugh. Recently, I found myself recalling his most celebrated pronouncement, 'the medium is the message', and wondering less about 'print versus screen' than how McLuhan's 'Gutenberg Galaxy' might apply to modern writers, particularly poets. The more I considered it, the more it seemed clear that the tools and means available have seriously affected style.

Beyond the historical cases – William Blake painting and etching his texts; Emily Dickinson shaping her hymn-sized 'fascicles'; John Milton being led by his own voice as he dictated to his daughter – the modern example that sprang to mind was William Carlos Williams. A practising doctor in New Jersey, he would jot down his poems on prescription pads as he was out on call. These were drafts, but it can't be a coincidence that the poems are predominantly short and narrow. A later American, A.R. Ammons, would run with the idea by putting a roll of adding-machine paper into his typewriter and tapping out:

> today I
> decided to write
> a long
> thin
> poem

Some 200 pages later, 'Tape for the Turn of the Year' concludes with a characteristically witty:

> so long:

Ammons's project* was a self-imposed aesthetic choice, but Dr Williams was merely reaching for what was available. Had he decided to write his much quoted 'This is just to say' in the available magnetic letters on the outside of an icebox – the same, perchance, that contained the delicious plums – one of the world's favourite poems might have turned out differently.

On this side of the Atlantic, meanwhile, as Williams was continuing his rebellion against Europe's pentametrical stranglehold into the 1960s, First World War poet Edmund Blunden was still dipping a steel nib into a pot of ink and producing perfect iambs that could have been written by Edmund Spenser four centuries earlier. Did he fear that a ballpoint might lead him to the no man's land of free verse? On the Western Front, the war poets had had to make do with what they found, since paper was at a premium, especially among those such as Isaac Rosenberg and Ivor Gurney, who were

Pen and inkwell.

not officers. This surely affected the way they wrote, adding more pressure for their verses to be intense, to load every rift with ore. What if the custom had been to write satirical verses on the cases of shells or tattoo them on their arms? British war poets might then have mastered the haiku. Rudyard Kipling came close with his pithy phrases of remembrance, such as 'Known unto God'. A gravestone has its own necessities.

The history of poetic style is a mixture of chance and choice. As a child, Vicki Feaver chose to write poems on toilet paper, then as a mature poet she discovered Sharon Olds – poems that, she says, 'don't just cover the paper'. But she never forgot the earliest influence, even printing the title of her ground-breaking collection, *The Handless Maiden*, 'in black ink on the brown cover of a notebook made in China that I loved because its thin pages reminded me of the Jeyes toilet paper.'* Derek Mahon in his poem 'The Drawing Board' gives the board a voice in which it stakes its claim in his poetry: 'it is I alone who let you sing/Wood music; hitherto shadowy and dumb,/I speak to you now as your indispensable medium'.* For James Merrill, the word 'medium' takes on its other meaning. Chance led him to the Ouija board, which in turn led to *The Changing Light at Sandover*. That the material from which this enormous verse trilogy grew had to be jotted down with a free hand, while the other was being swirled over a board laid out with letters and numbers, prescribes the manner of its composition. Sections begin with an **A**, a **B**, a **C**, etc., a **YES** an **&** or a **NO**. Voices from 'the dead' are all in capitals.

Poets often find such a liberating tension between what is drafted and what is typed, between what is in print and what is handwritten. Many like to type out their drafts and then annotate by hand – in the case of *The Waste Land*, one cannot imagine any other way of collaborating than Ezra Pound's scribbles over T.S. Eliot's typeface.

There can also be an obsessive loyalty to certain tools. Don Paterson tells us in *How Poets Work*:

Most poets are fetishistic about paper and pens, and at the moment I can't write on anything but grey Daler A5 sketchbooks with a Pilot Hi-Tecpoint V5 extra-fine rollerball. OK?*

And there are plenty of examples of contemporary poets apparently shaping their work according to the medium they employ. Philip Larkin showed in a rare appearance on television – a medium he generally shunned – how he had worked steadily line by line, stanza by stanza, page by page through each of his notebooks in writing 'The Whitsun Weddings'. By contrast, Peter Redgrove had 'germs' of poems scattered throughout different books which he allowed to 'incubate'. His method involved much use of literal cutting and pasting. The styles of both these writers reflect these methods.

Much more recently, at the launch of his 2025 collection, *The Shores of Vaikus*, Philip Gross explained that the form of the poems in his long sequence 'Evi and the Devil' came about through discovery of a particular 'Notepad' function on his new smartphone. He explained to me in an email that tapping a keyboard had always felt 'a little bit *other*', something practical, 'not an organic part of me'. Notepad even looked different: 'a small square block of words, no spacing'. He decided to copy his notes into Word and 'whoosh' them off to edit later:

The unexpected thing was, almost as quickly as I whooshed one on its way, another started forming in the space that whoosh had cleared. Not sequential, either. The next thing would come with the air of 'On the other hand...'

Novelist and poet Helen Dunmore credited her word processor and its metaphorical cut-and-paste with being 'the closest thing I can imagine to the sensation of being inside one's own brain', moving the process of writing

'beyond the mechanical into something as meltingly lateral as thought itself'.*
Chance has a hand (literally) in this, since she was forced at school to abjure her
left-handedness, and for the rest of her life – which was far too short – found
the physical act of writing awkward. Meanwhile, just as in the past a dodgy
typewriter may have led a poet to avoid certain combinations of letters, today's
older poets may find their computers like to insert capital letters where they didn't
think they wanted them, or that it has rearranged what they wrote because they
are not sure how to change the grammar and spelling settings. Seamus Heaney
was not alone in discovering late the creative possibilities in predictive text.

Such developments, even passing ones, have always attracted poets. A century
and a half after Arthur Hugh Clough's response to the penny post, *Amours de
Voyages*, Gwyneth Lewis was modelling poems on the fax; another two decades
and Sam Riviere's *81 Austerities* seemed to grow from the very language and layout
of social media. His poems reflect the medium in which they may be consumed,
too: I for one have them on my Kindle. The 280-character limit of Twitter/X has
an obvious appeal for wits, punsters, epigrammatists, and for some years Andy
Jackson has encouraged necessity to give birth to invention by posting 'Otwituaries'
whenever a celebrity dies. There have in fact been entire books of verse written
as Tweets, and George Szirtes has even posted long poems in stanzaic episodes.
On Facebook, too, the very interactive nature of the site fosters a different kind of
writing in which poets set each other challenges, collaborate, amend and judge.

Not all such experiments are so radical. As I will explain in the next chapter, my
friend Stuart Henson and I discovered that you can fit a sonnet on a traditional
postcard – or 'post card' as we liked to call it, preferring the 'vintage' spelling – and
for thirty years whenever we were on holiday we would send each other such greet-
ings in verse. That particular medium-driven collaboration became a collection
in 2021, *a Post Card to*; but seven years earlier Penelope Shuttle and I had worked
together on a book-length sequence of poems about Hounslow Heath which was
also driven and shaped by the writing medium. As Penny lives in Cornwall and I
am in Cambridgeshire, this project would have been impossible, or a very different
proposition, without email. We alternated contributions and even amended each
other's work, sometimes producing several poems a day. There was one poem
entirely co-written. But for me the real revelation was use of the iPad. The poems
came quickly and unwontedly: being able to research as I wrote, without delaying
the burst of energy, was crucial and demonstrably affected my style. Only a few
decades ago, such a poem would have required many visits to a reference library.
The freewheeling nature of the *Heath* poems, with their range of obscure local
history details is very much a product of the tool I was using.*

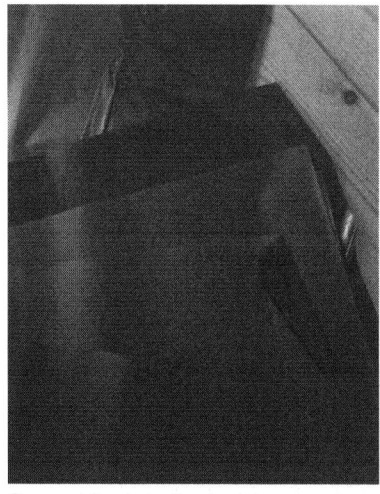

Rare surviving sheets of carbon paper.

The only equivalent experience was when I acquired my very first word processor, an Amstrad, in the late 1980s. I have always redrafted many times, and not needing to use carbon paper, not having to force myself to retype whole pages, was wonderful. It's quite possible that some readers will not even know what carbon paper is, as I was reminded today when I discovered a cache of crumpled sheets at the back of my desk and found myself handling their strange slippery skins again. I have attempted to take a picture of them here, but nothing quite evokes their troublesome necessity.

Certainly it didn't please the poet Ronald Duncan when I sent him a carbon copy of one of my plays to read, not being able to afford any classier form of duplication. Suffice to say, my fingers now bear the proof that copying in the olden days was not quite as straightforward as cut and paste.

But the most radical effect of seeing my words on that Amstrad screen was to make me experiment for the first time with a very long line. Indeed, it could

Computer looking down at pencil and notebook.

be said that Alan Sugar was at least partly responsible for firing me to write the thirty-two *Huntingdonshire Eclogues* and their sequels.

And yet – something that tends to astonish people – all my poems are still first drafted in pencil. There have been entire histories written about this humble tool, and even leaving aside its etymology there is something unavoidably Freudian about it. But I am in thrall to the slowing effect of the graphite, the need to regularly sharpen, the fleeting appearance of the marks it leaves, the way it is closer to drawing, hence perhaps to childhood. When I fly to Seattle next month, I shall pack several along with my iPad, and will hope to come back with a box of those lovely yellow American HBs. I'll give you my pencil when you pry it from my cold, dead hand.

Against Travel

Why rush round the world as if you have to see it
before your time runs out, like a tree
that knows it's reached its last season, so it branches

and flowers and fruits like never before, reaching
for the sun, the sun…? The world runs out,
but time won't. Hurrying to see all there is

is running further from what you think
you are seeing. Stay at home. Look harder
at what you have already. The ten thousand things

on your sim card will amount to nothing – no more
than the eight on a roll from your Brownie 127
judiciously snapped when there was all the time

in the world and everything was black and white –
once you have forgotten if you went to that place
or whether it's the picture you remember. Or whether

there was even weather in your heated bubble.
Now you're back, tell me about the road you live in,
the field beneath your home, that tree, this rain.

Flitting

There is something intriguing about reading what poets from one country have to say about another, especially if it's a poet you like and a country you know, such as your own. So, when the Irishman Dennis O'Driscoll publishes a long poem titled 'England', when St Lucia's Derek Walcott passes through Wales or Iowa's Amy Clampitt visits the Lake District or Yves Bonnefoy scrutinises Constable's Dedham Vale in French – this is delightful. We all know, or used to know, Robert Browning's 'Home Thoughts from Abroad': when I was a boy and snow covered the land one April, the newspaper headline was 'Oh, to be in England' – something unimaginable on a front page these days. But the line endures because it captures a certain creative longing – what the Welsh call 'hiraeth'. The Welsh language poet Waldo Williams lived not far from my home in Cambridgeshire during the Second World War, and taught, in fact, in the same school as me. In a village next to what is now the reservoir Grafham Water he wrote his celebrated poems about the bright field of his Welsh childhood.

It's one of the paradoxes of art that the most vivid evocations of home are often prompted by time spent away from it: think of D.H. Lawrence in Italy or Antonin Dvořák in America. Think, indeed, of Robert Frost in quintessentially English Beaconsfield producing all those quintessentially American poems. But the move need not be transatlantic. What a devastating difference a few miles made to John Clare. He was not alone in finding that different places stir very different kinds of poetry.

One of the first poems I wrote when Jane and I arrived in Upper Egypt would become the title poem of my first collection, *Westerners*. I could recognise that here was something genuine, but different. It's a poem that I still value, and if I have a signature poem this is it, but it's not quite the kind of thing I wrote most of the time when we were in Aswan. As I have hinted in the first chapter, I was under the spell of Imagism, and a lot of those poems were substitutes for the camera I preferred not to use as we explored the country.* The poems give the impression of being written on the hoof, snatched from the moment, which is how things often were for us, living like locals on the local salary. We were not tourists. We despised tourists.

I still have a certain resistance to touring of any kind, preferring to settle in a place then getting to know it. That's what happened when we went to New Jersey: we spent a year there and I found it considerably more of a challenge as a writer than Egypt had been. Possibly it was to do with the differences between the languages, but I felt I was losing a sense of who I was writing for. Should these lines be read with a New Jersey intonation (is that *ice* cream or ice *cream?*) and wouldn't it be better to let the American poets write this sort of stuff? But whereas I never really

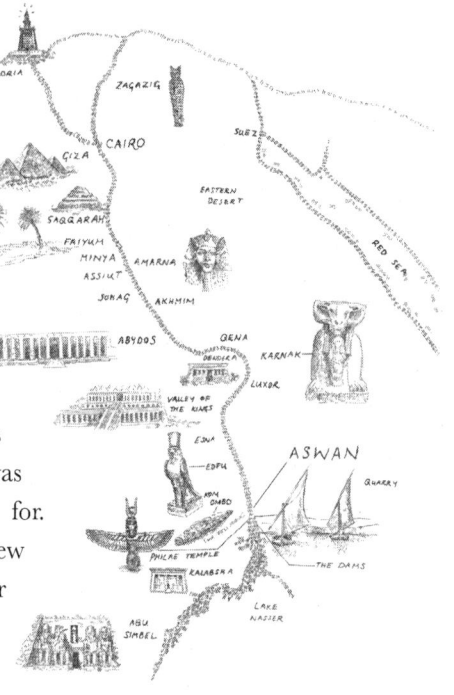

Map of Egypt by Rosie Greening.

grappled with the Arabic language poets, I was able to study the canon of modern American poetry, beginning with Helen Vendler's invaluable anthology, *The Harvard Book of Contemporary American Poetry*. Without her guidance I would never have come to love James Merrill, A.R. Ammons, Louise Glück and so many others.*

In Clinton, New Jersey and Aswan, Upper Egypt, writing about the place helped me become a part of it. Our eighteen months in Arbroath, in north-east Scotland, however, didn't quite have that effect, although they were crucial to my development. Having returned from Egypt, we were determined to get away from the troubled circumstances of family life in London and at the same time contribute something to society, but also I wanted to pursue my writing. So while Jane took a job teaching Vietnamese refugees, I sat and worked on plays and poetry, helped by a Scottish Arts Council award, hindered by the ice-*cream* van that circulated endlessly on our Arbroath council estate playing 'Popeye the Sailor Man'. In the end I had to confront the driver, but it turned out that he too was a keen amateur violinist, so I couldn't bring myself to complain further. And try as I might, the poems that came to me weren't very good.

I suppose I had hoped to respond in verse to the locality, but whenever I began to write about Scotland and its history everything fell apart. I still have some half-finished poems about Queen Victoria in the highlands and mountain hares

The mortuary chapel, western cemetery, Arbroath.

and a cliff called the Deil's Heid, along with some respectable lines about places we came to know such as Glen Isla and Arbroath Abbey.* There was also a long elegy I was proud of about a curious Scots Baronial-style mausoleum I used to visit in the town's western cemetery, pictured here. I proudly showed it to Douglas Dunn, who didn't think much of it – or, at least, I think he said it 'puzzled' him, which was a kindly way of saying the same thing. He was writer in residence at Dundee, then at work on his celebrated book, *Elegies*, and the first person I ever heard talk of 'flitting' – 'deracinated' was another word he taught me. My friendship with Douglas is probably the most enduring cultural legacy of that time in north-east Scotland, along with my discovery of Iain Crichton Smith. Douglas invited us to the launch of Smith's *Selected Poems* at the university in Dundee, and Jane and I were both mightily impressed by the Lewis man's reading. Forty years later I ended up editing a new selection of his poems myself.* And it's only now that I have at last managed some decent lines about that cemetery building in Arbroath, although I haven't dared show them to Douglas.

Looking back, the best things I wrote at that time were little poems about the refugees, whom I had begun teaching. I read a lot of Du Fu and Li Bai, and the poems adopted that Arthur Waley-esque manner. One or two I'm still happy with and they have been reprinted in my American *Selected*. Then there was a never-collected piece in the style of Beethoven's Op.133 *Grosse Fuge*, written after we heard the Fitzwilliam Quartet perform it in, of all places, Glamis Castle. Spookily, when we arrived in good time for the concert the castle was absolutely deserted; it only became apparent later that the clocks had gone back so we were an hour early. I also managed a poem about the Bell Rock Lighthouse, that needlepoint of light on the horizon, always in view and whose story as told by Robert Louis Stevenson intrigued me. It finally turned into a play, and I did make considerable progress as a dramatist during that stay. But the major development in Arbroath – which our daughters for many years heard as 'in our broath', some quaint expression meaning 'in the past'– was my above-mentioned sonnet sequence *The Winter Journey*. This had some local connections, as I explained in the last chapter, but was hardly engaging with Scottish culture and history.

The danger for the visiting poet is that you either entirely ignore where you find yourself or you end up writing a series of occasional pieces. The shorter the stay, the more likely this is to happen. I have judged enough poetry competitions to know how strong the lure can be to write a sonnet about the art gallery you visited or the sunset you witnessed. There's something of this willed quality, I have to confess, behind the sonnets in my Achill Island book. But as I have already mentioned, my friend Stuart Henson and I have turned the tendency to our advantage over the years by sending each other sonnets on postcards. It's a way of keeping our hands in as sonneteers and also making a holiday greeting more entertaining. The sonnet – originally an Italian form, but effective in many other languages – does seem to invite an international perspective, or it could be the other way round. The form is undoubtedly very good at containing powerful emotions, which is why it has conventionally been adopted by love poets, but it's also a handy vessel for whatever wry thoughts, sly observations or witty reflections feel apt in that time and place. If a poet's *Collected* is a tombstone and all those early poems become millstones, their occasional sonnets are best viewed as milestones.

Wherever I have lived (rather than merely visited) I have tried to go deeper. In fact, I wrote verse plays about all three places where Jane and I pitched our tent before we settled in Cambridgeshire. From Egypt came one about the building of the Aswan High Dam, since we knew people who worked on it, and had many Nubian friends displaced by Lake Nasser. In Scotland, as I've already mentioned, I wrote *The Stevenson Play*, involving the Bell Rock Light, which Robert Louis Stevenson's grandfather built on Robert Southey's celebrated 'Inchcape Rock'. Then, while living in New Jersey, I composed *A Ladder in Hopewell* about the 1932 Lindbergh kidnap, again drawing on the fact that we lived only a stone's throw from the Flemington Courthouse where the mistrial of Hauptmann took place, and a short drive from the Lindberghs' home in Hopewell. Although the Stevenson piece won a Best New Play prize at the Edinburgh Festival, only the Lindbergh script has ever been performed. Franklin (Lee) Harris, with whom I had previously undertaken a teaching exchange for a year, produced it with his Jericho Theatre Company in North Carolina, and I flew out to Asheville to attend the run, keeping a detailed journal, which you can read in a later chapter.

I will never forget the chilling effect of a very large semi-professional cast chanting the opening lines of the chorus, phrases darting from character to character, while the ghosts of Asheville's Black Mountain poets listened from the wings:

The world is wild tonight
    and the child lies
        all unsuspecting
In Hopewell
    The world is wild
       winds from Europe
Shake the dogwoods
    as they strain to blossom
        winds of myth
Sting the eyes
    and the rains
      of suffering descend
The world is wild tonight
      but the child in Lindbergh's house
In Hopewell
    is unaware
      is only suffering from a cold
Which is why
    although it is Tuesday
       the child is here
This once
    and only this once .
       not at his grandmother's
Mrs Morrow
    of Next Day Hill
       because of his cold
Because the night is cold
    because the world is wild
He will go there the next day
    only the next
      to Next Day Hill
And he will be happier
    in Hopewell
      in his maple-wood crib
In his nursery
    with its one shutter
      that will not shut

> But will clap
>
>   clap
>
>   clap
>
>   in the wind
>
> The world is wild tonight, Anne Morrow
> You were wise to keep him out of the cold
> Not to let him go to Next Day Hill
> But stay at Hopewell

Hope well, Anne Morrow Lindbergh

Although I frequently write about Englishness, and have recently co-edited an anthology of poems about it,* my heart keeps reaching out to other places we have lived. Usually it's somewhere across the Channel – often Germany, less often France. At one point we were actually going to settle in Brussels. I took the train and ferry there twice for two separate interviews at an international school, but didn't get the job – I sometimes wonder how that would have affected my poetry. Would there have been a verse drama about Waterloo? Would all my work on the First World War have happened at all? And if so, how differently would I have portrayed the conflict, having seen it from the perspective of 'gallant little Belgium'? Since Europe is once again so much in everyone's minds, it seems appropriate to make it the main focus for the rest of this chapter – although I will be taking us to its furthest fringes.

I must have started writing poetry seriously at about the same time, as I discovered that rather indigestible essay on Johann Wolfgang von Goethe by T.S. Eliot in *On Poetry and Poets*. Eliot suggests that a truly European author should demonstrate 'Abundance, Amplitude and Unity' (he also throws in 'Universality'), making it clear from his personal pronouns that this is a male preserve – just one of several elements in 'Goethe

Nightwalker's Song: *translations of Goethe by JG.*

as the Sage' that make it uncomfortable to reread. Eliot's boldness in canonical matters was not quite on the scale of Ezra Pound's or Harold Bloom's, but he doesn't hesitate to enrol Dante, Shakespeare and Goethe in his men's club. As well as women, he excludes big names such as Miguel de Cervantes, William Wordsworth, Friedrich Hölderlin on the basis – and this is his shibboleth – that in a truly great European writer it should not be possible to 'isolate' any one part and regard it as the essence of the work. Hölderlin gives us access to his fullness pretty much wherever you dip into him. Similarly, Cervantes would not do because he is 'for us entirely in [*Don Quixote*]'. As for Wordsworth, despite his greatness, 'he will never mean to Europeans of other nationality, what he means to his own compatriots'.

I have no idea whether in forty years I have come close to satisfying Eliot's criteria for Europeanness. Abundance I can claim, certainly. Just after the Covid pandemic Arc Publications brought out some of my own versions of Goethe, highlighting pieces with dramatic or musical associations such as 'The Sorcerer's Apprentice', along with poems English readers should really know, e.g. 'Harz Mountains, Winter Journey';* and during the actual year of Covid I had attempted something even more ambitious. I began translating both volumes of Rilke's *Neue Gedichte* into rhymed and metred English verse, a task which I have only just completed.* But before either of these projects came about, in my 2019 collection *The Silence* I had included several translations – versions? imitations? – from the German of Hölderlin. Perhaps this was a way of showing my own European credentials, but perversely it was also a means of reinforcing my allegiance to a particular 'country, and local culture', as Eliot put it, although he also adds 'race'.

This was especially true in my reimagining of the celebrated long poem, 'Homecoming', the original of which is a work of 'ambitious metaphysical scope', according to David Constantine, one of this poet's most distinguished translators. In my version I closely follow Hölderlin's narrative, which tells of his return to Nürtingen in April 1801 after a tutoring job at Hauptwyl. The opening, which Constantine calls in his biography* 'the most sustained and one of the densest of Hölderlin's poetical landscapes', evokes his thrill at looking back from Lake Constance and seeing dawn over the Alps. For me, it was looking up from the Great West Road at the air traffic coming and going over the old Hounslow Heath, yet that itself was a kind of link with a wider European aesthetic.

Such versions of a great German Romantic might be seen as a natural supplement to my even-earlier translations of Georg Heym, Georg Trakl, Ernst Stadler and August Stramm, poets who wrote about – or anticipated, in Heym's

case – the First World
War. These attempts
to stir some awareness
of the mere existence
of such writers outside
the UK had appeared
in a collection I had
dedicated to my old
German penfriend who
in fact stayed with us
under the flight path in
Hounslow. In *To the War*

JG at the grave of Jean Sibelius, Ainola, north of Helsinki.

Poets I chiefly engaged in dialogue with figures such as Rupert Brooke, Siegfried
Sassoon, Vera Brittain – a response, maybe, to a different kind of silence: that
refusal to talk about the trenches, something of which a post-war generation
of writers was acutely aware. But my versions of Hölderlin touch on certain
spiritual matters which preoccupy me too, and they are also a natural extension
of my musical obsessions, as so many of his poems feature in Austro-German
classical repertoire.

The long title poem of *The Silence*, however, comes from a different European
source – one as unique as its language. On the collection's cover is a bust of
the Finnish composer Sibelius, whose fame was such in his lifetime that when
an American sent a letter to 'Jean Sibelius, Europe' it quickly found its way to
his forest home north of Helsinki, where he lived and was buried. Ironically,
Sibelius's music has never quite been taken to the hearts of the leading European
nations, and René Leibowitz considered him 'the worst composer in the world'.
It wasn't until very recently that a French orchestra even brought out a complete
cycle of his symphonies. * And German orchestras have generally avoided
him, unless persuaded by respected champions – Hans Rosbaud, Herbert von
Karajan, Simon Rattle. My boss at the BBC, the Viennese musicologist Hans
Keller, had fitting words for every composer, whether it was Haydn, Beethoven,
Tchaikovsky, Schoenberg, Elgar, Gershwin, Britten or Dallapiccola, but he
told me that he would never comment on Sibelius because he simply didn't
understand him. Yet what Sibelius has to say feels more essentially European
today than anything by the Second Viennese School – and not only because it
is obviously in tune with contemporary environmental concerns.

I don't often take lines of poetry from my dreams, but when – as I explained
in an earlier chapter – 'the forest believes in you' dropped into my sleep, I knew

it had to be part of my Sibelius poem. Although I cut the original 1200 lines to almost half that length (I think Eliot might grant me 'amplitude'), those words remained, alongside words of Sibelius himself, which he placed at the head of his masterly evocation of the forest spirit, Tapio: 'Widespread they stand, the northland's dusky forests'. *Tapiola* was one of his very last compositions before that notorious 'Silence from Järvenpää' descended in the 1920s and lasted well into the 1950s:

Every day he pushes the envelope aside, leaves a new
emptiness and silence. Those you grew up with, they disappear
into the mouth that has nothing to say but will eventually devour
even Tapio's war whoop. The forest believes in you. *

In fact, it was in England, most deforested of countries, that Sibelius really found a devoted audience. Cecil Gray – a Scot, and partner of the American poet H.D. – wrote the earliest biography, which is still one of the best, and helped spread the word. Despite all Edward Elgar's Straussian credentials, 'das Land ohne Musik' had an increasingly troubled relationship with the Austro-German tradition after the First World War. Listeners looking for a fresh start responded wholeheartedly to the Finn, whose 'mosaic' approach to symphonic form would prove so influential on Arnold Bax, Ralph Vaughan Williams, Peter Maxwell Davies.

Curiously enough, when I wrote this long poem, I still had not been to Finland. We only managed to get there in 2019. I had originally planned to write the poem as a result of the visit. But on reflection, I am very glad it happened this way round. Travelling in the imagination has much to be said for it.

What is emerging already in this chapter is how much I am fascinated by those points at which European culture comes up against something different. My first collection, *Westerners* was so called because Jane and I *were* Westerners and among the few Europeans in Aswan, a unique environment, as much African as Middle Eastern, with a vibrant Nubian culture. We could not avoid becoming curiosities. But to ancient Egyptians 'Westerners' were the dead, because they were buried on the West Bank of the Nile, the side I used to cross to in my capacity as itinerant school inspector. I loved that creative tension, and its appealing doubleness.

Then, two decades after Egypt, I went to Iceland, researching my next collection, *Iceland Spar*, which would take its title from the strange quality of that calcite to make anything viewed through it look double. While there,

The tattered cover of JG's student play, Ragnarok.

I visited Thingvellir, site of the world's oldest parliament, and of a huge fault line where European and American tectonic plates meet each other. Again, the symbolism spoke to me. I was in Iceland for less than a week, but it is somewhere that made a deep impression. It has been of great importance to me, not only because I studied Old Norse at university and wrote my first play about Snorri Sturluson and the Norse gods – the tattered remains of *Ragnarok* are pictured here in all their immaturity – but because my father was stationed there during the war and his own silence on the matter fascinated me. There was clearly a cultural fault line as well as a real one. 'The place is full of Yanks' was all he would ever say.

Volunteering when he was eighteen in 1941, my father had left for Iceland at the end of 1942, finding himself firstly in what his diary describes – there was no blackout, unlike London – as the 'fairyland' of Reykjavík, though probably unaware as he wrote of how sincerely Icelanders believe in their 'hidden people', the *huldufolk*. He was posted to a place 'the name of which is pronounced Akarary (don't know how in hell the name is spelt!) – it's 300 miles from here and almost on the Arctic Circle!', sailing there on the *S.S. Gemini* – one of many

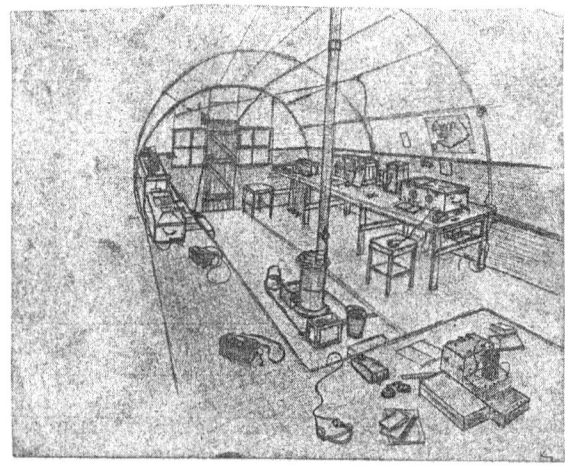

Drawing of the wireless operators' hut, Valhall Camp, Akureyri by Allan King.

curious 'twin' themes in this story. He would remain in Akureyri as a wireless operator until July 1943, enduring long cold night watches, coal-heaving, experiencing interminable blizzards and isolation; but also inspired by the scenery, the aurora borealis, the spectacular twilights ('red and ultramarine blue (also indigo blue) in the west and yellow and white in the east') stimulating conversation ('jawing about splitting the atom, etc... wireless is *the* thing of this century'), dramatic snow walks and cycle rides round the fjord, fishing, reading and film after film at the Nýja Bió cinema – which was still there when his son visited over half a century later, showing the saga of Bridget Jones!

Then there was the mail. My father had met my mother shortly before leaving wartime Kew and the beginning of their romance is a subtext to the poems I eventually wrote. The Akureyri camp was called *Valhall* but was only a corrugated iron Nissen hut heated by a coal-burning stove.* Here, the RAF recruits' main task was to receive weather reports from the tiny island of Jan Mayen and help protect convoys from German U-boats.

My father spent a further six months in Reykjavík, but this did not make quite so powerful an impression. I always had the feeling that the months he spent in Akureyri as a teenager were the most potent of his life.

It was only after his death in 1998 that I read his Iceland diary and began to realise quite how much it had all meant to him. He had never been back, never wanted to, he said; but the Society of Authors made it possible for me to go and see for myself the strange, sparse world he had occupied during the middle years of the war. The year of my pilgrimage proved significant, and a new kind

A page from Charles Greening's wartime Iceland album.

of 'war' was declared shortly after my return in the summer of 2001: it was unsettling to find myself printing off the final draft of the apocalyptic long poem 'Völuspá' ('Coming Soon'), with its disaster-movie imagery, just as news came in from America of 9/11. *Iceland Spar* itself wasn't published until 2008, the year of the financial crisis, when Iceland became known for entirely different reasons.

The land of Odin, then, always had a certain allure because of my father's silence, just as Sibelius's silence attracted me to the land of Kullervo. Both countries are cultural outliers, yet still recognisably European, although Iceland is not a member of the EU. My most direct assaults on the idea of European Union have been in two 'corona' sequences, which have nothing to do with Coronavirus, even though the more recent was published just as it was starting. The first was *European Union*, a series of fifteen linked sonnets (sometimes called a crown, or 'Hungarian' sonnets) each with a country for title, written in 1997, before the EU expanded.* The form demands that the last line of each sonnet becomes the first line of the next, and in the fifteenth all the previous last lines combine. It pleases me that that very un-European poet, Les Murray, expressed his admiration for the sequence. He would have appreciated the form, as devilish to handle as Brexit itself – but one I returned to in *Europa's Flight*.* This particular corona or 'crown' of sonnets is set on Crete, and its complexity might be less in honour of the Labyrinth, and more an acknowledgment of the maze of backstops and cliff-edges into which Britain threatened to disappear before the pandemic changed everything. Read in late 2020, however, it reflects a time when flying and indeed flitting were taken for granted.

A volcanic landscape in Iceland.

Off the Grid

It happens – you start
walking in the direction
your map unerringly
indicates you must take,
following the little red dots,

but where there should be a road
there's a fence, and where
a farm is marked it's
ineluctable bog:
there is no explanation, except

the polarity of your compass
has reversed, yes –
that's it, you tell yourself
as you glide on across
the reservoir, over

the scarpface, towards
a remembered dream
in which you fly or
fall using the map
as a kind of hang-glider.

Walking

If English poetry starts with Chaucer, then it also starts with walking. *The Canterbury Tales* is the story of a very considerable walk, with stories being told along the way. There have been many pedestrian poets since then, in every sense: not always those best equipped – think of Ben Jonson carrying his bulk from London to Hawthornden Castle in 1618 – and not always the poets we might expect.

The image of the American poet Wallace Stevens, for instance, is of someone utterly deskbound, quite un-Wordsworthian. In fact, Stevens never learnt to drive, and regularly took lengthy hikes for pleasure. On one typical Sunday in 1902 when he was in his twenties, he tells us in his journal that he walked over five miles along the 'Spring Valley Road', then another four to Ridgewood, a further mile to Hoboken, finally heading back in the Paterson direction for seven more miles. Ten years later he managed thirty miles from the Broadway end of the New York subway out to Greenwich, Connecticut. And so it went on, despite the cigars and the wealth. Even once he had joined the Hartford Accident and Indemnity Company, of which he was eventually vice-president, he kept at it. During the week, he would compose his poems during the four-mile round trip to work and back. There is definitely a connection between the process of writing poetry and the act of walking.

Although the footpaths were pretty well trodden during the Covid lockdown, in general it is rare to see anyone in the Cambridgeshire fields, and when I am out I feel very much that I am conforming to type by wandering lonely as a cloud. This is not Wordsworth country, however, but John Clare's and William Cowper's. Although I've written about Clare, I don't have his kind of eye for the detail of the countryside. I imagine him stop-starting when he walked, noting precise qualities of the flora and fauna – his epic walk home to Northamptonshire from his asylum in Essex was probably an exception. No, I have to make a conscious effort to look at things when I'm out for a ramble, but it's undoubtedly good for both me and my poetry when I do.

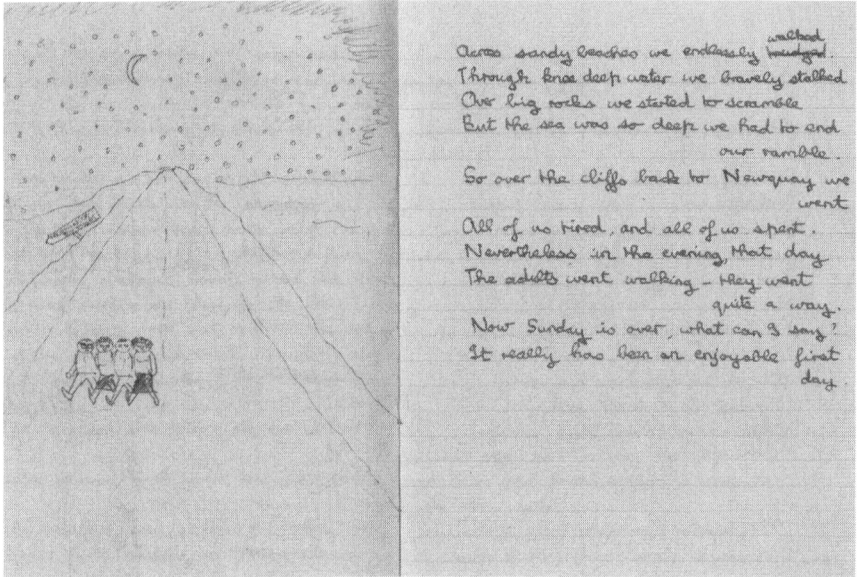

Pages from a holiday diary.

I must have grown used to writing about the adventure of a country walk in those holiday diaries my sister and I were encouraged to write when we were children – a typical page from one of them is pictured here – influenced, I suspect, by a once-ubiquitous poster advertising Start-Rite shoes. The advert showed two children, who could well have been my sister and me, walking

The Coastal Path. Lulworth Cove.

Jane and baby Katie, 1987.

down a long straight road into the distance. It struck a chord. Our family holidays were dominated by walking, and my pages are full of each day's progress, written up in illustrated straggly rhyming couplets.

The quality may or may not have improved, but as an adult I have been known to write verses on the backs of Ordnance Survey maps, trying to get down what I see and feel, the very act of composition making me attentive. My long poem 'The Coastal Path'* began like that during a holiday on the Dorset coast with our firstborn, Katie, when the excitement of fatherhood made me see everything in the light of that experience:

> This morning we were up and out before
> it had even dawned on the hotels
>
> that here was a fine day:
> by nine, we had carried Katie
>
> down to Lulworth Cove, where a seam
> in the membrane protecting
>
> the county of Dorset opens into
> a soft clay womb, and the buoys
>
> bob like coloured Easter eggs until
> one turns, as you watch, into a frogman.

I sent off the whole 240-line poem to the Arvon/*Observer* competition, not only because it was one of the few that had no limit on length, but because that particular year Ted Hughes and Seamus Heaney were judging. I had few hopes of being placed, but liked the idea of those two poets reading it. In fact the poem was selected to be among the final six and featured on the front page of the *Observer*. Though at the prize-giving I was pipped by Selima Hill, who was herself about to walk the Peddars Way, the competition was something of a turning point. 'Fotheringhay', which was also placed in a subsequent Arvon competition, arrived in rather a similar manner during a walk. It was a solo expedition this time, and the poem owes much to the intense beauty of a particular September day and the feeling that I had found a site not far from our home where lines of history converged, where history was 'now and England'.* I still have the scribbled-on maps from the 1987 coastal walk and the 1989

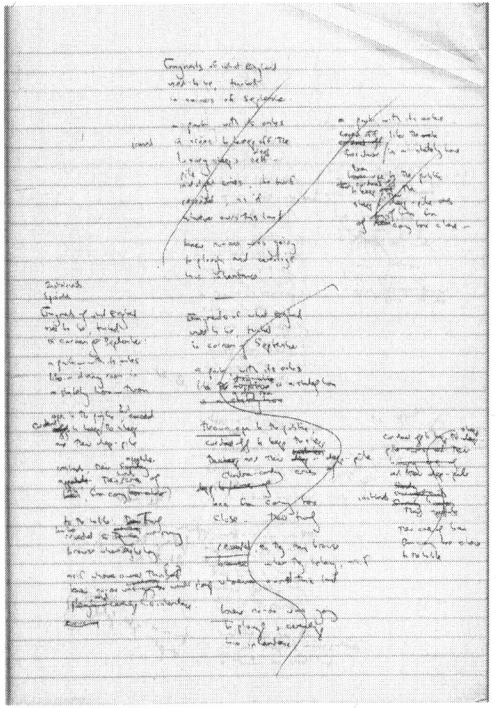

Early draft of the opening of 'Fotheringhay', September 1989.

round route to Fotheringhay. An early draft of the poem's opening is reproduced here.*

I suspect that a lot of Wordsworth's lines were written as he tramped across the hills, though allegedly he preferred a straight gravel path. There's no doubt that he composed in his head – most famously, the lines above Tintern Abbey – and there are reports of Cumberland locals seeing him, or hearing him mutter his way about the landscape. Wordsworth has always been important to me, and I like the kind of poem he favoured where the poet bumps into a stranger who imparts some kind of wisdom, as with the Leech Gatherer in 'Resolution and Independence'. What might be called the 'Encounter Poem' is almost a genre in itself, and it's something Edward Thomas developed in the early twentieth century, but it might equally apply to several of Eavan Boland's, notably 'The Achill Woman'.

I have tried a few of my own encounter poems over the years, including the title poem of *The Bocase Stone*, which describes a hike with our elder daughter when she was in single figures. We wanted to see a stone in Northamptonshire somewhat improbably associated with Robin Hood, but as we set out from the car a collie dog bounded up to us, followed by its owner, who shouted, 'That's the only happy thing you'll see today!' Or there was 'Making it Clear', about meeting an old man on top of a hill outside Perth, whose job during the war had been to locate the graves of bomber crews in Germany. These encounters tend to be with other men, for obvious reasons – the female encounters tending to be more distanced, in the vein of Wordsworth's solitary reaper. But I have expanded the genre in sequences such as the collaboration with Penelope Shuttle, *Heath*, or in the more recent 'Circles'*, a kind of 'Station Island' where I meet the ghosts of various people who have been important to me.

70

In any poem about walking, there must be a point at which the outer world recedes and the artificial lighting of the workshop predominates. That's when you discover whether you're just recycling 'Daffodils' or mimicking *Crow*. 'First follow Nature', wrote that most unnatural of poets, Alexander Pope, refusing to turn from the neat, paved way of his eighteenth-century couplets. Still, he had a point. Follow Nature, but don't chase it or give it a leafy stick to beat us with.

If Wordsworth is the best-known example of a head-down, hard-walking poet, there have also been strollers. William Cowper's epic *The Task* reveals a poet 'Happy to rove among poetic flowers' and features sections such as 'The Winter Morning Walk' and 'The Winter Walk at Noon'. His ambling iambics allow time for many an aphorism, some of which are largely forgotten – 'Nature is but a name for an effect/Whose cause is God', 'He is the freeman whom the truth makes free,/And all are slaves beside' – and some of which are very much current. When someone remarks that variety is the spice of life or claims to be monarch of all they survey; when they joke about tobacco being a pernicious weed or cry drunkenly, 'England, with all thy faults, I love thee still', before moving on to cups that cheer but not inebriate and lamenting the fact that their partner moves in mysterious ways, they are quoting William Cowper.

Cowper's rambling heirs would include a diverse collection of modern poets. Norman Nicholson, certainly, who came from and remained in Wordsworth's Lake District, but was drawn to Cowper's Home Counties Christianity and wrote a book about him. Anne Stevenson, too, whose 'Walking Early by the Wye' is just one of several she wrote on the subject. Charles Tomlinson describes walks in Gloucestershire and Italy. Jeremy Hooker favours Hampshire and Wales. Mimi Khalvati keeps returning to her Isle of Wight childhood and 'The Chine'. Benjamin Zephaniah used to jog through the Lincolnshire Fens, even if his subjects were drawn from the city. Then there are those urban wanderers such as Roger Robinson ('I walk through Brixton…'), Roy Fisher (notably *City* and *A Furnace*), Thomas Kinsella ('Nightwalker') – or almost anything by the gimlet-eyed C.K. Williams.

The Devil's Chimney near Cheltenham.

Ivor Gurney was also more in the Cowper than the Wordsworth camp, quite apart from his precarious mental health, noting how 'One comes across the strangest things in walks', more interested in the actual walk than the destination. The so-called Devil's Chimney, pictured here, was one of Gurney's favourite subjects, set in an area he returned to obsessively in his verse and indeed his music. I made a point of walking out to it when I found myself in Cheltenham for my first post-lockdown poetry reading in 2021. There was good reason why Gurney responded so enthusiastically in his London mental institution when Edward Thomas's widow, Helen, had the brilliant idea of taking him Ordnance Survey maps to study. As is well known, Edward Thomas enjoyed strolling with Robert Frost, and it was his indecision over which path to take that prompted one of the most famous poems in the American canon. But it is evident from many of his own poems and prose potboilers that Thomas was a serious long-distance walker, inheritor of Wordsworth's more determined approach.

We sense that instinct still in the work of older contemporary British poets – in the poetry and prose of Alice Oswald or Kathleen Jamie; in Simon Armitage's much-hyped traversal of the South West Coast Path or Lydia Kennaway's barely noticed *A History of Walking*; in Alistair Elliot's traversal of the Appian Way or P.J. Kavanagh's 'Severn Aisling' about travelling from the estuary to the source of the Severn.

But it is, I think, the Americans – though not Wallace Stevens – who have taken the poem-as-walk to a whole new level. With that in mind, I'd like to make a brief diversion from a somewhat eroded and too-much-trodden route to

JG and father, lost as usual.

introduce two American poets little known in the UK, poets for whom walking was vital: A.R. Ammons and Peter Kane Dufault.

The description of Peter Kane Dufault's work as 'nature poetry for grown-ups' was in fact P.J. Kavanagh's, made light-heartedly, no doubt, but the remark does say something about what we have come to expect from the genre. The English poet, critic and columnist Kavanagh described to me in a letter how he came across Dufault while out walking in upstate New York. He did not know him for a poet, but said cheerfully to the fellow chopping logs that he found all the No Trespassing signs about the woods rather daunting. Dufault was so taken with this word 'daunting' that they started chatting: he 'relaxed the wrinkles on his forehead, his eyes softened and he said, "What can I do for you?".' In fact, Kavanagh had been looking for a cottage which had belonged to the novelist John Cowper Powys and Dufault was delighted not only to show him where it was, but to give him a walking stick with Powys's initials on it, which he had received from the cottage's former owner.

Dufault writes in what is one of the most effective late twentieth-century modes for those who can manage it: 'prosody in the bedrock/and roll of the world', the ear guiding, the eye monitoring shape, line break; rhyme reinforcing where appropriate – sometimes rather eccentrically rhyming word-stem with prefix – and never any feeling of rigidity. There is something of the considerably more famous A.R. Ammons in his tendency to dense philosophical speculation, his exploration of science and science's big questions. He can even do 'really short poems' like Ammons. Americans philosophise naturally in their verse and Dufault is no exception. There is a real spiritual hunger in his writing, too. What is unusual is the wry, detached note that sounds even in his intensely inward-looking pieces such as his Dream Poem, 'Oneiric', in memory of his daughter.* In the poem he wonders, through intricate filigree of clause and line break, whether 'a single quantum' of her might still exist: 'the/particle *sine qua non* her/body had formed on, so in-/finitesimal a thing solidarity's/anyway never existed for it'.

Dufault could well have fitted into my chapter on dreams, as he is clearly attracted to them, like many American poets. His 'Trash', for instance, whose title might bring to mind Ammons's controversial and extraordinary late book, *Garbage*, is about 'the trash of thought… our oldest/waste-problem' and how dreams 'reach down, down/into whatever we've been,/and believe utterly buried'.

Whether it is the word 'trash' which makes me remember his comments on my own poems, I'm not sure, but in a letter from the late 1990s he first expressed doubts about my metres after which he explained how his came from sixty years of 'fiddling, banjo-picking and piping'. Then with almost audible emphasis he remarked on the undeniable fact that I'm a '<u>walker</u>', that nearly every poem I sent him seemed to involve 'a <u>walk</u>', before quickly reassuring me that he didn't mean my muse was wingless but like the American wild turkey 'it'll spread its wings when necessary, but it would rather walk than run, and rather run than fly.' I wish I had met Peter, but although we talked of it the occasion never presented itself and he died in 2013.

According to A.R. Ammons, who was roughly contemporary with Dufault, the universe is fairly brutal and unresponsive. Ammons's love songs tend to be oblique, as when he looks at 'Rings of birch bark' left in the woods after the wood itself has rotted, and imagines how this 'white song will/hug us together in the/woods of some lover's head'.* In other words, 'so long lives this and this gives life to thee'.

In the UK, Ammons's invisibility has been largely due to the fact that he has never been taken up by a British publisher, so his many books have seldom reached the bookshops. Norton's immense and immensely expensive two-volume *Complete Poems* is hardly going to change that. Yet Ammons should be easily appreciated by any reader accustomed to a Wordsworthian view of the world. For all the apparent severity, we are in good company on a walk with Archie Ammons, though we must expect him to interpret the landscape for us, to draw aesthetic guidance from it, as he does at the end of his most famous stroll round New Jersey's 'Corsons Inlet', where he concludes that there can be no 'finality of vision', that he has 'perceived nothing completely,/that tomorrow a new walk is a new walk.'*

Revealingly, one of Ammons's friends said that he had never known anyone who loved conversation so much and wondered if the poetry was in effect a concentration of his everyday talk. That he makes a good companion is particularly true in his long poems, such as the engrossing *Tape for the Turn of the Year,* * which I have already touched on in my chapter 'A Happy Medium'. You may recall that it began when the poet decided to put a reel of adding-machine paper into his typewriter and type a journal on it. In effect he was doing what Paul Klee did when he said he would take a line for a walk.

The Ammons style is essentially dramatic, and like good script writing it is economical. The knack of reading him – as with Dufault, as indeed with Gerard Manley Hopkins – is to catch the subtle turns and shifts of his syntax, to keep up with the games he plays with us as he breaks lines. One might say it's more of a tightrope walk: one must know the precise tension and balance. Ammons usually writes perfectly grammatical sentences, but the sense has to be hunted down.

Take 'Transfer', which opens:

> When the bee lands the
> morning glory bloom
> dips some and weaves:

The line layout leads us to expect that 'lands' is transitive, that the bee is somehow landing something; when our eye reaches the second line we realise this can't be so, unless it is somehow landing the morning glory. 'Bloom' can be a verb or a noun; so can 'dips'. It is only by the time we reach 'weaves' and have factored in the Americanism 'some' that we catch up with ourselves, the British reader perhaps lagging behind a little. That colon – invariably Ammons's punctuation of choice – gives us some breathing space, before the poem heads for home relatively straightforwardly: 'the coming true of/ weight/from weightless wing-held/air/seems at the touch/implausible.'

'Heading for home' could be the key to any walking poem. It's not unlike the progress of a symphony away from and back to the tonic or home key. With that in mind, I even called my 2003 collection *The Home Key*, though also because it had a long poem about the medium Daniel Dunglas Home.

I always associate my childhood home with walking because we didn't own a car. My father was a rather brittle diabetic, and my parents felt it would not be safe for him to drive; and naturally it was out of the question that my mother should be the one to learn. Wherever we went we walked. For a day out in London, we walked to Hounslow Central station, a couple of miles away. To get to school, I walked. And our holidays – well, you'll remember those holiday diaries I mentioned... If for example we were going to climb Snowdon, as we did one summer, it was accepted that we would have to walk a few miles from the guesthouse to the bus stop in order to get off at a point we could access the mountain; and then at the end of the day we'd have to get the bus back and walk again. The remarkable thing on reflection is that we had totally unsuitable shoes, and utterly inadequate bags. Rather than invest in rucksacks, or knapsacks as they were often called, for some reason we favoured the duffel bag with its thin cord, perfectly designed to cut into the shoulder. One of my earliest writing endeavours was a school holiday diary narrated entirely from the point of view of the duffel bag – illustrated here, just a little scarily.

1960s duffel bag as omniscient narrator.

75

There are innumerable poets who, like Wallace Stevens, never learnt to drive – so many, in fact, there was even a BBC Radio 4 documentary about them.* I doubt if there are many who don't walk, because there is no better way to clear the head. Nor is there a better way to get to know a place. Footpaths in particular hold a kind of sacred fascination for me, which can't be unconnected to what the Aborigines felt for their songlines. When I see a clear pathway cut through a wheatfield, starting apparently nowhere and heading apparently nowhere, I wonder what originally led people to walk that route. It usually turns out to be a church; but ley lines can suggest stranger reasons. 'Generations have trod, have trod, have trod', as Hopkins put it.

My family and I have followed in the footsteps of many poets over the years, from Yeats at Coole to Sorley Maclean on Skye, from Rainer Maria Rilke in Paris to Georg Trakl in Salzburg. The iambic walking rhythm, the slow engaging with a route familiar to the writer, the shucking off of modern surfaces and reroutings: there is nothing like it for reaching a deeper understanding of the poet.

P. GERARDUS HOPKINS OBIIT JUN. 8 1889 ÆTAT. AN. 44

A detail from the monument marking Gerard Manley Hopkins's grave, Dublin.

A footpath in Cambridgeshire.

Not surprisingly, when Jane and I were in Dublin a year or two ago for the launch of Dennis O'Driscoll's posthumous *Collected*, we not only took the bus out to Glasnevin cemetery to visit Hopkins's grave – or his name, at least, on the Jesuit memorial – but we also walked across the city to see where he had lived when at University College.

Dublin is an ideal city for poet-trailing, whether it's Patrick Kavanagh or James Joyce; and the very pavements have quotations embedded in them. One of the great poets of the urban walk is that distinguished celebrant of Dublin, Thomas Kinsella, who turns everything into a mythical quest.* This idea of walking through and out to the fringes of the city – like the stroller in Robert Frost's 'Acquainted with the Night' – is perhaps a hint for the future of what might be thought of as an endangered genre: pastoral.

Since Eliot first remarked on the smell of steaks in passageways, readers of poetry have been encouraged to distance themselves from the idea that there can be a modern version of traditional pastoral. Never mind that the entire corpus of writing about the First World War depends on it or that it is the kind of poetry readers really rather like – the New, we were assured, cannot mean the Natural. However, pastoral poetry is not the same as nature poetry. William Empson famously extended the definition of the genre to include virtually any literature that represented moral ambivalence. But one of its chief hallmarks is the tension between city and country, the mechanical and the natural, between what is fashionable and what has traditionally been thought to endure. Seen in this light, Stephen Spender's 1930s pylons are as much of the genre as anything by 1960s Ted Hughes, whose work, heavily influenced by the First World War poets, seemed to mark a return to it.

But in Hughes, even after he became a 'courtier' and planted his knot garden in *Rain-Charm for the Duchy*, there was never the sense that he valued the city and its ingenious artifice as the Elizabethans did, who were walkers without even thinking about it and to whom the pastoral was fundamental. What Hughes did offer was a new way of writing about the countryside which did not involve Georgian tropes, and was at least returning to Tennyson's 'nature red in tooth and claw'. Moreover, he was prepared to get his boots dirty, and understood that many of us – like the hero of his unforgettable short story, 'The Rain Horse' – are not. Now poets have had time to absorb Hughes's influence, now that they have also read the *Collected Poems* of his contemporary Geoffrey Hill, whose pastoral credentials are beginning to feel less costive, we can detect green shoots of a New Pastoral.

Lacking a Mary or Philip Sidney to provide us with an *Arcadia*, we might do well to follow two contemporary poets down a rather unprepossessing yet very English track. *Edgelands** is a series of 'journeys into England's true wilderness', taking us into a peculiarly twenty-first-century landscape, part ornamental maze, part wasteland. Paul Farley and Michael Symmons Roberts write in prose, but it's really only the line breaks that are lacking as we are guided through woodlands and gardens, past canals and on to piers, but also into retail parks and warehouses and airports and driving ranges, a landfill site,

On the downward path.

a container yard, a sewage farm. These are hardly the idealised rural locations one might expect, yet there is something idyllic about many of them. If pastoral is to survive anywhere today, it is surely in these collaborative fringes, and this is the kind of scrubby patch on which poets have begun pitching their tents. Pastoral as festival: park the car, start walking, escape the responsibilities of the 9–5 for the sake of mud and music…? Or begin to think seriously about it all – as John Wedgwood Clarke does in his collection *Landfill** or Angela France in her *Terminarchy.**

Next

There is always waiting: on the phone, online, or in a layby
at a bus stop that has no timetable, knowing the bus
has either gone or doesn't exist. Or with a crying baby

in the doctor's, name after name called, and the interfering
smile of one who talks and another you might have taught
who's waited all these years to tell you… Or you're standing in pouring

Monday outside the butcher's to Friday at the post office
or the bank or waiting for coal. Something will turn up. The golden
hosts (*please take your cash*) are pushing through clay and there are cafés

on the pavement again and we are ready to be served, to taste
a coffee that hasn't cooled, to get the bill, to pay
and let the lights change: home for an appointment and a fasting

blood test. The butcher is empty now. They are closing
the post office. We sit and wait for the news at 6
and 7 and 10. To hear how badly England are losing.

For the weather. And a trail for something on Egypt. Finish writing
your diary, lock up desire, let sleep make you drop *The God
Delusion* and enter your dream – the one where you are always waiting.

Waiting

One of my favourite poems is Matthew Arnold's 'The Scholar-Gipsy', which tells the story of 'the Oxford scholar poor… Who, tired of knocking at preferment's door,/One summer morn forsook/His friends, and went to learn the Gipsy lore', hoping to impart this wisdom to the world in due course. He, or his ghost, is regularly seen haunting Oxford and its environs still pursuing '*one* aim, *one* business, *one* desire', always waiting for 'the spark from heaven'.*

Arnold was talking about inspiration, a word poets try to avoid these days. It's tangled up with that problematically male notion of 'the Muse' and with clichéd footage of Wordsworth wandering among daffodils or Coleridge being interrupted by the person from Porlock. 'Footage' is the right word, I think, because films about artists invariably try and fail to show the process of 'being inspired'. Another reason for wariness is that you never know whether what you're feeling is actual inspiration or – well – 'fake Muse'. I have folders full of what I once believed to be major creative projects, dog-eared and yellowing now. Tennyson probably thought his unreadable verse dramas would confirm his reputation. Hardy felt he'd be immortalised for *The Dynasts*.

In spite of which, inspiration undoubtedly exists, and it's what even the most level-headed writers are quietly waiting for. It's the reverse of writer's block, but, like that block, it feels as if it will never end, which is another of the dangers. I can't be the only poet to have closed my laptop believing I could pick up where I left off, to find next morning I'm a mere empty vessel. When you're 'in form', you're like a cricketer for whom the ball curves away to the boundary with almost mystical ease. That feeling of being on a roll is hard to better. Until the rolling stops and you need the fuel marked 'I', which is where poets especially run into trouble and have famously found themselves drawn to dubious filling stations of one kind or another.

I'll resort to tea, but anything stronger would make things much worse. The likes of John Berryman or Dylan Thomas, however, couldn't cope without alcohol. For others it's been sex or the occult. Sylvia Plath found inspiration in the very proximity of death. Much less interestingly – as you will have gathered from the last chapter – I tend to simply go for a walk. Or read non-fiction. Some quirky fact, some detail of history, anything about the area where I live, or where I grew up, may spark a poem. Place is always an inspiration to me. Going on holiday can work, though you need to be open to the unexpected. Just because you're in Rome, it doesn't mean your poem is going to be about Rome.

I have had many conversations about this with my good friend Stuart Henson, often brought on by the question of fatigue. We taught together and would exchange news of our writings most days. We often fell back on a remark we attributed to Geoffrey Hill about how the state of exhaustion can be very creative. Well, it can be. But so can the state of relaxation.

Our 2021 collaboration, *a Post Card to** is made up of poems that simply couldn't wait, since we had solemnly undertaken to send them to each other when we were on holiday. I think it was I who started the exchange, with a sonnet about waiting for

Postcards featuring sonnets exchanged between JG and Stuart Henson.

inspiration. I am in Somerset. It is raining. 'Time passes/And nothing is on the page.' I imagine my friend saying 'one can't spout/poetry like rain…'

> One must cast
> gently into the stream, into that blue, fast-
> flowing moment when the mind is in spate;
> lean quietly on the Chinese bridge; and wait
> for the line to quiver, the reel to at last
> unwind, wrestling with – unable to see –
> this silvery form, a sonnet (from JDG).

Stuart was generally better than me at getting the postcard sent out, but in other respects he is very much a poet who is prepared to wait. While I incline to persistent battering at the rock in the hope that a shape will emerge, he prefers to sit and think about it. He brings a craftsman's eye to the task, inherited, no doubt, from his grandfather, who built a replacement Chinese bridge in his hometown of Godmanchester, even though there were no plans. He has a wonderful poem about this: 'Bridge' is a formal study in the patient processes of taking the old bridge down to measure it, then quietly putting a new one together. Naturally, at the opening ceremony, 'The men who built the bridge stood at the back./Nobody thought a workman worth the time/ to write an invitation.'*

The Chinese bridge at Godmanchester was a subject waiting to be written about, and Stuart knew it. All poets have topics they know – or don't yet know – they must one day explore. I always felt *Heath* would happen, but didn't guess it would be my friendship with Penelope Shuttle that would be the catalyst. Fotheringhay, Little Gidding – these were places tucked at the back of my mind, along with Kew Gardens; so were certain incidents from our travels such as my diabetic father's insulin reaction in the middle of a field of sugar cane near the Valley of the Kings (he was rescued by a taxi driver and taken back to the tomb-robbers' village of El-Gurnah). And Akureyri, where he was stationed during the war. You never know what will prompt the poem, but it might require nothing more than Norman MacCaig's prescription: sink into your favourite armchair with a glass of whisky and wait. For him, it was never long, and he was almost as prolific as his contemporary Scot, Iain Crichton Smith.

As I have suggested, though, drugs can be a problem for those not so productive. Unfortunately, no poet ever knows if or when the next poem is coming. We may begin to feel like frauds, to question our vocation. Who can blame us for our impatience, our eagerness to find some poetic Viagra? Remembering the examples of Berryman and so many others, it's undoubtedly safer, albeit expensive, to use holidays as a stimulus rather than depending on a resilient liver. If you were Philip Larkin, you'd grumble, listen to jazz and hang around the park. If you were Elizabeth Jennings you'd just keep writing and leave it to your editor to sift out 'the genuine' from the carrier bags full of drafts.

A cheap and reliable method of making the waiting time pass more fruitfully is to go back to forgotten drafts in old notebooks and rework them. A tiny fragment of good writing can do the trick. Things start to connect. And poetry is more than anything the making of musical and meaningful connections. But in the end, as a poet you are going to be doing a lot of waiting, constantly hoping for the Scholar-Gipsy's elusive spark.

When it happens, then there is a different kind of waiting. Horace's advice to poets in his *Ars Poetica* was (in Pope's words) 'Keep your piece nine years...', which may seem excessive, but I am old enough to realise that he knew what he was talking about. Certainly, it's as unwise to post a new poem directly online as it might have been in Horace's time to circulate it in the forum. An outbreak of feverish creativity can have one serious side effect: the inability to recognise whether something is fit to be published. Pope knew all about that, besieged as he was by would-be poets asking his advice:

> 'Nine years!' cries he, who high in Drury Lane
> Lull'd by soft zephyrs through the broken pane,
> Rhymes ere he wakes, and prints before term ends,
> Obliged by hunger and request of friends:
> 'The piece you think is incorrect: why take it,
> I'm all submission, what you'd have it, make it.'

Many pieces of writing feel like a work of genius to the genius who has just finished them. That feeling can last quite a while. We all feel like geniuses when we are writing fluently. But realisation will dawn, and it's better that it dawns on the author than the reader.

What Horace is really saying, what Pope was saying when he quoted him in 'An Epistle to Dr Arbuthnot', is make sure your poem is actually finished.

I have lost count of the number of times I have completed my pencil drafts, typed up the poem, redrafted it on the screen, and felt Yeats's audible 'click' that seemed to say the poem is ready to go. At that point I'll print it off and put

Hourglass.

it in a punched pocket in this year's chronological lever arch file. I have just disconnected the computer and am about to lock the study, when − wait − that second line... isn't it lifted from Ted Hughes? Or it may be an obvious blunder such as putting the wrong number of lines in a sonnet, or missing some syllables out of my syllabics. Those little things drop into the head, often when one relaxes and stops thinking about the poem − sometimes during the night. I have occasionally got out of bed and come in bare feet to my outside study in order to check something I have written. If it's not a technical detail it could be a factual one, which may be harder to correct, especially if rhyme is involved. Or a spelling. Or just some little tweak that will make the poem better. Wait. Be patient. Allow the brain to sort the problem out even if you don't think there is a problem, rather as we have learnt to let computers sort out their glitches. 'PLEASE WAIT. DO NOT TURN OFF YOUR PC', where PC stands for Poetic Creativity.

Assuming you have waited long enough to check that the poem is actually finished or to discover whether what felt like a landmark in contemporary verse was just a piece of phoney rhetoric, you may then want to see what editors think of it. Most of the waiting a writer experiences is waiting to hear back from editors. Nine times out of ten – and that's if you're lucky – what you will hear is formal words of rejection. Three or four times out of ten you will hear nothing at all. Once or twice in your writing life you may get a swift enthusiastic acceptance. That's wonderful, except that such a lightning strike of praise can blind you to a poem's true quality. There are poems I have clung to, insisted on including in a collection because a big magazine once published them, but really they are not up to the job. Maybe the editor accepted it because it was the right size for the space available or because it fitted the theme of the issue. 'Fools' approval stings', as Eliot said. And there are fools among editors as there are fools among poets. In an effort to avoid the obvious follies, there are questions I always ask myself when deciding whether or not to use a particular poem in a collection. Is it what Sylvia Plath called 'a book poem'? Is it Eavan Boland's 'poem to grow old in'? Have I waited long enough? You have to allow space to trust your own judgement and to remind yourself that there are bad readers out there, and overworked selectors.

Poets who don't give up in the early stages quickly come to recognise that their work will be regularly rejected. Climbing Parnassus you have to acclimatise yourself. Take regular breaks to survey the waste land you haven't written. You may never get to the top, but it's thick mist up there anyway. And those who have reached Parnassus's peak are all dead anyway. Patience and resilience are at least as important as learning how to handle a sonnet or blank verse.

In the days before the online 'Submittable' system, you'd wait for the brown A5 envelopes to return, the ones with your own handwriting on them (a cruel touch, that), hoping as you picked them off the mat that they wouldn't weigh too much. Sometimes there would be a standard rejection slip. Howard Sergeant of *Outposts* would write in courteous detail. Alan Ross of *London Magazine* or Jon Silkin of *Stand* would sometimes put a few lines, more usually a brief 'Almost' or 'Not quite' or something similarly upbeat. Just occasionally there would be a full-on critique. Now and then, blunt disapproval. Once I received a post-card that simply said in purple felt-tip: 'Er... no.' It's a ritual: and not without its pleasures, especially when you find a handwritten note from a well-known poet. Of course, they themselves will have gone through this, and I do have a certain respect for those who do the rejecting. I like to think there are editors out there who are brave enough to say no to a poem by a famous name if it's not good enough – and all of us write poems that aren't good enough. Anyone

A small selection of JG's rejection slips.

who's judged a poetry competition or simply put together a poetry submission will know that only by rejection can anything half decent emerge. And accept-ance isn't everything. The most depressing magazines to find yourself in are those where everything and everyone has been granted admission.

So what should you do as a writer when you've waited and waited, and then the answer comes back: 'Sorry, but...'? With poems sent to magazines, that's life. But when it's your lovingly curated collection, or the novel you've redrafted three times, or the play you've dreamt of seeing at the National, that's another matter. Friends – if you dare tell any friends – will console you with stories of *Lord of the Flies* and goodness knows how many other classics that were endlessly turned down. And you will be assured that rejection will make you stronger, which is true. If there's one thing any author needs it's persistence. Another is hope. If a manuscript is rejected, send it out again as quickly as possible – then there is always the thought that someone might at least be reading it. It's all about the waiting.

But as the rejection slips mount up, other than telling yourself that tastes vary, that you don't like their list anyway, that it's them not you, it's worth just making sure that it *isn't* you. The most beneficial effect of a 'with regret' note is that it does encourage you to reassess your work, to read it as a stranger has read it, who's maybe spotted something quite obvious that you overlooked.

So, dear reader, if you recognise this scenario and would like my advice: by all means be angry with editors, but don't write off to them and say so – and don't write off the advice they give you either.

Eventually someone accepts your work. That's when the next period of waiting begins, because they are already committed to the year x, so the earliest they can possibly produce it is… My second book, with Bloodaxe, took several years to come out after acceptance, and as luck would have it we were living in the USA by the time it appeared. In fact, we weren't even there, but on holiday across the border in a suburb of Toronto. I remember our hosts coming down the garden with a package containing *The Tutankhamun Variations*. I don't think the fact that I was out of the country did my sales any good, and in 1991 there was no social media to promote the book. It's always been the case that you have to think on a geological timescale when publishing poetry, and the shrewdest publishers will be prepared to keep volumes in print or at least ready to be printed on demand. I concur with Geoffrey Grigson's belief that we have to think vertically about the popularity of certain poems: there may be few readers at any one point in time, but over the years they mount up.

Of course, the nimble pamphlet is rather a different case from the oil tanker of a full collection, and while pamphlets were in decline from their extraordinary abundance during the 1960s and 70s, the Michael Marks Award single-handedly made them fashionable again. I have been lucky enough to have had a few very swift pamphlet appearances. One was published by the superbly

named Carnivorous Arpeggio press – rivalled only by the poetry magazine, *Spectacular Diseases* – and it consisted merely of two short translations of Oskar Loerke. I was very pleased to see this at a time when not much else of mine was appearing, but unfortunately Loerke's German publisher somehow found out about the 'pamphlet' – a single sheet folded into two pages with a poem on each, plus a green cover – and sent a chillingly formal letter ordering us to withdraw the book. The publisher told me he had already sold almost the entire print-run (of fifty copies), so it hardly mattered, but I've been very careful about permissions ever since.

I would say that the most memorably swift appearance was my *Achill Island Tagebuch,** which I

Achill Island Tagebuch *(Redfoxpress, 2018).*

sent off for consideration just after Christmas 2019 and had accepted on New Year's Eve. I was holding a copy by February. This was a handmade limited-edition hardback too, with illustrations, my twenty-four sonnets stitched together in a cottage on a cliff above Silverstrand beach, Doogort. Ironically, it would have been well worth waiting for. But the advantage to the publisher of moving quickly is that there is no time for the poet to revise anything. The advantage to me was that this was the record of a trip that had just happened.

We poets live permanently under the sign of a feather being dropped into the Grand Canyon – and no editor ever suggests that our books might actually sell. *You think your feather's so special it's going to echo?* Even the major poetry lists tend to need support from, say, an Andrew Lloyd Webber musical. Nevertheless, verse *can* find a market, particularly when there's a powerful human story, or if it taps into some current obsession. And occasionally because of the actual words.

The small world of the small press, where most poets huddle, depends heavily on the writer's willingness to help with marketing rather than to sit and wait for reviews or sales figures. It's not always very glamorous, but it's better than the alternative, which is oblivion; so poets will usually have a story to tell – and some, like Ian McMillan, have poems to tell it for them – about their experience of readings. Dennis O'Driscoll wrote a marvellous essay on this subject in which he quotes Thomas Lynch's remark that 'for poetry readings, the general rule is that if the poet is outnumbered it is a success'.* We have all known what it's like to be introduced by someone who has no idea who we are or what we've done, and cares even less. Or to listen to apologies because there's a rival event in the next town. Or to hear how so-and-so, who can't be with us, usually never misses. Every poet worth her or his salt has attended an unlikely event in the unlikely hope that someone at the library/town hall/village fete might be looking for poetry – their kind of (not very easy) poetry. Or has been allowed to sit in a corner of their local bookshop, if it still exists, ignored for an entire afternoon. Poets who are very hands-on may even have taken their cue from Jon Silkin, who used to buttonhole people in pubs, approach cinema queues, engage with anyone whose eye he could catch and somehow convince them that *Stand* magazine was what they needed to make their lives complete. But Dignity usually intervenes: would Geoffrey Hill have done this?

So much depends not on a red wheelbarrowful of books in the high street, but on the Internet. Forty years ago, when my first collection came out, book promotion involved literal cutting and pasting, photocopying, sticking leaflets in envelopes and putting stamps on them. I still send publicity postcards by snail mail to older friends. But the alternative email-shot is a pretty intrusive kind of advertising, so it comes down to Twitter/X and Facebook, Instagram, Threads, Bluesky and even TikTok – ideally something where there's a link to be clicked for a quick sale. And what about the blurb? As a poet you might even have to write your own, especially if you're the only one who understands the book. Easier than that other operation: the request for an endorsement. The rule used to be that your slim volume would only quote published reviews, though you'd sometimes see a phrase cropped from a celebrity rejection slip: 'very ambitious' or 'unlike anything else I have read'. But who can wait for that these days? So the commissioned puff began its rise.

Station sign relocated in bus shelter at Adlestrop.

We are all waiting for a train that very probably won't arrive. Or perhaps it's arrived and we don't even know we are on it. Did Edward Thomas have any idea what the result would be of that brief stop on his journey from London in June 1914? He was dead within three years and wouldn't have expected to be remembered as anything other than a writer of reviews and potboilers. He could hardly have guessed that 'Adlestrop' would become one of the most popular poems in English and an archetypal poem about waiting.

Those few poets who do achieve anything like fame in their lifetimes don't seem to have been any the happier for it. Poets Laureate are frequently struck dumb. Even getting on to the exam syllabus just means you are constantly receiving emails. Many of the poets who matter most to me are anything but household names, and never will be. Although they may briefly have been acquainted with fame, it's not what Michael Drayton, George Gascoigne, Walter Savage Landor, Edmund Blunden, Wilfrid Gibson, Kathleen Raine, Sheila Wingfield, Vernon Watkins, Kamau Brathwaite, Charles Tomlinson, John Haines, Freda Downie or Molly Holden are waiting for: it's people to go on reading them, even if there's only a handful in each generation.

Pavement Artist

Rain has filled all the streets
With mirrors
CHARLES TOMLINSON

Looking through holes in the road
into the sky, I walk back
from the doctor's. Too many old
poets are still trying to dance

round chimney pots. Faking
cheery grime in their emissionless
cartoon world, they weep free
verse for the children, the homeless and pigeons

when they should be putting their feet up
or resting their repetitively strained
imaginations. But it's the holes
in the everyday that set us off –

like Mr Banks flying his kite,
or that other Tomlinson, who looked
until the light went out of his eye,
and showed us the way in.

Watching

These days people tend to watch more than they look. 'Watching' suggests the action is elsewhere, probably on a screen. The distinction is a subtle one, however. Birdwatchers might just as easily be said to be 'looking at' movement in the hedge or above a copse. But the word 'watch' carries some suggestion of 'watching over', of staying awake and alert, which is what poets need to do. I admire those who can, like Edward Thomas, Geoffrey Grigson – or Molly Holden.

Rather a forgotten figure today, Holden was one whose attention to her immediate environment was second to none. Obliged to slow down by her multiple sclerosis, she produced a distinctive body of poetry about the natural world, low-key but of high quality. She could write an entire poem about the difference between the bark of a pear tree and a crack willow. 'It is not bred in me to overlook/the close at hand, the particular', she wrote, lamenting that (given her condition) it's 'just as well'. Holden is part of that community of poets who are happy to sit back and watch the others court fame and acclaim. Some of the best are still watching from the antiquarian bookshelves centuries after their deaths. Holden's own work – she died in 1981 – has been long out of print, the individual volumes resting with other 'Phoenix Living Poets' (Bowden, Broade, Couroucli, Earley) awaiting their resurrection from the ashes of oblivion. An illustrated fine press limited edition of the work appeared in the US in 2021 at around $1000. The 1987 Carcanet *Selected* is only available second-hand for around £50. That suggests there is a demand out there for her kind of attention to minutiae. It also suggests that we may have been distracted from some genuine poetry by glitzier, noisier, more 'relevant' alternatives.

By the late 1980s, having spent some years watching over classes and then sinking down in front of a TV, I had myself rather lost the art of looking. A decade earlier when Jane and I were working at the BBC, we'd had a number of artist friends and were always being encouraged to look closely at their work or pictures they recommended. It sometimes felt as though we were being drawn into their vision – literally so when on one occasion we found ourselves coming down a footpath near Mapledurham House towards distant figures with an easel. It turned out to be our friends, Gill and Ian Edwards, who were painting the view we had walked into and who didn't even know we were in the area.

We had a particular friendship, too, with a Russian couple, exiles Jane came to know through the BBC Russian Service: Oleg Kudryashov specialised in etchings, and presented us with a series of them which he had titled 'Windows'. They are memories of Moscow, but also a reminder to stay watchful, and to keep looking.* Living in Egypt for two years, we had no choice: the experience forced one to take note of everything and put it on paper. I wrote, but I also sketched in pen-and-ink, as my grandfather had done before me (his were caricatures, chiefly, like the one reproduced here from when he worked for Mercedes) and as our younger daughter, Rosie, still does.* Thereafter, the habit rather fell away. Was it just laziness? Or growing up? As a child, a teenager, even as a young man, I had been able to look without knowing I was doing so, which is perhaps why so much of the imagery in my poems is from those Hounslow years. How was it that in the late 1980s I suddenly remembered the importance

A drawing by JG's grandfather, Clarence Melville Greening.

of using my eyes? Could it have been because baby Katie had arrived and I was watching her as she studied the world for the first time?

In autumn 1988 I began writing my thirty-two *Huntingdonshire Eclogues*, consciously trying to make myself look properly at where we had settled, whether I liked the place or not. That place happened to be Cromwell country, and while there aren't many lessons on the art of poetry to be learnt from the Lord Protector – Andrew Marvell would be a better guide – his remark that he should be painted 'warts and all' is sound advice. I don't have a bad eye; I can still draw a quick sketch on a jotter or a chalkboard, but I haven't always described effectively in my poetry. My imagination is such that when I look hard at something, say an apple, rather than seeing the 'appliness' that Paul Cézanne would have seen and tried to capture, I tend to begin making comparisons. The apple turns into a face, a planet, a bomb, a ball, or takes me to Eden, to Avalon and Robert Graves's 'Apple Island', to the Beatles' last LPs, to Isaac Newton or Alan Turing.

I can date my first 'proper poem' to March 1977. I remember composing it in an orchard beside the bungalow where I was living with two fellow postgraduate students in Brampford Speke, near Exeter. It was a magical place, more convenient for Dartmoor than for the university, and with little else nearby other than The Agricultural Inn. This was essentially the front parlour of an elderly woman's cottage, and remains the most extraordinary pub I've ever visited. Our bungalow was perched on the banks of the River Exe, which flooded regularly, rising dangerously close to my bedroom window as I sat reading Ted Hughes's *Crow*. That experience was diverting enough, and something I would later write about, but it was the orchard that fascinated me at the time. The area of west London where I grew up had once been orchards, and the two apple trees in our garden were thought to be survivors, so it could be the word made me feel at home. Anyway, I wanted to convey what I was feeling by capturing what I was seeing, and I sensed there was poetry in those trees. I watched them develop, willing myself to look closely, to *attend*. Wasn't it D.H. Lawrence who described poetry as 'an act of attention'? There wouldn't have been any apples in March, but I certainly recall staring very hard at the patterns the twigs made, sensing that I had finally found what I was looking for. It wasn't just the tree coming into bud.

'The Orchard' was published in *Bananas*, and was one of my very first appearances in print. It felt like a watershed, and the publication seemed to impress Ted Hughes when we exchanged letters a few months later, but that may have been because he was having an affair with the editor, Emma Tennant. I still have a copy of that striking tabloid-style magazine, from Spring

1979, No. 14, priced 50p, and about the size of today's *Daily Mail*. Its yellowing cover carries a photograph of the same Edwardian model of typewriter I had worked on at home for years, alongside the names of some contributors: Jenny Joseph, Alan Sillitoe, Martin Booth... And inside are Maura D. Dooley, William Scammell, Helen Dunmore, Yehuda Amichai, Peter Redgrove, whose glorious poem 'The Apple Broadcast' appears in full for the first time, and puts mine to shame.

I had never reprinted 'The Orchard' until Kevin Gardner chose to include it in my 2023 American Selected, *The Interpretation of Owls*. I had preferred to begin my earlier selection, *Hunts*, with a later poem,

A copy of the literary magazine, Bananas, *ed. Emma Tennant.*

'Baby-arctic', which appeared alongside it in the same issue of *Bananas*. Looking again at that original smudgy typed-out A4 sheet (yes, A4 had just about replaced foolscap) there are things I still like about it, such as the opening nine lines:

```
      The Orchard

Passing by an orchard at a distance
The trees may be seen to grow in lines
Certain inches at certain times

But climbing over the stile
That separates the road from the trees
Where the speed-limit drops

And winding down my windows
That are misted up with travelling
I see now:
```

Typescript of 1977 poem, 'The Orchard'.

Thereafter I am showing off too much – something else to watch! – and it betrays the influence of Eliot in the declaratory, sermonising manner. Then

A reel of Standard 8 cine film.

it veers towards the Georgians, whose verse dramas I had been reading for my dissertation, and the Metaphysicals must be behind the ersatz computing conceit which I will refrain from quoting. There's also an uncomfortable mixture of colloquial and rather fastidious diction. Yet I'm quietly impressed by my efforts to use, as Ted Hughes might have put it, both sides of my brain. And I'm pleased by the wit of 'two twigs that make an equals sign', by some nice use of internal rhyme, by verse that does feel genuinely free. Some of the phrases even linger in the memory. If we happen to spot a bird hopping around our fruit tree, Jane can still be relied on to quote the ending: 'pecks all the eaters/and sings'.

I think of myself as a listener, for whom music is the crowning art form; but I have applied myself to a fair number of arts that involve watching. For much of my youth, for instance, I was determined to be a filmmaker, and did indeed make many films on our family cine camera – 8mm rather than 16mm, and reel-to-reel 'Standard 8' in preference to the more popular cassettes of 'Super 8'. This camera arrived when I was still in single figures myself and when we didn't yet have a television, so it's not surprising I was hooked from the start. The Standard 8 format made editing possible, and it was always the editing I loved. For a good while I was preparing to train as a film editor after I left school; I even visited BBC Ealing Studios, where all those famous comedies had been made, and was shown by a professional how studio video was interwoven with film for exterior shots, which was the only option in those days. But it turned out that since I was colour blind, I was ineligible. And as no one suggested I do otherwise, I gave up the idea and applied to university instead.

But I left behind me a body of work that Stanley Kubrick would be proud of – at least, I did what he did and, once I had got over my Dalek animation phase, tried my hand at every possible genre, from horror, to sci-fi, to spy* as well as various homages: silent film for *Hilarious History* and Ealing Comedy itself in *Six of the Worst*. This *Kind Hearts and Coronets* rip-off involved my friend Stephen Hanvey playing all six villains. His considerable acting skills were put to better use

Stephen Hanvey in Gordon *(1984) at Edinburgh.*

later on a much-reduced scale at the Edinburgh Fringe, when he performed a one-man play I wrote for him about Gordon of Khartoum. There was a certain occasion when it proved to be a one-man play performing to a one-man audience.

The skills I taught myself with a reel-to-reel editing machine, a razor, some film cement and nail polish remover may seem a far cry from those needed by a poet. But if there is one piece of advice I never tire of giving to young poets it is: don't be afraid to cut.

A favourite film of mine from those days, and the last one I ever made, was my 'mash-up' of cine I had shot during a walk through Glencoe, along the old route used by the MacDonalds who escaped the Glencoe Massacre. It was grim, misty, atmospheric weather, foolishly dangerous conditions to be fell walking, but as I climbed I kept on filming. Although I could only take silent footage, I always prepared a carefully timed soundtrack on tape, but in this case I wanted the film to illustrate the music. I had recently discovered Jean Sibelius, and in particular his late tone poem, *Tapiola*, virtually his final masterpiece before the thirty-year creative silence. Rearranging so many short lengths of celluloid to fit the music was the bridge to my work as a poet. Little did I know then that nearly half a century later I would be writing a long poem about Sibelius and that celebrated silence (discussed in the chapter 'Flitting').

The films I never got to make still niggle. One came close to being done and might even have been in 16mm. My adaptation of Wolfgang Borchert's wartime short story about a kitchen clock stuck at half-past two should really have happened. I had a cast and a camera. But rather ridiculously, I simply couldn't find a suitable clock. The other film, which was fully scripted in the approved manner with screen-shaped sketches of each shot, was my Standard 8 version of Milton's *Paradise Lost*. I had it all planned, down to the choreography of the falling angels to Bruno Walter's performance of the scherzo from Bruckner's Ninth. In this case, the problem was finding an Eve, especially given the fact that she would probably have had to remove her clothes.

Model theatre in action.

If my interest in film can be put down to lack of a television, it survived the arrival of our first, which was I believe a portable model – at least, I remember I used to lug it upstairs to my room to watch *Star Trek*, or *The Man from U.N.C.L.E.* But at the same time I was developing a love of theatre, and that can only be down to the pantomimes our grandfather took us to each year in Richmond. Panto was just about the only theatre we saw, but it was enough to stir my imagination and set some very disturbing dreams in motion about ogres in our garden shed – imagery that still finds its way into my poetry. My sister and I had been writing and performing plays for our parents since we were small. There is a photo which I hesitate to publish of all our teddies and dolls arranged on the lawn ready for the latest production. But it was my home-made model theatre that was the focus of my dramatic interests as I was leaving that ageless age which I somehow associate with *Just William*. William Brown is the better comparison than Wilhelm Meister, although Goethe's hero was as

Items from the model theatre.

passionate as I was about his puppet theatre and the genre of the puppet show has a significance for German writers unparalleled in English literature.*

As with my films, there would always be an involved soundtrack for my miniature productions, and the emphasis was on the Variety Show. The theatre itself was built from a design in my *Boy's Own Book of Hobbies*, which was the Bible of my youth. I had won it from *The Boy's Own Paper* for sending in a newspaper clipping spotted by my sister, Valerie, who should really have received the prize: 'The fire at Manchester was said to be a clear case of arson by the Chief Constable.' The structure was fairly sophisticated for the time, with a plywood proscenium and a rack where various drop-scenes could be raised and lowered, next to a highly dangerous bar of hot lightbulbs. There were footlights and a working curtain, too. The characters were all hand-drawn and attached to little blocks of wood on lengths of absurdly thick coat-hanger wire. They were wiggled as the script was read. Apart from the variety shows and a bizarre adaptation of a dull one-act play called *The Spinsters of Lush*, there was my version of *A Christmas Carol* and a full-scale *Alice Through the Looking Glass*, both with many stage effects. Marley's face appeared on Scrooge's front door; the Cheshire Cat's smile hung in the air. I would invite friends and neighbours to each performance, the tiny lit proscenium arch wrapped around with our living room curtains to conceal all my busy workings, so that it became in effect a tiny television screen.

I wrote a sonnet about those days after discovering the old equipment in my parents' attic:

> We pull my model theatre from the eaves –
> a plywood proscenium, boxfuls of scene
> changes, cut out and painted to the whims of teen-
> age imperative, characters heaped like leaves
> from thirty seasons: Beatles under divas,
> a Scrooge on an Alice, the Tiller Girls' obscenely
> sellotaped kicks, ghosts of Dickens, the Red Queen...
> Creativity's forgotten shuttle weaves
> on this quaint loom, amazed at all it made
> just to be glimpsed by friends for a gasp or two
> then swapped for the next backdrop, lit, voiced over,
> the world in a little room, pieces of card
> consummately slid and wriggled by one who
> no longer exists, imagination's lover.

How did all this feed into my poetry? Perhaps, as the sonnet suggests, it was a way of taming my imagination. I was learning ways of combining words, music and action, and as in a poem, there was only one person in charge, operating all the scene changes, doing all the voices. I only got involved in proper theatre when I was at secondary school, with a brief appearance as Barnardo in *Hamlet*. But generally I was 'callboy' for several enterprising productions by our young English teacher, who specialised in drama: *The Royal Pardon, The Knight of the Burning Pestle, Coriolanus.* Essentially I had to summon the actors from the classrooms where they were changing, but I had plenty of opportunity to watch and learn from what was happening on stage. I also kept writing my own plays, veering now towards the full-sized stage.

Best of them was my satire of 1960s politics, *Haroldianus*, which rather delighted Mr MacGibbon, but he left it to me to stage, and I didn't have the courage or the resources to put it on.

```
G.Browne) Would you proceed especially against bruvver Haroldianus
          Wilsonium ?

First P) Against him first: He's a very dog to the public!

G.Browne) Consider you what services he has done for his country.

First P) Very well. Perhaps you are satisfied with the nationalisation
         of HP sauce, check raincoats and tobacco - but for that he
         pays himself with being proud!

G.Browne) Noe, but speak not maliciously bruvver.
```

Part of the script of Haroldianus, *a spoof from JG's school years.*

At some point my love of poetry and my love of drama converged and I began writing verse plays. Although I turned increasingly to prose for the stage, verse drama became the main focus of my creative output through my twenties and thirties. My enthusiasm all seems so distant now, but my suspicion is that I was blinded to the obvious disadvantages by the fact that Shakespeare and his contemporaries had made it work so well. I wasn't alone in mistaking a pantomime horse for Pegasus, and even Yeats realised that we couldn't simply recreate Shakespeare; in fact, his verse dramas hold up well and are among the most effective written since Elizabethan times. Unlike Eliot, he believed that the audience should be aware that they were listening to verse. I read everything to be found on the subject, beginning with Eliot's essays and commentaries on his own experience of shifting from pure poetry to the poetry of the stage. His 'true Penelope' was Noël Coward, however, and I found more drama in *The Waste Land* than *The Elder Statesman*. It was downhill from *Murder in the Cathedral*, which is more like a masque.

From Eliot, I moved back and looked at earlier revivals of the genre – the plays of Tennyson, Hardy's *The Dynasts* – and by the time I came to write a dissertation on the subject* I knew of verse dramas that no one else had bothered to remember. These ranged from the huge Edwardian hits of the utterly forgotten Stephen Phillips to various Georgians such as Gordon

Bottomley, then post-war curiosities like Ronald Duncan's *This Way to the Tomb* and John Arden's controversial *The Island of the Mighty*, whose RSC premiere he and Margaretta D'Arcy picketed in 1972 because they considered the production too pro-imperialist. There were the prep school-style entertainments by W.H. Auden and radio features by Louis MacNeice – notably *The Dark Tower* – and all those forgotten Mercury Theatre productions by E. Martin Browne. There was Christopher Fry, Anne Ridler, Norman Nicholson, Charles Williams. All this was before Tony Harrison arrived and showed us on the national stage and indeed on television how it might be done better, how Eliot's idea of the verse drama that conceals its verse was not the only way. And then came Derek Walcott, Glyn Maxwell, Carol Ann Duffy, Simon Armitage, Peter and Alice Oswald, Christopher Reid – all showing different possible directions for effectively continuing the Shakespearean tradition.

During my verse drama years, I corresponded with several of the key players – you will remember Ronald Duncan berated me for sending him an ill-typed, barely legible carbon – and even met up with John Arden and Margaretta D'Arcy in a pub after a performance of *The Non-Stop Connolly Show*. On that occasion, I was berated for my political naivety. It was Ted Hughes who responded most positively when I sent him some verse plays of my own, the *Three Devon Plays*, and he expressed sympathy for the 'near-impossible' task

Programme of The Voyage of the Argo *(1993) produced at Kimbolton School.*

of writing a satisfactory drama in verse. He also told me how he discovered that both written scenes and individual speeches were almost always too long, and that scenes which seemed to read naturally as dialogue became on stage 'interminable journeys on narrow rails'. Every page, he said, had to contain the equivalent of a new dramatic surprise, 'a lump of action' and went on to make a very Hughesian analogy: the words in a play, he suggested, were like a Japanese woman married to a frightening, irrepressible Samurai.

Not that I subsequently had a great deal of success with my plays, other than a few prizes for scripts and a staged reading at Riverside Studios of *The Isis Myth*, a somewhat Eugene O'Neillish application of Egyptian mythology to my parents-in-law's story. Then there was the American Lindbergh production discussed in the following chapter. But when I was teaching, I regularly wrote scripts which I could 'test drive' in student productions. The best may well have been *The Maskes of Oliver Cromwell*, but *The Voyage of the Argo* was by far the strongest production. And I suspect the audience who experienced *Domna*, the story of Septimius Severus, in the open-air courtyard of Kimbolton Castle, won't forget it in a hurry. I still bear the scars.

Kimbolton

13.3.13

On an icy morning, I shiver past
the portico where a dead colleague

staged an open-air *Julius Caesar*
(all boys, of course). In Rome,

the cardinals have flown the green room,
hoping for a curtain before the Ides

of March. The dreamer passes,
but Catherine lay here, staying loyal

to her King and to her religion,
a single spot, behind her the monasteries,

like flats from an old-fashioned musical
being struck. My daughter spoke

those words – *Tell him in death
I blessed him.* Girls had arrived

by then and she was standing only
twenty feet from where the Queen

gave up the ghost. There is a ghost,
the cleaners will tell you. And I have

my own encounter to relate. But let's
go back to the Sistine Chapel and wait

beneath commissioned nudes for the scarlet
flowing up from steerage, anticipate

the funnelled smoke machine, the Latin
power ballad, blackout, chorus

of deckchairs (with halberds), 'Save our Souls',
and the white-clad figure entering.

Asheville Journal, 2002

Shakespeare set the challenge: how can we make poetry effective on the stage? Poets have been trying and largely failing ever since. The lyrical interlude that follows (which might be subtitled *Journal of a Play Year*) is an on-the-spot account of one theatre group's attempt to navigate the choppy lines of a verse drama. I include it as proof that poetry can sometimes be tempted out of the shadows and to show what might happen when it (and the poor devil who wrote it) have to face the public.

Suddenly I find myself in North Carolina, because of something I wrote twelve years ago, a verse drama called A Ladder in Hopewell, *which I had consigned to the reject heap. It wasn't until my old exchange partner Franklin Harris asked me if I'd anything suitable for his theatre group that I remembered it and wondered whether it might be salvaged. That conversation only came about by chance, too, since we happened to be sitting next to each other at a dinner in Kimbolton Castle, celebrating the tenth anniversary of the Fulbright Exchange we'd initiated at the school. This year's visit by American students had gone ahead, even though the attack on the World Trade Center occurred just a few weeks back. It was a strange time to be planning anything for 2002 and I'm so delighted that this is happening at all, particularly as it was in Franklin's old clapboard house in New Jersey I wrote the play, that very hot early summer of 1991 as we were emerging from the yellow-ribboned anxiety of the Gulf War. Now here I am in the South, under the creeping shadows of a ceiling fan, the cardinal birds calling, the trees clustering up against the Harrises' precipitous deck outside, July 4th on the horizon… and I'm wondering how this English interloper's play is likely to be received.*

Meanwhile, Franklin and Judy rush to order enough bottled water for the interval, take all the calls for tickets, nip out to buy a last-minute item of costume, collect the programmes… Franklin said I was welcome to follow the track through the trees down to the creek, but take a stick and put on stout shoes. 'I've only seen a snake twice in six years…' I didn't go far. No Lyme Disease here, at least, but it wouldn't be the occasion to mess with poison ivy. Judy tells me that 9/11 is still very much on everyone's mind. It was certainly on mine as I flew in over New York. She told me about a Turkish friend of theirs who was in a café in Hendersonville he had frequented for years. The proprietress called the police to say he was acting strangely. And then all the panics about spilt powder during the anthrax scares: police teams in space suits and elaborate traffic diversions because of spilt sugar in a grocery or plaster of Paris in a mailbox. I'm not sure how A Ladder in Hopewell *fits into this mood. We changed one line from the final chorus to refer to the twin towers 'of evidence and truth', since it was all about the time that had passed since the kidnap, and mentioned other key events such as the Gulf War – which, of course, Norman Schwarzkopf, son of the kidnap investigator, was to lead.*

I shall be intrigued to see how the chorus works. Franklin says they each have a little bin beneath their chair, with items in it they need to 'become' their next character. He also says they have used the ladder in all kinds of imaginative ways. He took it as his starting point.

Well, in an hour or two I shall have to go and face the music (thirties jazz, actually, rather than my original suggestions of Barber, Copland and certain American minimalists). Here comes the Englishman who dared to malign America's greatest hero. No worse than Robert Altman dissecting the English Country House in Gosford Park, *which I watched on the plane over.*

Thunder in the distance. A terrific storm last night. Not an omen, I hope. But then the first lines of the play are: 'The world is wild tonight...'

***

We arrive at the front of the theatre, which I assume is the back. Not easy to locate, tucked down an alley, beside a large and smelly garbage container. But it's very well equipped inside, although Franklin would like more lights. This is only the second or third production here and it looks very new. The audience is curved around the stage in three sections. The tiering is effective. The main problem is a couple of pillars which could affect sight lines. But they've only had one rehearsal in the actual venue.

Poster for A Ladder in Hopewell, *Asheville, 2002.*

I meet several actors. Stage staff scurry around. Lighting cues. The period slides flashed on to the two 'scrim' screens at the back – made from tobacco growers' cloth, apparently. And there's the crib that will become the ladder.

Franklin gives a pre-performance talk, and a prayer. Now they go through a warm-up procedure. Shaking their hands, waggling their heads, all ages, laughing, joking, limbering up, twisting and stretching. In the middle of all this, the absent partner, Tom, calls on Franklin's mobile. He's stuck in Colorado surrounded by out-of-control forest fires and wishing us all good luck for the opening. A rising mood of excitement. Outside, thunder clouds are thick and dark. Inside, the lighting changes and changes. Fragments of my lines come back to me. Warm-up games. Zap-zap in a circle. A great sense of the group bond. Seventeen actors who know each other intimately. Wisecracks from the cast. Ninety-nine seats in the auditorium. Can't we find that extra chair? It's for Hauptmann! Now vocal preparation: wobbling the jaw, humming, haaing. A surreal scene: Sour-sap. Wee Willy Winkie. Babababbee. Dadadadadie. Gegegegeie. Red Letter Yellow Letter. Unique New York. *Next a cacophony of favourite lines. Then they introduce themselves to me in character, with one fact about themselves. A slow circle. I respond as best I can.*

Before they all disappear, I throw out some clumsy words of gratitude at which they break into applause.

This huge tree that has grown up from the cone I planted with so much sweat (it was a hot, hot summer) those many years ago in New Jersey. Trees grow exceptionally tall in North Carolina, Judy told me yesterday.

I think of that strange psychic occurrence we read about last month, where someone had been taking pictures on the London Underground and when they were developed they found the image of Hauptmann in the electric chair superimposed. It turns out the shots had been taken as the Tube train was passing beneath the Chamber of Horrors at Madame Tussauds.

In the programme, the date of my birth has been changed to 1945. I have lost or gained nine years. 'We are the years that pass...' as the final chorus says. And really I thought this was all in the past, but then I discovered that Anne Morrow Lindbergh only died last December. And I keep hearing of people who have some personal connection with the story.

Governor Hoffman, played by the dramatically named Jennifer Szczesny, tells me that this is the most difficult part she has ever had to do. And she's the most experienced actress in the cast. Perhaps it's because she has to shift from chorus to member of the audience, to narrator and then to Hoffman as a character in the plot.

It's 7.30. I feel like I'm the condemned man. Programmes are out. The sandwich board is out. The audience filter in early. Middle-aged to old – those more likely to know the story already. I can hear them talking about what's written in the programme: my introduction, the director's comments… Franklin warns those in the front row that actors will come right up to them and they should move if that bothers them. 7.35: ten people in their seats. 7.40: twenty. Asheville's a big place. 65,000 or so. No other theatre showing anything downtown tonight, so this could be good. A broader range of ages now. Some teenagers; all sorts. It begins to feel like an audience. 7.45: thirty and rising. Sweaty palms. Plenty in the central block, but none in the two side sections. I think the theatre manager, Jackie, keeps those for latecomers. Southern drawl on all sides. 'How are y'all?' The two long syllables of the word 'South'. Individual voices vanish (thankfully) into the general chatter.

What if they hate it? Asheville is what Franklin calls a 'word-of-mouth' city, and our audiences depend on this first-night reaction. Five minutes pass and no new people. 7.55, a late surge. Seats are filling up.

Franklin has appeared to give his introductory spiel to the audience, tells them I'm somewhere out there. A few heads turn. His cell phone rings and it's a reminder from his stage manager to tell the audience to turn off theirs.

He's gone. The lights go down. Jazz and the black-and-white slides of Lindbergh and his family alternate on the tobacco-cloth screens.

***

Dawn birdsong: something – cardinals, someone said – making that strange electronic call; and a woodpecker. Others I can't identify. The same exotic delight I wanted to convey in that scene where Lindbergh sits at Sissinghurst and listens to the birds. A lyrical moment in which he hears the cuckoo and it becomes a symbol of loss and displacement. So sharp and accurate in his understanding of engines and flight patterns, he is completely at sea in this natural environment. The cuckoo is the only English bird he can identify before he's distracted by a more familiar one: a Messerschmitt 109. Ironically, Franklin couldn't find a cuckoo effect and put in a mockingbird, which threatened to make a mockery of my lines, but in fact added a piquant, surreal significance, although it's ornithologically dubious. I wonder whether it's a scene that an English audience would have 'got' more easily. Our late replacement Lindbergh seemed ill at ease with the address to 'Sleep' with its echoes of Henry IV.

Cardinals, golden orioles, a tiger butterfly and a brilliant monarch fluttering to its death at my feet. As good a metaphor as any for what I'm feeling.

We drive out with our two quarters and wrench open the first newspaper box we find – such a distinctly American experience, like putting your mail out to be collected and raising the little metal flag. I stand in the blazing heat in front of the convenience store, empty pickup trucks coming and going around me, and I read the Citizen-Times *review:* 'A Ladder in Hopewell: *historical, innovative'. Delighted, Franklin and I sweep back to show Judy, pretending it's not special and saying nothing of the fact that she gets a mention for doing 'a bang-up job with fedoras and 1930s women's hats, argyle sweaters, British rainwear and women's stockings with seams'. When Jane gets to see the review, she's amused by the reference to my use of 'the original lyrics to 'Rock a bye Baby'' ('all that education comes down to this...'). The reviewer likes the chorus ('fascinating and quite practical') and notes the allegorical reference to the execution of a carpenter on a Friday (a fact which upsets one or two of our more conservative audience members).*

We get a huge yellow copy of this write-up from a most amazingly sophisticated copy shop on the way to the theatre. It will be displayed in the foyer.

It's warm-up time again already. Swinging hips and touching toes. 'I can't reach the ground from here.' 'Let the ground reach you!' All in a circle: take it in turns to mime an activity, the first person asking 'What are you doing?' and the next replying by saying something they are not doing, which the questioner has to mime, before themselves being asked, and so on. Much hilarity. Now it's Ge-ge-ge-ge, gurragurragurra, red letter, yellow letter, unique New York...

The cast cluster around the reviews, looking anxious or thrilled. About sixty in the audience again: a little disappointed it's not full, but the review didn't give times and location. Some people are arriving in a state of irritation because they haven't been able to find us. Franklin calms them with his front-of-curtain speech, then the jazz starts up.

***

The actress who plays Anna Hauptmann does it very movingly. I spoke to her after last night's performance. She revealed that: (a) she has a master's in criminology and so has a particular fascination with this case; (b) her grandmother's name was Schoeffler, which was Anna's maiden name. She's evidently researched that part with a passion. In fact, many of the cast have become deeply involved in the historical (and not so historical) issues. Others are gushing with enthusiasm – our French cabaret singer/psychiatrist, for instance, who's a Native American and is very excited to meet a 'real writer' but has herself had quite a career as a singer. I'm just impressed to meet a Native American!

A good audience last night. About sixty again. I sold three books, and spoke to a guy who had brought his three children with him (eight, ten, eleven), all of whom were enjoying it. They'd done a project on Lindbergh at school. I spoke to little Abigail (eight), who told me the number of gallons of fuel he carried in the tank at his back when he took off!

Judy asked why Lindbergh says 'You're gonna burn baby, you're gonna burn'. In that brief soliloquy he almost becomes Hauptmann (as later Hauptmann uses language of the aviator as he approaches his death) and in the intensity of the loss of the baby, summoning all his old stoicism and determination he finds that the fears return as well.

It's my old preoccupation: the tension between opposites who are in fact twins. Cromwell and Charles I. Gordon and the Mahdi. Osiris and Seth.

I was more attentive to the minutiae last night and fully appreciated how skilfully Franklin has directed it: all that shrewd choreography, carefully balanced set pieces, constant variety of angle and mood. The choruses are really imaginatively done, with much use of the twin 'scrims'; and I like the way he has chosen to break up the lines (this is left entirely to the discretion of the director), especially that 'su-per-con-duc-tiv-i-ty' in the final chorus. The one where they list all the elements of the injustice is beautifully staged, with Hoffman moving in and out of the chorus groupings (it's quite a broad stage). And it's fun to anticipate the moments when the audience is shocked and stunned by the 'Kill Hauptmann!' outbursts. I was watching them wondering what would happen next.

Hauptmann's ability to suggest the build-up of frustrated rage inside him is impressive, though I wish he'd tone down the accent. It's still impenetrable at times.

Lots of tears during the performance, apparently: the actors get so involved and are so moved by it.

I'm moved by the fact that they are.

A quick glass of wine in a bar after tonight's performance: bongo music and salsa dancing. Then the winding half-hour drive back into the mountains.

* * *

Strange to think I put the play in a drawer for eleven years, exceeding Horace's advice to budding writers by two. Then just a couple of weeks after 9/11, this whole idea comes up. Yes, I had my reservations about letting a specifically Christian group take it on, but that's only been a positive influence and simply makes me realise how steeped in Christian symbolism my work is. I suppose a lot of my early pieces were openly so: there was one dreadful Biblical piece, which Jane laughs at, titled A Lot Falls. *About a man with two daughters… Well.*

There have, it's true, been many occasions in the run-up to these performances when higher powers seem to have come to our rescue. Franklin said that he was on the point of giving up, but knew he had to go on because I had invested so heavily in my airfare and the other members of the cast were so keen. Maybe it's like the success of Charles Augustus Lindbergh himself: triumph against the odds. In this case, the single engine is Franklin (or Lee, as I have always called him).

On the deck as the day wears on. It's like being at Treetops or some observation platform in the jungle. Two mosquito repellent burners on the table. A large earthenware chimney and wood burner, purely for 'aesthetic effect', they tell me. The inevitable rockers.

Halfway through the run.

Cicadas like the buzz of the dynamos on Hauptmann's electric chair.

Some problems with the sound cues last night – someone else was in charge – only when he'd been electrocuted did we hear it happening. And then the lights didn't go down. Poor old Hauptmann had to get up and walk away. But he comes back on as a ghost anyway. A few other late sounds – a telephone that didn't ring in time, a church bell and a Messerschmitt.

A dogfight behind me.
  Apparently Franklin was attacked by a dog when he was out jogging some months ago. A bite in the groin, just missed a main artery. The woman concerned was not concerned.

A buzzing cry; something pigeon-like; a repeated dee-dah dee-dah. Now a distant American train hooter, evoking all those old movies.

I wish the young man who plays Lindbergh would really listen *in that scene. Attention to the world, analysing it, trying to make out how it works. It's probably too late to try and convey anything of that to him, although I made one or two suggestions yesterday.*

Still can't quite grasp that I'm in North Carolina. Not far from where the Wright Brothers took off. And precisely where Edward Buncombe first gave a word to the English language, which I hope won't be applied to A Ladder in Hopewell*: Bunkum.*

This is a strange dream-like segment of time. Building something with the spirit while the bodily processes of my usual life go on 3000 miles away. A touch of the 'near-death' experience about it all, sitting here among these trees.
  That three-headed dog barks on.

The old man who plays Condon ('Jafsie') had to ask me how to pronounce Lethe. The only word anyone has asked me to pronounce.

Carl Sandburg's house before tonight's performance. Everyone stared at me as we walked in and I only realised later it's because Sandburg looks rather like me in the photos on display. He plays a one-string fiddle as far as I'm concerned, as well as his guitar. He was one of the most popular poets of the 1960s, but I wonder if he will survive. His Collected *already has the overweight, dusty feel of a Greenleaf*

Carl Sandburg's house, Flat Rock, North Carolina.

Whittier or a Longfellow. He was a poet of the people, who thought that the worst word in the English language was 'exclusive', but who should have excluded rather more from his work. The tour round his house takes pains to emphasise how his wife was just as important – as an acclaimed goat-keeper. She also constructed their bed. But Franklin points out that Judy made their filing cabinet... Mrs S. clearly kept Carl ticking over, but I only have a limited interest in goats. Franklin took a photo of me beside the rear of one, anyway. And we took a look at the 'Flat Rock' after which the settlement is called (such literally named places abound) and I sat on it. Here is where Carl Sandburg came and wrote many of his poems. I reckon he should have taken Auden's advice and found himself a windowless room instead. Thousands of books in the house, which seemed to amaze our tour guide, as did the fact that Sandburg spent so little time watching the 'idiot box', even though he had a Zenith TV in every room. Turns out he was friends with the director of the company and received a free one every year. The picture we were invited to imagine was of a cosy family spending its time folk-singing round the piano or engaging in other equally wholesome pursuits. Bring on The Simpsons. *Actually, I couldn't restrain the pangs of envy at this huge mansion and did begin wondering what would happen if my play were a hit... As Anne Morrow said, 'Fame is a kind of death'. Most of Sandburg's fame and wealth was earned by his massive biography of Lincoln, and I ain't going to do one of Churchill or Mrs Thatcher. Nor is this considered more than a modest dwelling, anyway. 'Big' is the Vanderbilt chateau up the road, which costs $30 to visit, and is something of a Citizen Kane erection, from what I've heard.*

***

Standing room only last night. Afterwards, I was introduced to the woman who'd driven from Long Island with her little boy ('She's a freak'). She had one question, predictably: did I really think Lindbergh was a villain? Everyone has their own theory about this case, one of which is that he was behind it all. Someone suggested to me that the baby had learning difficulties and this did not square up to Lindbergh's eugenic ideals, so he arranged for the baby to be removed. Then there's the one about his crazy sister-in-law. Yes, he had his dark side – most troublingly his involvement with the Nazis – but he wasn't 'evil'. The same naive single-mindedness that carried him across the Atlantic made him incapable of seeing what a moral fog he was flying into.

Most extraordinary of all was meeting the son of the man who analysed the timber of the ladder for Arthur Koehler, a character in my play. He and his wife were very uneasy and almost hostile to the idea that Hauptmann could have been framed. They didn't seem to know Ludovic Kennedy's The Airman and the Carpenter. *They were very dogmatic about the handwriting evidence, but that is pretty disputable. There was so much pressure on the leading experts, who'd been assured by the police that Hauptmann was guilty with 100% certainty. Who's going to deny it in the face of that?*

Anyhow, lots of interest still and another full house tomorrow. Four thousand dollars this production has cost, and Jericho are inevitably going to make a loss, but Franklin feels that it will boost their reputation considerably. Tomorrow's audience will be older, because it's a matinee, and therefore more knowledgeable about the history. Perhaps less easily convinced of Hauptmann's innocence?

What is an Englishman doing telling this to the Americans?

Underpinning the play is a whole structure of differences, and my play is entirely artifice in the way that audiences accustomed to movies often forget. The difference between McLuhan's cool and hot media, I suppose. I am inclined, when asked about the rights and wrongs of the case, only to talk in terms of this as a play. The actors filter the director who filters my script which filters Ludovic Kennedy who filtered all the innumerable springs of accusation and rumour which flowed from some distant truth somewhere seventy years ago. For all its American themes, it must be a peculiarly English work. Just as Ives doesn't convince as Brahms or Wagner for a moment, even when he's quoting them, but is the quintessential American, so I am repeatedly revealed as an English playwright. I have certain spiritual sensitivities and a puritanical streak which help me into the American camp – a woman last night said she was probably the only person in the audience who knew that Huntingdon was where Oliver Cromwell was born – but this is no more American drama than Hamlet was Danish. And this is no more Hamlet *than I'm Francis Bacon.*

Breakfast on the deck: still, birdsong, scents and odours, the woodpecker climbing the oak. Where am I sailing? Into obscurity, of course. Is that a mockingbird?

Something poignant about plays: so many prepared and put on, some of them masterpieces, brilliantly produced, superbly acted. A few people go and see them. They are forgotten. Like that monarch butterfly.

Verse drama was a real obsession of mine in the 1970s. When I went to Mannheim on a studentship, I took a huge silver trunk with me (not to mention that reel-to-reel tape recorder), laden with heavy hardbacks of the obscurest Georgian verse plays. John Drinkwater, Lascelles Abercrombie, Gordon Bottomley and the Andrew Lloyd Webber of his day, Stephen Phillips. I was going to Germany to study English verse drama. No wonder they all thought me mad. That was one of the loneliest periods of my life, though I did get to know the operatic repertoire while I was there and saw a complete performance in Heidelberg of Goethe's Faust *(Part II).*

Birdsong. One like an alarm clock being wound, the others like the alarm going off. A weird repeated electronic warbling. Judy comes on to the deck and we talk of fires. She can smell wood burning and is unduly conscious of the dangers since their partner, Tom, is currently cut off in Colorado. Americans always live within a hand's reach of the elements. North Carolina's had its fair share of natural disasters.

***

The final performance was the slickest of the week: it had pace and authority. Lindbergh had really got on top of the part. One or two details which irritate after the fourth time: that newspaper with an AOL ad visible, a paperback *copy of Lindbergh's book, those jarring Keystone Kops, the use of 'etcetera' instead of reciting the whole of 'To be or not to be...' But I have to remember how it struck me the first time round. We had a full house, slightly more elderly, as predicted. One old timer had known Anna Hauptmann in Pennsylvania and had inherited her children's swing set. Another refused to actually come and see the play ('I lived it') but stood around in the foyer being rude to everyone, because there was no question that Hauptmann was guilty and he wasn't going to listen to any darned arguments to the contrary. I chatted to a few more of the cast because I knew they would all be disappearing soon after the performance. No cast party, alas.*

Willy, who plays Fisch, revealed that he is descended from a victim of an equally celebrated miscarriage of justice, the Sacco and Vanzetti case of 1927. He is really interested in the play and wants to do something similar to put the record straight for his ancestors. He visualises a two-hander of some kind. Willy's a terrific actor and his little Fisch monologue is one of the highlights of the evening.

Some very fortuitous names in this story: the fishy Fisch. Red and Violet, two suspects who defy 'infrared analysis' and 'ultraviolet scanning'. Hoffman who really is a 'man of hope'. Morrow of 'Next Day Hill' – and if Charlie hadn't been kept until the Next Day, he might never have been kidnapped. Hauptmann ('head man' or 'captain'). Schwarzkopf ('black head').

Before the last performance, Franklin went through individual successes with his cast and I had a brief word, simply telling the story I'd read that morning in a volume of Marianne Moore's prose Franklin bought for me. George Bernard Shaw sent a young actress who'd appeared in one of his plays the following cable: 'wonderful, marvellous, superb', to which she replied 'Undeserving such praise'; and he 'I meant the play'; and she 'So did I'. It raised a laugh. Then I muttered, stumbled my way through some thanks and they flocked on stage for their usual high-spirited warm-up.

Unique New York. Unique New York. Good day, bad day. Good day, bad day.

It turns out that the sister of one of our crew was in the World Trade Center on September 11th, but escaped, though she was knocked down several times in the rush to get away before the towers collapsed. I think of our own single visit there, with Ruth, a survivor of Auschwitz. Franklin's son says that one of the most moving sights was all those unclaimed parked cars in the suburb where he lived.

Much talk of more impending attacks because of July 4th.

I remember my father's note in his Iceland diary of 1942 just before returning to England, reminding himself that the threat of U-boats was a very real one. The same diary mentions how he saw GBS at the National Gallery: 'Sensation!' I know how he would have enjoyed this play, but he was always suspicious of Americans after his Iceland years.

* * *

A misty Monday morning with the usual rich depths of birdsong. It's all over. It's been a refreshing time: like drilling a well and feeling the pure water come up or cutting a hole in the ice. I shall miss these early morning sessions. It's like a stage set here: the backdrop of trees comes out of Wagner, Siegfried listening to the Wood Bird. The deck itself is wide enough to present an opera.

The flying Dutchman, Johan, who plays 'Jafsie', is going to give me a lift to the airport later. I wonder how he reacted to 'Put that Dutchman in the hot seat!' shouted by the chorus night after night… A wealthy guy who's worked in international development and arranged for every female member of the cast to receive a single rose at the last performance.

So they are scattered now; that particular combination of individuals will never come together again. As if a bomb has fallen. Meanwhile, the woodpecker ascends.

Something drops with a thud just beside me on the deck. I lean down and turn it over with my pencil. It is a bright green scarab beetle. Symbol of… Well, where do I begin? It reminds me of Rosie, who requested a scarab cake for her last birthday – our birthday. Ibsen's birthday.

What is left of this grand venture? A bit of excitement to feed one's middle years. My horoscope in the paper today says it's a good time to take a project further… The strangest thing is how I put the play aside for so long. It was originally sparked by a conversation with a composer we met at a Syracuse symphony concert, Crystal LaPoint, who was interested in trying her hand at opera. So my early drafts were to be set to music. Then it became a full-blown verse drama. And eventually I turned it into a radio script, thinking that might solve the problem of the large cast, but it immediately killed the theatricality. Finally, I proceeded to lose the original. The play put on in Asheville was re-adapted earlier this year, with a little cut and paste. Yes, the scarab symbolises resurrection.

The fruits fall from the trees. Wood ants weave across the deck. A spider hides itself (remember that vast one we saw hanging across our pathway at the arboretum). Is that a little scorpion crossing the table? Could be, says Franklin. Will it harm the dog? (Meaning me.) He won't touch it, says Franklin. Ziek lies at my feet, ready to lick and leap. Now he goes out with Franklin to get used to his new electric-shock collar. 'Das also war des Pudels Kern'.

The cicadas buzz.

These woods are a paradigm of the poetic process. Dense, inviting, but shadowed with anxieties (snake, tick, bear, fire). A beam of sun will shaft through, then go again. Aspiring instincts – woodpecker, squirrel. Brilliant insights – oriole, cardinal. Then a fruit will drop, a seed, a cone. Or a spider. A scarab beetle.

In my play, I tried to use the whole range of possible resources: lyrical chorus, lofty chorus, jokey exchange, rhetorical outburst, dark meditation, bright dialogue, allusive monologue, song, parody, chant, satire, ritual… No wonder the cast was bewildered at first.

Cranberry and orange juice on the deck. The sharp tang of another culture. Like hearing that Southern accent. I thought the character of Arthur Koehler was playing up and exaggerating the voice, but it seems the actor speaks like that naturally. I like the long silence as he watches an imaginary tree grow, then: 'Arthur Koehler is a patient man'. I wonder how the guy who knew Koehler reacted to that? I suspect some of the audience were waiting for a prompt.

Before I leave, I suggest to Franklin that having a large family (he has five children) is like putting on a lifelong drama in your house. Perhaps that's how he learnt to direct? That and being a schoolteacher for so many years. He really is such a fine director, giving the actors leeway but always knowing what he wants. He hugs me and tells me to make sure I experience the white rocking chairs at Charlotte airport. I will. I'll rock there reading A.R. Ammons, North Carolina's finest poet, as the thunderstorm passes. I'll rock as they announce that the Pittsburgh plane has been struck by lightning, 'but we don't think there's any damage'. I'll rock and think about Johan's comment that he'd like to have known what became of all the characters in the play: how Anna kept on campaigning for her husband for sixty years and Anne became a recluse… I'll think of that departure into the unknown and the dark on a single Whirlwind engine seventy-five years ago. And I'll try and prepare myself for sudden obscurity, for the predictable synchronicities: the name of Lindbergh on the front page of tomorrow's Guardian.

I attempt to express some of my gratitude before I am handed over to the Dutchman.

Lindbergh's The Spirit of St Louis
(Rosie Greening).

Clink

Red wooden gate
with a latch
like a thumbs-up

whose clink as the
milkman brings
his ensemble in

and takes the empties
yodelling a street
cry at blue tits'

top-of-the-silver-
morning under our gold
rush of laburnum

through our aroma
of creosote and cut
privet, his crates

rattling away from us
as if churns were
longing to be freed

on that whining float
still just within
earshot – open!

Listening

When I was younger, classical music had such a hold on me that I eventually needed to withdraw from it in order to compose decent poetry. I soon came back to it once I could hear more clearly where I was going, but unlike some fellow practitioners (Daljit Nagra, for example, likes to write to 'lively rock music' as a way of escaping his 'normal logical mind')* I can't produce poetry while listening to anything else. Indeed, I can generally do nothing but listen when there's music playing, and it's certainly not a relaxing experience. The only exception was once on a nervy flight to Crete when – maybe for the same reasons as Daljit Nagra – I let the impenetrable sounds of Iannis Xenakis play through my headphones and began to write a crown of sonnets.* It's hardly news to suggest that music has a unique potency and that most religions have done well to bring it into their sanctum rather than let it set up as a rival.

Much as I delight in songs (and have been strongly influenced by the Schubertian song cycle), the enormous appeal and cultish power of rock and pop remain a mystery to me. I'm unnerved by the way everything has to be reduced to a song track, as if there were no other kind. I prefer music that asks me to work a little more, and takes me somewhere beyond words. But our society seems to have lost interest in those longer forms, and it's no longer considered embarrassing to dismiss them. Confessing a love of symphonies (let alone string quartets) definitely wouldn't help a modern politician get elected. The opposite in fact, as Neil Kinnock understood when he lamented the highly electable Tony Blair's deficient musical appreciation. Keir Starmer is a trained flautist and enjoys classical music, but he knows it's not going to win him any votes. He too has seen all those TV dramas in which a character's interest in such music warns us what to expect. There is a general suspicion if not bafflement today at the very idea of music lasting more than five minutes, where there are no words or accompanying pictures, where it's not the tune that matters but the way it's transfigured.

Violin, little used.

Music, for me, has always felt like a powerful rival to poetry. The relationship between them is extraordinarily complex and not to be taken lightly. Gilbert and Sullivan would have told us that; so could Bob Dylan. But the two art forms really don't need each other at all. Milton's 'blest pair of sirens', Voice and Verse, can indeed raise the spirits; but it could be said they are at their most potent when permitted to go solo. Poetry on its own, and music on its own can... well, to suggest that they literally 'raise spirits' would be going too far, but it can sometimes feel that way. There is a terrifying force at work in each. Together, they seem to temper each other, which perhaps makes their force more bearable, an alternating current. The art of the German *Lied* is not something one would bring up in friendly conversation at the Dog and Duck. Opera, though, might be more sympathetically received, as it was when Puccini's aria 'Nessun Dorma' was used to introduce the 1990 World Cup. It is virtually the only high musical art form acknowledged by the news media, often as a synecdoche for all elite culture (while the elite sports teams go on being celebrated). Yet music without words or images, non-programmatic orchestral, chamber, instrumental music – this is surely the most potent art form known to humanity, one to which poetry itself aspires, one that takes the listener to the nucleus of things.

If architecture is frozen music, then music is not quite defrosted architecture, but something to do with aural structural design: how one sound relates to another, connecting with otherwise inaccessible emotional and intellectual patterns and achieving that sense of 'rightness' every artist will recognise. Words have their own rhythms, their own dimensions, which have to be compromised when set to music. A.E. Housman's verses are cut to suit Vaughan Williams's 'Is My Team Ploughing?'. Wilhelm Müller's lines are repeated or reorganised to fit Schubert's strophes. Shakespeare's *The Tempest* is completely rewritten for the sake of Thomas Adès's opera. The truth is that Beethoven's late quartets will always go deeper than even his Ninth Symphony or the *Missa Solemnis*.

Behind this feeling that one is being drawn into a mystical web, towards whatever lies at its centre, there is mathematics. Here I feel obliged to step back, since all my former maths teachers would affirm – as would C.G. Jung's, I'm reassured to note – that while their subject interested me, it defeated me; but it's clear Pythagoras of Samos and his heirs were on to something when they saw in music the key to the universe. It's connected with the number seven and the details are all explored in Jamie James's eruditely entertaining book *The Music of the Spheres*,* in which he writes of the Pythagoreans that they 'did not simply discern congruities

Meeting the ancestor. Elgar statue in Malvern.

among number and music and the cosmos: they identified them. Music *was* number; and the cosmos *was* music.' Suffice to say that Apollo was for good reason regarded as one of the wisest of the Greek gods.

Long before I began exploring the literary canon, I was working my way through the classics of Western repertoire with the help of *Westerman's Concert Guide* and Tovey's *Essays in Musical Analysis*. For one of my teenage birthdays I requested the complete Beethoven string quartets; for Christmas it was Bruckner's Eighth Symphony. Even now I'm not sure where this all came from. My parents were quietly interested in music, my mother an amateur pianist, my father having attended appreciation classes. We were allegedly related to Elgar, whose mother was a Greening. I learnt the violin and led the school orchestra, but I didn't have many actual music lessons there. Our music teacher and conductor was a very eccentric man, known to Imogen Holst. I discovered recently that he had studied with Anton Webern. I had more encouragement from a young English teacher, who shared my enthusiasm for Shostakovich and was highly amused when I expressed admiration for a certain Paul Hindsmith rather than the better-known Hindemith.

Within a few years I could recognise most of the familiar concert pieces and must have been very irritating to my family – as I still am when I identify what's playing in the background on a film or in the bus station. But, yes, I did have friends, I did 'have a life', even the odd encounter with a girl (tricky when you're at a boys' school) though the excitement and cultural upheaval of the 1960s rather passed me by; in fact, I have yet to be convinced that they were anything more than an eccentric side-slip, like the decadent 1890s. I was writing all the while, between discs, beginning to learn where poetry could take me, and by the time I was at university it was obvious that record collecting was distracting me too much from my own creative resources. I was listening to them, not to myself.

When Jane and I married, I was separated overnight from my father's top quality hi-fi equipment, so it was that much easier to quit the record habit. But at the same time I was plunged into a world of music, because I took a job in BBC Radio 3's New Music department as Hans Keller's 'Clerk, New Music'. Hans was about to retire, and what really tickled his fancy was the fact that I had been trying to make a living as a children's magician.* He was interested too in my aspirations as a poet, although he claimed to have no understanding at all of poetry. That was a relief, since anything Hans did claim to have knowledge of he would pursue relentlessly to ensure you were not being in any way a phoney (he had a particular suspicion of so-called 'dodecaphoneys' among twentieth-century composers). Anyway, he gave me an empty room, where the telephone rang about once a fortnight, and told me to get on with writing my poetry.

So the spirits of words and music worked happily side by side during the eighteen months I was at Yalding House. I took dictation of letters to Anna Freud and Thomas Szasz, I filed the scores sent in by composers obscure and not so obscure, I brought coffee to the score-reading 'panel' – usually just Edmund Rubbra; occasionally Richard Arnell or Susan Bradshaw instead – and I discovered a long-lost Benjamin Britten score when I was clearing out Hans's cupboard, the *Third Programme Overture*, which Britten had given to Hans and asked him to hide. Other than that, I didn't write much good poetry.

But I did have a triumph with a spoof anonymous letter which I circulated round the BBC, oblivious to any breach of protocol. We were much afflicted by road repairs outside Yalding House:

Dear Mr Keller

RODE: WORKS (outside)

These works by B. Rode were recommended by the panel of the 1950 Young Compressors' Forum, and we have been asked by Mr Rode himself to submit them to your Pneumatic Department.

Although Rode works have appeared repeatedly in the repertoire of certain street musicians ('Stillheit', 'Serenade for Pick and Earplugs', 'Infuriation' etc.), none has yet found its way into the concert hall or on to your national wavelengths: as a result, although widely disseminated, his works are not particularly popular with the public, perhaps because they have not been given a substantial opportunity to come to grips with the deep, exploratory essence of Rode.

The critic, Taylor Woodrow, says of his most difficult work, *The Leak Sonata* (which has only just come to light): "To the unwary or unwilling listener this may sound like so much noise, but on closer acquaintance (such as is these days more and more possible) he will perceive in it a subtle yet unmistakeable machine-gun-like rhythmicism, whose probing insistence continually breaks through the cliches of convention (the Kerbstohns, Macadams and other established names on which modernity smoothly and contentedly runs)."

Rode himself has claimed that his aim is to compress as much as possible (of anything) into the smallest space, to disturb, to disrupt, to revolutionise, to "shatter the rock-hard conventional consciousness, even where it is at its most rock-hard" in order to lay down his own ultimately fresh, ideal surfaces.

Perhaps he achieves this most perfectly in his *Excavation No.9*, where the phenomenal structure and remarkable orchestration (three-foot diameter gaspipe accompanied by a small pipe orchestra) are rivalled only by the sheer time it takes to perform: three weeks at least for the first subject ("Gas") and even longer for the second ("Dig") to appear, and then several months before even the exposition is completed. Repeats are, of course, vital. It cannot be denied that a neo-classical achievement of this kind deserves more of a hearing than it has so far received.

It should not be difficult for the BBC to mount a performance: he writes for small forces of unskilled labourers whose aural and vernacular background makes them particularly suited to this role. He favours a percussive instrumentation, although his recent *Diversion* is scored largely for irate car horn.

Naturally, Rode is eager to hear his works on the BBC: he has been trying for twenty years, but your department has shut its doors and windows on his appeals – and has even gone so far as to install double glazing!

We are taking the liberty of staging a live performance of one of his longest and noisiest creations outside Yalding House this month.

Thanking you for your interest

Yours sincerely

Musical Engineering Division

Hans was delighted, as I'd hoped he would be – after all, he had himself played an almighty practical joke on the BBC when he passed off some random bashing noises as an avant-garde work by 'Piotr Zak'.* The critics who waxed lyrical about *Mobile for Tape and Percussion* were not happy when they found out the composer was fictional and the music was simply Hans and friends having fun. For a long time he couldn't work out who had written the Rode piece, but decided in the end it must be by Robert Simpson, the eminent symphonist and musicologist, one of several big names working at Radio 3. When he found out it was mine he was full of praise. But when I subsequently showed him a longer serious piece about Solzhenitsyn it came back covered with his characteristic annotations and the comment: 'While your Rode piece was masterly, this isn't'.

Nubian Dancing, Aswan, c.1980.

Meanwhile, despite my separation from the family hi-fi, poetry was still only flowing sporadically, held back either by the daily commute or by the thought of that High Dam of Deutsche Grammophon and Philips and EMI and Decca LPs. So we left our BBC jobs – Jane had been in the Russian Service, in the office next door to Georgi Markov who was murdered by an umbrella assassin on Waterloo Bridge while she was there – and headed for Egypt with Voluntary Service Overseas.

The two years in Aswan became a proper starting point for my mature poetry, I think, not only because of the location's exotic appeal, but because I had so little music available to distract me. Yet what I did hear has evidently made its mark. The call of the muezzin went deep, and it is a sound that never fails to stir me when it drifts into a news bulletin; but Nubian dancing, Egyptian wedding songs, and the singing of Umm Khalsum can have that effect too, even if I've no idea what she sings about. Odd things caught my ear in Egypt. On one occasion a beggar with a squeeze box was playing a tune used in Rimsky Korsakov's *Scheherazade*, whether poached by him or somehow returned to the streets of Aswan I do not know.

Schubert's song cycle *Winterreise* was just one of a handful of cassette tapes we took with us to Egypt, and for all the firecrackers I have thrown so far in my discussion of song, German *Lieder* have profoundly affected me – perhaps for the very reason that they are not in the language I use for poetry. But it's hardly surprising that I was moved by listening to Dietrich Fischer-Dieskau's wintry travels while we were trying to survive temperatures heading beyond forty degrees; or that it all came back to me a few months after our return when I wrote *The Winter Journey*, my Captain Scott sonnet sequence. What a delight when the composer Cecilia McDowall chose to set one of those sonnets as part of *Three Songs after Schubert*.* The poem she selected was written to follow the precise metre of the first song in Müller's cycle, but she managed to make the setting entirely her own, playing with my lines and including dramatic repetitions, as a composer must.

There have been further collaborations, two of which were to have been premiered in 2020, but fell victim to Covid. For Philip Lancaster (composer, poet and Ivor Gurney scholar) I had provided a series of poems about poplars, *Fallen*, which he set for tenor and violin ready for the Ludlow Song Weekend.* The other was by Roderick Williams, the acclaimed baritone and composer who premiered Cecilia's Schubert songs. He had texted me just as I was sitting in Jubilee Hall waiting for my reading to start at the 2019 Aldeburgh poetry festival. The message asked if I would – and I jest not – consider writing an extra stanza for John Keats's 'To Autumn'. He had been commissioned to set the 'Ode' for the Waynflete Singers to perform in Winchester Cathedral, but felt he wanted to bring a contemporary perspective which emphasised current ecological concerns. When walking in the area near Winchester which had inspired Keats, he was particularly troubled by the amount of pollution, especially noise pollution. I promptly wrote the stanza – mostly on the slow train home – keeping Keats's verse form and his surprisingly irregular rhyme scheme:

After Autumn

Season of fumes and fine particulates,
Whose sun inclines to put you in a home
Then turn the heating up; to banish gnats,
And manage hedge-crickets: robin won't come,
Nor lamb be served, but cuts of twittering news
With opioids. Across your bee-less land
The smart new networked motorways advance
On a different season; their husky wind
Growling from under Keats's laden boughs
Grows louder, like a Harvest Home for us
Who reap, as darkness gathers, our last chance.

My earliest potential musical collaboration was with the late Peter Anthony Monk, whose work I came to know when I was at Radio 3. I wrote some poems for a song cycle about marriage (since I was a newly-wed) but nothing came of it, and the poems wouldn't have been the equal of his strikingly original music. Then, much later, there was the possibility of an opera about Lindbergh, as discussed in the last chapter. It was soon after our return from America that I found myself in contact with Evelyn Glennie, the deaf percussionist, who lived in a village quite near us. I had written a poem about her and she suggested we meet to discuss whether we could work together. Although the proposed collaboration never took place, I did finish a sequence of poems designed to complement her playing. These were inspired by the array of musical instruments she showed me at her house, an experience which was second only to being shown the sound effects department of the BBC Drama department by a friend who worked there. On both occasions it was a case of trying to guess what sound the object might actually make – and in the case of Evelyn Glennie wondering how she

Scotland's distinguished vocal ensemble

WIGMORE HALL, LONDON   *W*IGMORE HALL

Thursday 8th June 2000 at 7.30 pm

Music by Strauss, Mahler, Britten and Mottram (world premiere)

MORRISON

Dunedin Consort performance of Falls, *Wigmore Hall, June 2000.*

could tell one from another. The answer to that question is in her absorbing memoir, *Good Vibrations.* *

The first such joint enterprise to get off the ground was around the time of the Millennium: a major commission for an engineering company who wanted a choral work for the Dunedin Consort to perform at Wigmore Hall. The composer Paul Mottram asked me if I could provide texts for him to set, and he needed them quite quickly. I couldn't think what to write, until I remembered a book of photographs I had bought when we visited Niagara Falls. It showed people doing all kinds of ridiculous stunts over the Falls – going over in barrels, crossing it on a tightrope. I took these as my cue. The cycle was a great success and toured Canada – though whether it was done at Niagara itself I'm not sure – later being taken up by the National Youth Choir and performed at Snape Maltings.

Probably the most entertaining of the various commissions I have undertaken was for teacher and composer David Gibbs to perform with his Kimbolton School Choir in 2010. Thinking it might amuse the students, I came up with *Orrery*, a series of linked planetary poems. As a schoolboy, I had been enthralled by astronomy and the notion of extraterrestrial life, even going so far as to join BUFORA, the British UFO Research Association; and I still remember certain random facts about the universe I was able to draw on for the libretto. An orrery is a working model of our solar system, and in my sequence the turning of the handle to operate the machinery offered a way of linking the separate sections. During the performance we had a model orrery on stage, its handle turned at key moments, and there were projected images on a screen:

Turn the handle…

> dark and silver
> dust and peace
> war and water
> moon and ice

131

*Turn the handle
and the planets...*

> cloud and lava
> ring and gas
> day and distance
> year and mass

*Turn the handle
and the planets
begin to revolve...*

> dark and silver
> dust and peace etc. [*ad lib*]

*Here's the mechanical
answer to mysteries
we can't solve...*

> Is there anybody out there?

After this opening invocation, there was an allusion to Orson Welles's 1938 *War of the Worlds* broadcast and 'Venus' evoked climate change, before Mercury came dashing through, a spoilt brat with an over-protective parent. It was all as un-Holstian as we could manage (Holst was more interested in astrological meanings anyway). Our Jupiter was no Bringer of Jollity, but a giant server 'processing God's raw materials'. Saturn was represented by its moons (many more have been discovered since), a wonderful opportunity for fugal interplay, although the school choir might disagree:

> Titan, Dione,
> Hyperion, Phoebe, Enceladus
> and Rhea and Miras
> and Tethys

> Prometheus, Atlas,
> Pandora, Telesto,
> Calypso, Helene,

Epimetheus
Janus
Pan

Kiviuq, Ijiraq, Paaliaq, Siarnaq,
Erriapo and Tarvos and Albiorix

Skathi and Thrymyr
and Ymir and Suttungr

Mundilfari
and Narvi

Methone, Pallene,
Polydeuces

Daphnis

The outer planets were cooler, increasingly cynical. Pluto, after all, was still unknown when Holst was writing his suite. By the time Gibbs wrote his, it had not

Gustav Holst at Cheltenham.

only been discovered but had since been declassified and only recently reclassified as a dwarf planet. By the end of *Orrery*, the question at its heart remained unanswered: is there anybody out there?

Poets, then, are often asked by composers to write. But they may well be independently moved by music to write too, and that was the idea behind *Accompanied Voices*, a bulky anthology I finished editing in 2015 after ten years gathering poems, largely by contemporary poets, about specific composers. Poets frequently seem to be casting an envious eye at the structural resources available to those who write music. Some have used compositions as a scaffolding for their poems: Anthony Hecht's Haydn-inspired 'A Love for Four Voices', for example, or Joanna Boulter's *Twenty-Four Preludes and Fugues on Dmitri Shostakovich*. T.S. Eliot's *Four Quartets* is indebted to Beethoven's A minor Quartet Op.132, whose playful gestures he reproduces in some of the question-and-answer passages. Eliot turned more than once to Beethoven, tracing the structure of one of his overtures in 'Coriolan', for instance, but it was clear that the final quartets offered him a new way forward. He told Stephen Spender in a letter* that he found 'a sort of heavenly or at least more than human glory' about some late Beethoven along with feelings of reconciliation and 'relief after great suffering', and then suggested he would like to express something similar in his own later verse.

Basil Bunting's *Briggflatts* is one of the most distinguished examples of a poem rooted in music. It is a work that aspires by the poet's own admission to something like the fugal effect of Bach's *The Art of Fugue*, but draws more immediately on Scarlatti – the B minor fugato sonata (L.33). Recordings were issued of Bunting reading the poem with a Scarlatti sonata between each 'movement'. He drew an accompanying diagram to demonstrate the kind of sonata form he was exploiting and according to his first biographer, Victoria Forde, he honed the 700 lines from an original 20,000. Bunting had been an amateur music critic, so he knew what he was doing, although he recognised the art's dangerous allure when he remarked it was fortunate he knew Scarlatti rather than Corelli or he might have ended up trying to imitate the latter's heavenly largos and dancing angels.

I remember Martyn Crucefix telling me how he once wrote a series of poems inspired by each of the seven Sibelius symphonies.* Long before I myself became preoccupied with Sibelius, I was immersed in the music of Johannes Brahms. In the mid-1970s I was studying in Mannheim and managed to visit several places associated with him, most memorably the house in Baden-Baden where he worked on his first two symphonies and the *German Requiem*. It was the end of the day and the house was completely empty when I looked round it. At that time I was writing plays rather more than poetry and was determined to write one about Brahms – another verse drama. But as I began to research young Hannes's somewhat seamy life, and his painfully frustrated obsession with Clara, who had been Robert Schumann's wife since Brahms was a small boy, it became apparent that this was always going to be the Schumann show. *Schumann* was indeed the play that was staged in Exeter when I was barely twenty-two – my rather intense portrait of the composer was used on the poster.

SCHUMANN

Detail of poster for Schumann.

That student production stays in my memory partly for some embarrassing incidents and incompetent stage management, though also for a very fine performance of the title role by my friend Miles Harper, whose tastes are really more in the direction of David Bowie. We took trouble over the incidental music, even if Schumann's works didn't have the same visceral effect on me as Brahms's. Yet the life was fascinating, a veritable showcase of Romantic emblems, involving a tyrannical 'Barrett of Wimpole Street'-style father, forbidden love and heady impulsiveness, featuring syphilis and mercury treatment and consequent insanity, culminating in that suicidal plunge into the Rhine, a river which winds throughout Schumann's writings from the magnificent *Rhenish* Symphony to the songs in *Dichterliebe.*

Although I have made the case against the primacy of song in our culture, those song cycles – as much as Schubert's – were an undeniably powerful influence on my development as a poet. I took to them half a lifetime ago when I first heard Ian Partridge perform them on a bargain *Classics for Pleasure* LP. Robert Schumann wrote enough songs for several lifetimes – almost 140 in 1840 alone, including several complete cycles. His *Dichterliebe* from that year has been called the greatest song cycle by any composer. Schubert's *Winterreise* must rival it, but the poems are not so good: because he was a writer himself, Schumann knew to choose fine verse.

Apart from Ezra Pound, poets have not generally aspired to compose music, but there have been plenty of musicians who think they can write. Many undoubtedly can, from Thomas Campion to Hector Berlioz, from Ivor Gurney to Joni Mitchell. Some of them were even poets. It's surprising how often one turns to an obituary of a musician and finds – as happened with William Alwyn and Robert Tear – that they were closet poets. The conductor Andrew Davis, who died in 2024, appears to have spent much of lockdown translating Virgil's *Aeneid.* The composer Michael Tippett was encouraged by T.S. Eliot to write his own libretti and got away with it, although whenever I listen to Tippett's choral music I wish he had employed a professional. There are not as many musicians who can't write, I suspect, as writers who can't play an instrument, but there are some uncomfortable cases. Hans Keller had one of the most remarkable minds and an unsurpassed understanding of the musical repertoire, but when it comes to his prose style it's another matter. Reading Hans, one is always conscious of the author at work, especially when he plays with the language as he often does, bringing his wicked Viennese wit to English's homonyms and idioms. Even his fellow Austrian, the late Alfred Brendel, prince among pianists, doesn't sound entirely natural when he writes. But one practising musician, whose books are a constant delight and whose approach has influenced this writer, deserves a cadenza at this point.

The pianist Susan Tomes has found a way to take apparently trivial aspects of the professional musician's life and show how important they really are. In her books, what might have been fragmented and esoteric turns out to have considerable momentum, shifting from pianistic matters such as how to choreograph the walk to the stool or why only older pianists are expected to play Schubert's B Flat Sonata or the nature of mistakes ('it seems that I have practised getting it wrong') to knotty issues such as the changing convention of playing from memory or the possibility of over-preparation. She knows that to be an entertaining writer she must drop in revealing snippets of autobiography – how she used to enjoy playing tennis more before she learned you had to hit the ball so someone could *not* hit it back – and is at ease, as good writers are, with bizarre anecdotes, such as discovering at US airport security that her fingerprints have been worn away by piano practice. Very often such experiences lead her to some conclusion which may affect her own performance: a chance visit to Kilmainham Gaol darkens her playing of Mozart; snapping ivories caused by swelling wood set her imagining an 'underlying template located under the keys'. Piano playing is compared to diving, cycling, cooking, drystone walling, the purring of cats and even quantum physics. She touches on the uncanny aspects of music making, too: how a conductor and soloist can start together even though they aren't looking at each other. But Tomes has a particular understanding of humanity rare in music writing, looking 'beyond the notes', title of one of her best books,* to reveal how the world perceives musicians. Sometimes they are treated as servants, sometimes as honoured guests. Mostly, the public regard their profession as imprecise, unstructured, undemanding, an indulgence in difficult times. Even concert-goers can be horrifyingly insensitive: a woman recognises Tomes at the airport, says nothing about the music but rants about the chipped piano and the scruffy orchestra; or a friend says she has bought a recording of Beethoven trios but doesn't care who the performers are.

If there is such indifference to matters of musical interpretation, perhaps we should not expect audiences to care much about a composer's choice of text and a performer's ability to convey the words clearly. It has to be said that for some composers it's better if we *can't* make out the words, although it's true that very often it is second-rate poetry that works best. What makes Wilhelm Müller's poems so effective in Schubert is that same par-baked quality that weakens them on the page. But there are certain composers who can be relied upon to choose badly.

Elgar, for example, except when he opted to set Newman's *The Dream of Gerontius*, had consistently poor taste in verse. Benjamin Britten, by contrast, not only showed superb literary judgement – there is a published anthology of the poems he set* – but he evidently recognised the same quality in Schumann when he chose to record his little-known late setting of scenes from Goethe's *Faust*. Britten knew how few composers (only Mahler?) have succeeded in setting Germany's greatest poet and dramatist. What makes Schumann succeed with Goethe is the same quality that makes him a great writer of song cycles using poems by Heine and Eichendorff. He is a master of organic structure: one song leads to another, much as they do in Beethoven's only cycle, *An die Ferne Geliebte*. As in Beethoven, there is always a writerly sense of an underlying narrative, rather than just a surface story about, say, a lovesick miller. Moreover, there is never a note wasted. If the words demand a tiny scrap of a song, he'll give us one. But he can do masterly strophic settings. Or even an eight-minute monodrama, such as *Die Löwenbraut*.

The song cycle, I would suggest, has been more influential than we give it credit for. It could even be argued that the modern taste for poetic sequences from *The Waste Land* to *Station Island* emerges from a familiarity with German *Lieder*, carefully filtered through the Victorian front parlour. Yes, naturally the Elizabethan sonnet sequence has its say, but the sheer dramatic variety of the sung narrative in Schumann's many lyric groupings – and the unsung plots behind many of his instrumental pieces – must have fed those very musical Brownings and Tennysons and Rossettis, for whom the voice and piano were a natural accompaniment to their middle-class existence. Anyone searching for the true pitch of late English Romanticism would do well to listen to 'Ich Grolle Nicht' rather than wade through 'Maud'. And Schumann's repugnance at the trivialisation of high culture surely played accompaniment to Matthew Arnold's big scenes. The composer knew what he was doing when he concluded *Carnaval* with a protest march against the Philistines.

Maze at Saffron Walden.

O

Nothing has been written,
yet there is something
at the point of take-off:

a child's mouth gaping
as the *Cordelia* enters
orbit and numbers

begin to lap each other
round a speedway
circuit. Absent

father begins his
race for the crown –
it hangs with its promise

of meaning, though nothing
on paper, except
barren multiplication.

Meaning

Lewis Carroll's Alice can be relied on to take a sensible view on most matters and her attitude to poetry is always enlightening. When she discovers the text of 'Jabberwocky', for example, her reaction is that it seems 'very pretty' but '*rather hard to understand*', which is not unlike the reaction most people have to poetry, especially with Carroll's added brackets: '(You see she didn't like to confess, even to herself, that she couldn't make it out at all.)' Later, she asks Humpty Dumpty's advice on the meaning, and he certainly knows all the vocabulary, but he leaves her none the wiser and is merely keen to ply her with yet more verse: '"I can repeat poetry as well as other folk, if it comes to that—"/"Oh, it needn't come to that!" Alice hastily said...'

Alice is one of those rare readers who has the courage to ask what something means, whereas most of us prefer to nod sagely and say nothing. T.S. Eliot was once asked what he meant by the line from 'Ash Wednesday', 'Lady, three white leopards sat under a juniper-tree', and responded by saying it meant three white leopards sat under a juniper tree. Browning remarked of his 'Sordello': 'When it was written, God and Robert Browning knew what it meant; now only God knows.' Considering how long poets will take to pick and unpick a line, it's surprising how nervous we can be about explaining ourselves – something very evident in Don Paterson and Clare Brown's anthology of mini-essays by poets 'in their own words': *Don't Ask Me What I Mean.** Archibald MacLeish overcame the problem by suggesting in his 'Ars Poetica' that a poem 'should not mean/ But be', which cleared the way for a great deal of meaningless verse, little of it as good as 'Jabberwocky'. Picking up the cue from Humpty Dumpty, there has been a considerable university industry in taking poems apart and putting them together again, and a sympathy for views such as Medbh McGuckian's that 'too many poems are all meaning and no reserve'.

Nowadays it is very difficult to know whether poets mean what they say or say what they mean, but it's not a pressing concern in a free society where sales of poetry are hardly registered anyway. It's quite another matter if you are living and writing under a dictatorship. Ambiguity is a very useful way of passing comment on a regime without appearing to. Why else would Yevgeny Yevtushenko have had such a following, and how else could Eastern European poets such as Marin Sorescu fill rock music stadiums for their readings? It wouldn't have taken Stalin long to realise he was being mocked when he heard about Osip Mandelstam's 'Kremlin mountaineer', if only because of the allusion to laughing cockroaches above his lips, but in fact the poet titled it 'The Stalin Epigram' anyway, and was consequently arrested.

When I was a teacher, children would occasionally want to know (like Alice) what a line meant, which Craig Raine once suggested was the most intelligent question you can ask of a poem. They would also regularly demand: what is a metaphor? The two questions are usually related, and neither is as easy to answer as you might think, although referring them to any poem by Craig Raine or to that cockroach moustache would have been a good response to the latter. Much of the English language is metaphorical and we don't even notice the fact: the leg of a table, the ghost of a smile, the mouse of a PC, the track of an album, which you might rip or stream.

One of the reasons that politicians are generally deaf to metaphor (John Major famously said 'When your back's to the wall, there is only one thing to do and that is turn around and fight') is that too much alertness to it can breed a sense of insecurity and instability about the very words one speaks. This is not what the government requires of its politicians. They must pretend that there is no threatening marsh around us all, no ignis fatuus, no toxic gas, and that no one is lost. Their way of talking must be as straight and simple as a waymarked boardwalk. They may wave something cheerfully that they regard as a metaphor. Our Future is Green. Drain the Swamp. Fair is Worth Fighting For. Don't Turn Back the Clock. Labour Isn't Working. If they happen to meet a genuinely potent metaphor along their wooden way, it will no more hinder their progress than knots in the planks under their feet. One recent Prime Minister was rather different in this respect, since he has a literary bent and will cheerfully lurch into the metaphors like a child in a sandpit. Sometimes they are vivid, sometimes inappropriate, but they don't make for the kind of clarity that is required during, say, a global pandemic – when we were told by the Welsh First Minister that a firebreak could turn the tide.

What the politicians generally ignore, however, poets embrace. And even by using that everyday, overworked metaphor, 'embrace', a dozen possible lines of metaphorical development pop into my head. Some of them are cartoonish

– metaphor is one of the political cartoonist's most effective weapons – but others could become poetry. Poet as tree-hugger. Russian poets greeting each other. Intertwining love poems, or even poets – say, Robert and Elizabeth Barrett Browning. The word 'embrace' starts to repeat itself in my mouth; I hear its elements; I want to know its etymology. It has something of the word 'embarrass' about it, but there's also a comedic note that brings in braces or what Americans call suspenders. And there's that lippy opening 'em' sound. I start to imagine some kind of silent film sequence involving birch trees and vodka and kissing and comedians' trousers falling down… But the image has become something else entirely since those months when we were not allowed to hug anyone. There is a new poignancy. Our younger daughter, who writes children's books for a living, even produced one during that time called *Can I Have a Hug?* The very metaphors change their meaning from year to year.

Ash keys.

My poems often begin with a double meaning, and I reassure myself that this is fine since Shakespeare also loved puns. The titles of my books do much the same. I have already explained in the chapter 'Flitting' about my choice of *Westerners*, but the title of a much later collection, *The Home Key*,* also has underlying meanings beyond the fact that it contained many poems about the place where I live and 'place' is the key to understanding my poetry. Firstly, the 'home key' is a common term for the 'tonic' to which a sonata or symphony returns. Secondly, there was a lot of occult writing in that book, including a long poem about the medium D.D. Home.* What he may have achieved in his seances is a key to all kinds of questions we want answered. No poet can use the word 'key' without being aware of its many metaphorical associations. Some of those recur in my work – the so-called ash keys that form in bunches on ash trees and endure through the winter. Then there are piano keys. The keyboard I am writing on now. Or the key to a map – I love maps and often write about them.

As I have mentioned, my 2008 collection *Iceland Spar* had the idea of doubleness keyed into it and my 'Selected' from the following year I called *Hunts*, partly because that is the official abbreviation of the county we live in and partly because it contains so many poems about searching – whether for an emperor penguin's egg or a pharaoh's tomb. *Knot* (2013) was a labyrinthine book, in which lines from one poem connect with lines from another. I was thinking of knot gardens, and love-knots – but there's a bird called a knot too. And I always kept in mind the fact that *knot* sounds like *not*; there was a subtext in the book about things *not* happening. Then what about that 'knot in a plank' I mentioned in my discussion above of the way politicians speak…? (And how tempted I was to take that 'wooden' metaphor further.)

If there's any satisfactory definition of a poet it might be someone who is inescapably attuned to the metaphorical. Splitting a word in a pun or play on meaning is often where it all starts – the poetic equivalent of splitting the atom. The result can be a Waste Land, but it can also produce concentrated energy, as in the case of the Emily Dickinson Powerhouse. One of my good friends from university is the writer Michael W. Thomas, with whom I used to have what we once agreed must be called a 'joke relationship'. Every conversation was a pun, probably as a way of avoiding a darkness we both saw and feared, particularly when we found ourselves one night negotiating with our landlord as he held a gun to his children and his wife hid in our room. As Shelley put it in 'Julian and Maddalo', for us it was 'Talk interrupted with such raillery/As mocks itself, because it cannot scorn/The thoughts it would extinguish'. Wordplay has been at the heart of many of my friendships. But I wonder where this comes from…

It may be something to do with my father's dubious sense of humour, his fund of quips from the war years. He was always very quick to spot a double meaning, and would dart back with 'as the actress said to the bishop' or 'heard in the blackout'. Since we were a rather buttoned-up family, loath to talk directly about sex, this was one way of dealing with it. Strangely, he worked for a while in the obscene publications department of the Home Office and did tell us (with some relish) about the locked safe where Donald McGill's saucy postcards were kept – that master of the double entendre. Consequently, I have a soft spot for comedians who are quick with a pun – Ted Ray, Frankie Howerd, Paul Merton, Sandi Toksvig, Milton Jones – and for poets who explore the possibilities of multiple meanings in their work.

I have to confess, however, I'm not drawn so much to the density of allusion Geoffrey Hill made his own: his puns can feel laboured and relentless, fit for a crossword clue rather than a singing line. But *Mercian Hymns* is irresistible and a good place to start for readers unfamiliar with Hill. In the second hymn, for example, Offa's name is punningly transformed to 'offer' ('Best-selling brand… A specious gift') to a 'curt graffito' (as in 'F off!'), to 'the starting cry of a race' ('They're off!'), where 'race' also has another meaning. The brilliant and frequently stinging critic William Logan, who has always been interested in his work, has said nevertheless that he finds Hill's attempts at humour 'frightening'. But I find in this early sequence the light and the serious cohabit harmoniously. On balance, though, my taste is more for the sparkling cleverness of D.J. Enright, U.A. Fanthorpe, James Merrill, A.E. Stallings.

I have a particular affection for those artists who position themselves halfway between the serious and the popular: sounding accessible, but plumbing depths. It's a very English habitat, explored further in the chapter 'Genius', and some of our bestselling poets graze there, such as John Betjeman and Wendy Cope. One or two end up irritating more than they illuminate, although this tends to be in their prose. I'm thinking of Stephen Fry and his *The Ode Less Travelled*, but even Clive James, for all his erudition, can leave the reader feeling in need of someone who doesn't scintillate quite so much. Yet who could not be pleased by Victoria Wood or, from my own childhood, Flanders and Swann?

Michael Flanders had a wonderfully acute ear for metre and rhyme – 'if your parents don't mind, we'd... inextricably entwined we'd... said the honeysuckle to the bindweed' – and was formally (and grammatically) ingenious, as when in 'Madeira M'Dear' he repeatedly lets a single verb control four nouns: 'put out the cat,/The wine, his cigar, and the lamps', 'raising her glass,/Her courage, her eyes, and his hopes.' Donald Swann knew exactly how to showcase Flanders's lyrics with his flexible semi-improvised accompaniments. The titles invariably play with language, and there will be a brilliant throwaway pun somewhere, such as 'It's simply a case of *chacun à son gout*' – the 'gout' pronounced as in the illness brought on by drinking... madeira.

The danger with puns and hyperconsciousness of etymology is that you can end up writing poems that 'blunder round about a meaning', and if Pope were to visit our age, he would find plenty of examples of that – in Cambridge, no doubt, but also in America in the wake of John Ashbery, who once told an interviewer that he wouldn't put a hidden meaning in his poems because the reader might find it. I wonder what Pope would make of Jorie Graham, whose poems are a challenge even to read aloud.

In her introduction to *Best American Poetry 1990*,* Graham describes hearing a poet read immediately after a writer of fiction. She tells of her discomfort at this new music which seemed to 'begin out of nowhere', moving 'irrationally', a poetry which was 'not a little story told in musical rhythms' and how it only gradually started to get through to her: a sense of words chipping away at the silence, increasing in volume, then eventually 'cutting into an element that was crushing in its power and weight'. I suspect other readers have had a similar experience in their first encounter with Graham's own work. It can feel as if we are trapped in the poet's formidable mind, that we are being carried through the process of a poem's manufacture, never actually experiencing a finished poem. There are doubtless good theoretical reasons why this should be so, but the reader's reaction much of the time is to wonder where the poetry went. The truth is it left when all those other clever words came in. When she is more restrained, there is certainly something in Jorie Graham's work to allure and intrigue. It is best to begin with the earlier poems and the shorter poems – certainly not the aptly named *Never*: possibly 'At Lucia Signorelli's Resurrection of the Body' or her fascinating 'Short History of the West'.*

Thus it is with Jorie Graham. At the other extreme, there is Billy Collins, another American, but one whose products are pure surface and which read like the work of someone who sits waiting for them to happen – the kind of fate Larkin spent his life trying to avoid. Billy Collins is famous and enviably popular, although he has the distinct advantage over Jorie Graham of being accessible at a first reading and of being essentially a comic poet. His languorous, occasionally winsome style might well catch the fancy of non-poetry readers in the way that e.e. cummings once did, offering lashings of spring and love for all, though without anything approaching cummings's virtuosity.

But even Collins's superficiality seems like utter profundity compared with some of the poetry that is nowadays filling the shelves where one used to find Patience Strong or Charles Bukowski or Mary Wilson or Felix Dennis or Pam Ayres or Sue Lenier ('better than Ted Hughes and Sylvia Plath', if you recall). Plump modern tomes are the work of latter-day scribblers who have evidently never blotted out a line, who appear to be uninterested in or oblivious to what has been achieved before them, and who make only one thing clear: that the achievement of meaning within a coherent and grammatical sentence remains for them out of reach.

Billy Collins can write – that is never in question – and when he writes about taking off Emily Dickinson's clothes, for example,* he knows what has been done and what he is doing. Jorie Graham's decision to be difficult is a conscious one too. Like Eliot, it could be she feels that difficult times demand difficult poetry. Like Andrew Motion, she knows that poetry speaks 'for what cannot be spoken, as well as what can'.

But it's as true today as it was three centuries ago when Pope was writing *The Dunciad* that the work of certain bestselling scribblers bears little or no relation to poetry. For these notables – our Flecknoe, our Shadwell – whose collections I recommend you do not open, poetry itself remains a closed book.

Edmund Blunden by Rosie Greening.

There is a middle ground, a poetry where there is a clear surface meaning, and it's because surfaces go so deep, as Hugo Williams said,* that things can be made interesting. This is literally the case in a once-popular poem by First World War poet Edmund Blunden.

'The Midnight Skaters' is set in Kent, where Blunden grew up – an area famous for hop-growing. It's apparently about children skating, and used to turn up regularly in school anthologies. I reproduce it here with the kind permission of Margi Blunden and the estate of the poet:

The hop-poles stand in cones,
    The icy pond lurks under,
The pole-tops steeple to the thrones
    Of stars, sound gulfs of wonder;
But not the tallest there, 'tis said,
Could fathom to this pond's black bed.

Then is not death at watch
    Within those secret waters?
What wants he but to catch
    Earth's heedless sons and daughters?
With but a crystal parapet
Between, he has his engines set.

Then on, blood shouts, on, on,
    Twirl, wheel and whip above him,
Dance on this ball-floor thin and wan,
    Use him as though you love him;
Court him, elude him, reel and pass,
    And let him hate you through the glass.

It's not about the war at all – on the surface, at least. But listen to the language, and you'll hear the terminology of the modern battlefield, notably that 'parapet' and those 'engines' suggesting something more than an icy pond. We think of mines and shells and wire. Even hop-poles, while very Kentish, are at the same time like defences of some sort – and they became so in Blunden's own pen-and-ink sketch of the scene which appears on the cover of my Oxford edition of his war memoir, *Undertones of War*. Blunden was always trying to hold back his memory of the First World War trenches, but it lurked there like those large invisible fish about which he had a 'constant instinctive terror'.*

'The Midnight Skaters' can be read as an allegory of the poet's own remarkable *Totentanz*.* Like these nimble skaters, the young recruit deftly eluded death – his nickname was Rabbit, perhaps because he was so quick-witted. The very idea of a 'crystal' parapet is absurd, but so was much of what went on at the Western Front. We are back with Alice, whose adventures were popular among Tommies on the Western Front.

Meaning is in our poems whether we like it or not. The apparent contents may not give much of a clue, but Louis Simpson had the right idea in his poem, 'American Poetry' which begins: 'Whatever it is, it must have/A stomach that can digest/ Rubber, coal, uranium, moons, poems…' In other words, it must be a poetry that is ready to face up to the industrial realities and to the 'Anxiety of Influence'. Simpson does not stop there: 'Like the shark, it contains a shoe…' Are we meant to recall the hero of *The Glass Menagerie* stuck in his shoe factory? Or to remember all the Willy Lomans? We are certainly meant to think that American poetry must have teeth. 'It must swim for miles through the desert/Uttering cries that are almost human.' Is that the cultural desert? And those cries – like Ginsberg's 'Howl', like 'the wail' of Charles Simic, like the cry Frost heard 'over the houses from another street/But not to call me back or say good-bye'…

Edmund Blunden's grave, Long Melford.

Missing a Trick

I learnt to square the circle
but left it at that children's
party and never went back.
I must have forgotten to pack it up
with all the other equipment,
ribbons, cards, sweets, debris
from a cake made out of dates
torn from a calendar, 'flower', nuts
and bolts. So I lost a way
of working that moment when you say
the right word, of making steel
yield to magic, so-called.

Magic

Magician at work.

Poetry is a kind of magic and Prospero is our figurehead; if you can't manage to summon the real thing, then you must at least learn to be a competent stage magician. I'm not quite sure whether I have ever achieved real magic, but I have been known to put on a decent show. And I mean that literally. For much of my teens I was an amateur conjuror.

It's not unusual for young boys and girls to learn party tricks, generally cracker jokes or novelty after-dinner gags, and somewhere in most childhoods there has been a magic box of one kind or another. But once I had tried it – inspired, maybe, by a trick my father did with a shilling in a nest of boxes – there was something about the mixture of performance and secrets and powerful language that drew me somewhat obsessively into the world of amateur magic. My Christmas and birthday present requests almost always came from the Davenports catalogue, a wonderful bumper volume published by the magic shop in Coptic Street, near the British Museum. On one occasion, my parents even took me up to a specialist supplier, Oscar Oswald, an immense Dickensian character whose 'Magical Mart' occupied a flat in Soho where he demonstrated possible tricks that might interest a beginner. It was from him I acquired Colour Change Cords, one of my most enduring and ingenious tricks.

One day at secondary school I was summoned to the staff room where a PE teacher asked me if it was true – knowing by then I had no interest in PE – that I was interested in magic. It turned out his neighbour had been a professional stage magician; he had recently died and his widow was looking for someone to take all the equipment. You can imagine my reaction. It was like being in a *Just William* story. Within a few days I was taken in my teacher's car to collect the hoard – and a hoard is what it was (*William and the Box of Magic, William and the Treasure Trove*): Elusive Rabbits, Squaring the Circle, Multiplying Billiard Balls, The Floating Zombie, Run Rabbit Run... Mind you, there were a few dodgy items mixed in with the fake eggs and silks and rubber doves – the occasional naked woman on a playing card, and not all of the instructions quite matched up to the tricks. But this was a packing case full of top-quality magic equipment, in gleaming chrome or beautifully crafted from lacquered wood, together with a proper conjuror's table, velvet-topped, with a concealed pocket.

I promptly put an advert in the local paper – YOUNG AMATEUR MAGICIAN – and asked a friend who was keen on printing if he'd make me a card:

THE GREAT JADY
GIVES
CONJURING SHOWS
FOR CHILDREN'S AND O.A.P.'S
PARTIES. REASONABLE FEE

Smile though you may at the name this young amateur magician gave himself, soon the queries started rolling in. The biggest gig was for a Christmas do at Fairey Aviation, Heathrow, but most were local birthday parties. Occasionally the kids were rowdy or it would be hard to persuade the parents to pay up, which at least meant I quickly learnt a persistence about money which was later useful in literary journalism. My friend, Mark Fricker, who had featured in several of my home movies, acted as my assistant, and goodness knows what we looked like: he must have been one of the tallest boys in the school; I was definitely the smallest.

There was no poetry involved as yet, but there was a little money, and we had fun. In those days I had no interest in literary matters, and most of my reading other than those *William* books (and some Willard Price adventures) was non-fiction, how-to guides, research for my latest hobby. I still have a

large stock of magic books, including some beautiful Victorian volumes by Professor Hoffmann – *Modern Magic*, *More Magic*, *Later Magic* – picked up at the local Red Cross fete and illustrated with enticing engravings of the workings of elaborate stage illusions. These felt to me like veritable books of spells. I fantasised about building some of the equipment, including how to make a lady float or how to saw her in half, but they were beyond me – even if I had known any willing ladies. I had the instinct to make things out of wood or metal, but lacked the skills. As for social skills, they were a long way off.

Advancing into my teens, I became more bookish, more interested in writing, and the magic shows faded away. Farewell to the endless rabbits and paper streamers and production goods. Farewell to the cake made out of eggshell, 'flower', nuts and bolts, dates (from a calendar), and burning methylated spirits for flavouring. I now earned my pocket money at the EMI record factory in Hayes or, appropriately enough, at the local fire-extinguisher factory. It wasn't exactly that I had grown cripplingly self-conscious, though that colour-change trick would soon strike a sympathetic chord, but I sensed that conjuring was simply

The Floating Lady.

The cake trick.

153

too undignified a pursuit for a would-be writer. I devoted myself more and more to stage productions and to music.

But by the time I had finished university and needed a job, it occurred to me that one source of income could be by giving magic shows once again. I had applied to work in Hamleys toy store over Christmas, demonstrating tricks, and even had an interview, but turned down the job offer because I felt the whole business was deceitful. It was one thing to entertain children; quite another – and here I must have remembered a certain Christmas morning – to fool them into parting with their money for a mere secret. I would go it alone, and would at the same time make a virtue of my growing passion for poetry.

By then I knew Eliot's distinction between poetry and verse, and understood that not everything in rhyme and metre had to be designed for immortality – as many successful poets can testify, from Jessie Pope and Robert Service to John Cooper Clarke and Brian Bilston. So I wrote some patter myself in rhyming couplets and learnt it off by heart, incorporating one or two classics: for Eliot's 'Macavity' a vanishing rabbit trick was converted into a vanishing cat, and one of Ted Hughes's children's poems about the moon fitted well with the Floating Zombie. As I've already mentioned, Hughes seemed to brighten when he heard I was giving magic shows, though I'm not sure I ever confessed to hijacking his moon poem. Responding to some plays I had sent him, he said he thought conjuring was a skill much admired and envied by theatrical people and that it proved I was willing to throw myself into a battlefield – to stand up and improvise a stage show, in peril of 'being laughed off'. I knew already the dangers of such a reaction, having been among the laughers in the first ever professional magic show I saw when I was at primary school. 'Competent' doesn't even come close to describing that performance, which was one failed trick after another, including a Cinderella whose coach never arrived, leaving her in rags on the stage.

The theatrical people who rejected my plays clearly didn't share Hughes's point of view, but the BBC's Hans Keller did when I was interviewed for my clerical job at Radio 3. Performance, after all, is performance. I remember him saying he hoped I would be able to keep up the magic, and muttering apologies about the 'bloody salary' the BBC was offering me. It's odd to think of ultra-rational Hans even mentioning magic, but he knew its power, and had indeed entered into a debate with his friend Benjamin Britten over whether magic in music is analysable. For Hans, everything was analysable if you felt you had some understanding of it – as to the rest, he agreed with Wittgenstein that it was better to remain silent. In a radio talk* about 'Britten as Interpreter' he responded to the composer's comments on the experience of returning to perform Schubert's song cycle *Winterreise*, 'the extraordinary mastery of it... the renewal of the magic; each time the mystery remains.' Hans suggested that 'in all valid performances, it is the instinctive understanding, the feeling of the magic, that comes first. Analysis cannot replace it; but it does make one aware of the logic of one's emotional experience... all intellectual analysis without emotional basis is sham.'

At the time when I was giving my own last performances to rooms full of young children, I had that instinct for the magic not of the tricks, which felt now more like sham (really just wrapped up mechanical actions), but of the words which were driving me on. As any magician will tell you, the most powerful moment is when you get the room to shout out the magic word, the more polysyllabic the better. It's very useful, too, for concealing the sound of a click or a slide. The *abracadabra, hocus pocus, shazam* and the so-called patter are all designed to divert and misdirect: these are the vital elements. It's what every actor knows – and doubtless what Shakespeare knew, who himself turned more and more to the theme of magic in his late plays. If Hamlet gives us a portrait of the young Shakespeare, then Prospero is surely the ageing artist, the word-magician who is fully aware of the potency at his disposal. When I came to compose my long poem, *The Silence*, I was well past the age at which Shakespeare had stopped writing and become his works, but I was very conscious of his masque-like late creations as a model. As I have explained in earlier chapters, my poem is about Sibelius's thirty-year creative silence. But one of his last major works before the drought was incidental music for Shakespeare's play, and the final third of my long poem is full of allusions to *The Tempest*.

For decades I kept quiet about my conjuring years because I feared the reviewers latching on to the fact and applying it to my books – 'mere trickery, not real magic'. There are other 'magician poets', such as the American David Wagoner, who died during the pandemic and had long been a favourite of mine before I learnt of his parallel career. Apparently the only organisation Wagoner admitted to belonging to was the Society of American Magicians, where he learnt skills essential for his novel *The Escape Artist*. Most of the poems about magic have been purged from his *Collected*, although 'The Inexhaustible Hat' remains, and there is a new one in 'My Passenger', a splendid anecdote about a drunken policeman and a carload of conjuring equipment. The critics have generally been kind to Wagoner, putting a positive spin on this biographical gift. Sanford Pinsker, for example, simply notes that the way Wagoner makes something pop out of nothing 'is the essence of the magician's art', and comments on the importance of 'astonishment' in his verse. Perhaps it accounts for Wagoner's interest in 'performance', in 'exhibition' – nature as a grand show, the 'circus-act' of a bird climbing a stalk, the mockingbird's impressions, the peacock's display – and certainly lies behind such fine late work as his version of the Orpheus-Eurydice myth. Unlike Rilke's version to which it is indebted, this Orpheus turns round because he is so excited at the new music he is writing as a result of his visit to Hades.

But neither Wagoner nor I have gone down the James Merrill route and devoted ourselves to the Ouija board. Nor have we followed in Yeats's footsteps by attending seances, consulting mediums or joining the Society for Psychical Research. That I left to my wife, who has an inexhaustible appetite for such things, though you must put out of your mind any similarity to what Mrs Yeats (George Hyde-Lees) did for her husband with her automatic writing. Brenda Maddox's brilliant and fascinating book *George's Ghosts** laid out her underlying motives in unsparing detail. Nevertheless I suspect I have read more widely in the literature of the occult than those scientists who dismiss it, and I can't resist true stories which involve apparent magic. Therefore I suppose I may also be regarded as 'silly' – to quote Auden's elegy for Yeats.

Among the stories I have put into verse is that of Daniel Dunglas Home, whose name – it's pronounced Hume – I mentioned earlier. There was a sequence about him in my collection *The Home Key*, but also I wrote an uncollected piece designed to be set to music, called simply *Home*. This was originally conceived as something halfway between an oratorio and a one-act opera. It concerns the life and activities of this nineteenth-century Scottish-American medium, one of the most extraordinary characters of his time. His fame coincided with the rise of Spiritualism, which was partly a reaction to the intense materialism of the age and the traditional Church's stubborn resistance to such supernatural possibilities. There were plenty of willing participants whenever he held a seance. Home was regularly denounced as a fraud and thoroughly detested by many of his contemporaries, including Robert Browning, who composed one of his longest and least effective poems about him, thinly disguised as 'Mr Sludge, "The Medium"'.* Although he was rather a weak and indeed 'homeless' individual, he passed virtually every 'test' he was ever set and managed to confound the wisest moguls of the industrial revolution, much to the dismay of some – though not all – of the Victorian scientific community.

That notion of a search for a spiritual 'home' appealed to me, and is one of the punning preoccupations in my verse/prose text, which mixes narrative with a series of dramatic set pieces – various seances, the investigation by physicist William Crookes, a set-to with the Brownings. I felt there was a great deal of musical and theatrical potential in some of the more bizarre incidents recorded, where apparently bells rang, tambourines were shaken, grand pianos floated across the room.

Here's the opening:

A seance is in progress as the lights come up.

CHORUS
At home. The candles sway and dim.
The carpets seem to rise. He's come.
He joins our circle, smiles.

HOME AS A BOY (*could be invisible,*
a high voice from the seance)
                                    Papa!
There's a heart beating in my chair!

CHORUS
Silvery glow. Icy gales.
Rap! The table. Distant bells
and wave-break, pipe and creak
of rigging. A gull's cry. You shake,
as warm and human fingers clasp
your hand, tap out the names you ask
while he sits in tranquillity
tight-lipped and far away.

HOME (*grown up, steps into light*)
They call me fraud.

CHORUS
But if he is, he has fooled the world.

HOME
They call me cheap.

CHORUS
But if he is, he has charged no fee.

HOME
They call me crook.

CROOKES (*suddenly visible on other side of stage*)
But if he is, then so am I.

CHORUS
Crookes the scientist has seen
his accordion play one-handed
'There's no place like home…'

CROOKES
And if he hid a harmonica
behind his bushy moustache,
I did not spot it.

CHORUS
Transported by an accordion
in sweet discord with all
good sense and learning
'Home, Home, Sweet Sweet Home…'
(*etc. Continues beneath narration.*)*

In the 1990s, I was much impressed by a book called *The Airmen Who Would Not Die* by John G. Fuller, and immediately knew I had to write a poem based on it. *Gascoigne's Egg** brought together several of my interests and coincided with a period when I was forced to confront mortality as my father was slipping into his last decline. It tells the story of the fatal maiden voyage of the *R101* airship, which was built in and launched from one of the two mighty sheds at Cardington, Bedfordshire, a few miles from our home. In fact, our neighbour had watched the hydrogen-filled airship pass at the bottom of her garden back in 1930 on its stormy flight to exotic places – it crashed in Beauvais, killing all on board.

Cardington happens to be the birthplace of one of my favourite Elizabethan poets, George Gascoigne, author of anthology pieces such as 'Gascoigne's Lullaby' and 'Gascoigne's Farewell'. The remains of the manor where he grew up can still be made out on the edge of the village. These things might seem to be entirely unconnected, but Fuller's book – well written and researched, and not at all trashy, despite the publisher's best attempts to make it appear so – is a ghost story.

The Cardington sheds.

Essentially, Fuller makes the highly convincing case that there were warnings from the spirit world that the airship was going to come down. Taking this idea a little further, I had Gascoigne's ghost narrate the story and at the same time turn it into an allegory of the history of English verse. Although it is seldom acknowledged, and for most readers his name might as well be Anon, Gascoigne was the first poet in English to use many verse forms and genres we now take for granted, as the poem makes clear: 'our literature's first/blank verse is a blank in the memory;/the first tale of modern life, a blank;//the first masque, sonnet sequence, satire/— all blank. Deleted.'

The poignancy of this was emphasised by the fact that in the second hangar at Cardington (the sheds are enormous and visible for miles) another airship was being built by private enterprise, the *R100*, and one of those working on it was the bestselling author Neville Shute. The stanza continues:

> I am famous for all
> that is unknown. *Ferenda Natura…* fame is
>
> not the second hangar at Cardington,
> the quietly virtuous and unblemished Vickers,
> never in service to the state, and nowhere
>
> commemorated. Master Shute is read by thousands.
> My little Robin keep close your coin.
> My lullaby sleeps tight in the anthologies.

I dedicated the poem to John Gurney, a poet who lived in Bedford and had an interest in the *R101*. Tucked in my reading copy of *Gascoigne's Egg* I have his own poem about the ship. But it is John's epic, *War*, which I think really goes to the heart of things magical.

As an account of the First World War this long poem is highly original in that it is written from the point of view of an aviator. John Gurney had himself been a fighter pilot and might be expected to know what he's talking about when he describes the apparently 'civilised and clean' life of airmen 'compared with our unholy infantry'. But it is the cosmographic scope of the book that makes it feel like a real epic. The narrator, a neurasthenic squadron-major, is also a medium and spends many of his non-flying hours in conversation with William Blake, visiting different spiritual planes in his astral body, learning the shape of life to come. In this, the poem resembles James Merrill's *The Changing Light at Sandover*, but it is written with such a cool, manual-like precision, in such predictable and well-tempered iambics, and with such a lack of irony, that disbelief hardly occurs any more than it would in reading Dante or Milton.

Take, for example, the description of how a soul departs from a body in Book XIII. It is curiously surgical and characteristically unemotional in tone, yet its poetic precision – note that spondee in the penultimate line, and the specific nautical use of 'springs' – proves very moving in the context of this book, which deals with the death of the narrator's mother:

> I reached out with my leather-washer stick
> and tried, to Blake's annoyance, to entwine
> the cable round its shape. I saw at once
> my wire rod passed straight through it, just as if
> the line were but a filament of light
> without the slightest substance. By degrees
> the cord appeared to fray. I watched it part
> like strands of hemp that slowly snap apart
> in springs that tie a steamer to a quay.
> They splay, and crack, and detonate, until
> one thread alone is left to take the strain
> of a big wave, whose ship is carried out,
> and breaks the hold forever.

War is in some ways a spiritual handbook, a twentieth-century Book of the Dead. Unlike Merrill's trilogy, there is nothing of the circus about it: what compels us to read on to the end is partly a strong narrative, building to the ultimate single-combat between the narrator and the German ace, Von Streich, and partly the feeling that this book is going to tell us something about ourselves. One of John Gurney's last long poems is on Freud, although Freud would have detested the 'black tide of mud of occultism' that surges through these pages. At *War*'s heart is a mythic quest through the unconscious for the sources of evil. As the narrator searches for his newly dead and spiritually scarred brother, we witness the complex structure of the afterlife, its many hazards, but also the various opportunities for healing; and we are shown 'the great task', which is, as Blake puts it in the poem, 'to introvert all war'.

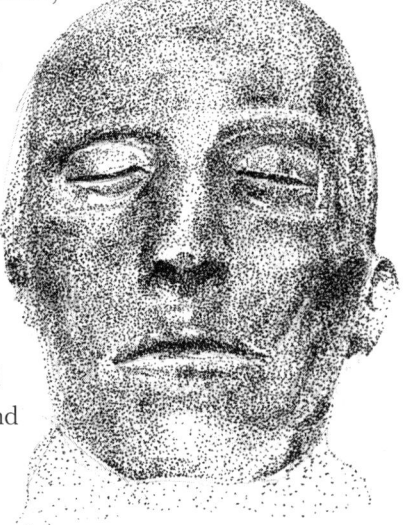

Gascoigne's Egg was published the very year John died, and perhaps because so many of my friends seemed to be departing prematurely, I was once again drawn to the occult. This time it was an unexpected yet predictable return to Egypt. When we lived there, friends had told us about their visit to the Temple of Abydos and their meeting with a strange old woman called Omm Sety. She was something of a legend in the country.

Born in Blackheath as Dorothy Eady, she tumbled down the stairs at the age of three and soon started to believe that

Sety I by Rosie Greening.

her real home was far from London and a good deal further back than the early 1900s. Through visions and recurring dreams the idea took root that the child had in a former life been a temple priestess and consort to Pharaoh Sety I, whose face is still one of the best known among the mummies.* Young Dorothy would not rest until she had made her way out to Abydos and indeed found a suitable Egyptian man to marry – 'someone like *him*' – which she did, although he soon left when he realised that her strangeness involved some very intimate encounters with the dead Pharaoh. The archaeologists at Abydos were astonished at how much Dorothy seemed to know about their site, and could not deny that her visions kept pointing them towards new discoveries. She set up home near Abydos with a reputation, a menagerie and a clutch of friends, and became a tourist attraction in her own right. Omm Sety was still there in 1980 when Jane and I lived in Upper Egypt and when we visited Abydos itself, although we never met her.

My poem, *Omm Sety*, was constructed to represent the structure of a key building at Abydos, the Osirion, with equivalent numbers of stanzas to pillars, for example. The narrative juxtaposed imagined speech by the Pharaoh in rhymed italics with passages about Omm Sety and glimpses of our own time in Egypt, set out to represent the so-called 'djed' pillar. Nobody quite knows what this is (maybe Osiris's backbone?) but it features on many Egyptian temple walls, and it makes an interesting syllabic stanza shape. *Omm Sety* is one of the most arcane things I have ever written, yet it is one of the few poems that people have come up to me and enthused about. It's also a good performance piece. When it appeared as a pamphlet from John Lucas's Shoestring Press in 2001, we

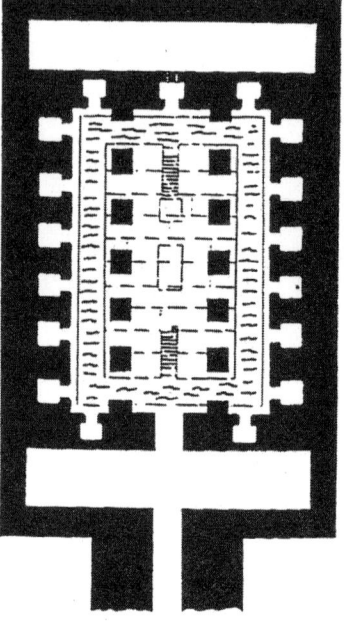

The Osirion at Abydos.

premiered it in Kimbolton Castle dividing the parts among the voices of the late John Gohorry, Rennie Parker, Stuart Henson and me. I've often thought it would work well on radio.

Reading from The Tutankhamun variations *at Beacon Hill, Highclere*

When I give a poetry reading, I wonder how much has fed into my performances from those old conjuring days. There is no fancy equipment, no collapsing wand, or silly hat, no cane that turns into a silk scarf; and the trickery is all on the printed page, apart from those improvised bits of crowd-pleasing patter in between. No misdirection is needed, though a good reading is the best possible disguise for a bad poem. Is there a magic word for the room to join in? No, I'll leave that to John Agard. For me there's only that barely audible sigh and knowing nod that Dickens describes somewhere in *Nicholas Nickleby* as the typical reaction to a literary reading. Now, there is a man who knew about performing, and who was also no mean amateur conjuror.

To C.G. Jung, Probably

If as I'm sitting at Böll's desk an email
arrives out of the blue of thirty years
from one who taught me Böll or if I talk
about Łódź with A only to discover
B, whom I meet that evening, has a photo
of its main street on his mantelpiece, because
his family came from Łódź: how do these
synchronicities help me live my life?
How even can I explain to anyone
their strange personal potency? You cross
the beach at Goa and *Hello!* a voice calls,
calls again as you cross the Pont du Gard.
So what? It's none of it the slightest use,
though just as X is in your thoughts, X rings,
or as you read Y's works, the death of Y
is announced. Give us more to get hold of, gods,
while Jane sits with the Greek anthology
and I recall how on an impulse we drove
to Z's grave, stood there, then saw her husband
approach from nowhere... like that empty seat
beside me at a formal dinner, filled
suddenly by one who knew the whole story
from A to Z, each particular name.

Coincidence

Kimbolton Castle by Rosie Greening.

It is some time in the 1990s and I'm on the top floor of Kimbolton Castle, home to the school where I teach, typing up a selection of my poems for an American press, who will shortly reject them. About halfway through, I reach 'Sestina for the Six Wives', one of my more intricate pieces of work. As I type the lines about Anne Boleyn dancing in a yellow dress on the day of Catherine's funeral, the computer crashes and I lose the poem. So I restart, reach the same point, and it happens again. On the third attempt I lose everything. Strange enough? Even stranger when you recall that it was in this castle that Catherine of Aragon died.

It's a good story and I know it's true, even if no one else thinks anything of it. And whatever the explanation, it is a reminder that poetry does tend to inhabit a curiously twilit world. Unlike T.S. Eliot's Margate Sands, where nothing connects with nothing, in the poet's head everything connects with everything. You might even say that poetry is a state of hyperconnectedness. Every poet, every artist has a story about synchronicity, and I have noticed, curiously enough, that they often seem to involve birds. Not only much-quoted examples such as Sibelius's encounter with the cranes that prefigured his death, but little things that you might miss if you aren't tuned in. I think of the blue tit that kept tapping at my study window when I was writing a series of bird poems and an owl that was brought into the pub where I was having lunch in Camelford on the day the *TLS* first published any poem of mine – about an

167

owl. And I also recall how I was manning our school bookshop in the old mews area of the castle one day, when I picked up Neil Astley's bestselling anthology, *Staying Alive*, to browse through. I noticed there was a poem about a heron by my colleague, Stuart Henson, lines I knew well. But I had no idea 'The Heron' had been included in Neil's book. Since Stuart was working just along the corridor, I took it to show him and find out why he hadn't told me about such a notable literary acceptance. It was the first he knew of the book, since the permissions request had disappeared into the great vacancy that was Harry Chambers/Peterloo Poets. But the heron in question, he told me ('dead by the stable door/at the foot of the wall, in the snow, in the drain.') had actually been found just below the window in the drama studio where we were standing.*

As it happens, just today Tom Chivers posted on Twitter/X – the more appropriate name in this case – that he had been up all night finishing the last chapter of his book when he glanced through the window and saw 'a grey heron flying straight towards me from the river, then lifting its wings into the sky. The last line I wrote: "The heron scans the water and is gone."'

One of the most striking such bird stories was told me by the poet Annie Fisher, who lives near where Edward Thomas heard chiffchaffs when he was 'In Pursuit of Spring'. On the very day a century later, she went to the same spot hoping to hear some herself, and on returning home was told that a bird looking very like a chiffchaff had just flown in and perched on her computer. It's

Edmund Blunden's copy of Keats *by Edward Thomas.*

an extraordinary tale, which I can never resist telling, and although I tried to make it into a poem, it's really much easier to take ordinariness as your starting point. Which is why 'The Ancient Mariner' – the ultimate ominous bird poem – is such an achievement.

The writings of Edmund Blunden are full of strange synchronicities and ghostly encounters, although he seldom draws any conclusions. One of the most curious personal experiences came when in 1918 he found Edward Thomas's book on Keats down the side of a bunk in a billet where Thomas had himself been staying. Blunden was always convinced that it had been the author's own copy.

I was fortunate enough to see and hold this little book (pictured here) when I visited the Blunden archive at his daughter's home before it was transferred to America. I only ended up editing his *Undertones of War*, in fact, because Margi Blunden chanced upon my study of First World War poets* and liked how I had written about her father. This war memoir, which has never been out of print since 1928, presents a phantasmagorical world of tragedy into which the coincidences of everyday life are continually drawn. Brothers seemed to be especially afflicted, as in Chapter VI, 'Specimen of the War of Attrition'. Blunden has just greeted a young and cheerful lance-corporal making tea, when a shell bursts nearby. He thinks at first they have been lucky – Blunden had the most astonishing luck – but there's a shout and he turns to find, where the boy had been, only blackening flesh, pulpy bone and 'the eye under the duckboard'. He continues: 'At this moment, while we looked with intense fear at so strange a horror, the lance-corporal's brother came round the traverse.'

The only one among my friends who has been a fighter was John Gurney, whose epic, *War*, I discussed in the previous chapter. He was also very drawn to the Jungian world, to crossing paths and intersecting contrails, something I referred to in a sonnet written after our paths unexpectedly coincided one day at the local station:

> Bedford Midland. A stooping Horus hawk
> above the mind's abandoned aerodrome
> checks at the barrier. *John?* Our shock
> dumb-synchronised. *John!* I in monochrome,
> pain-striped for a funeral, you travelling
> light to grandparenthood. And suddenly, in
> one surprise roll, we are unravelling
> a rainbow, enter an inverted spin
> through ether, phlogiston, prana, to where
> Egypt opens its lotus chute. Aerial
> displays that – like the station signs we tear
> past blindly – soon prove immaterial,
> as King's Cross/St Pancras brakes all dreams
> but yours: you sit there, gliding to the Thames.

One always felt with John that things were happening on a different – well, different *plane*, for lack of a better word. He seemed to inhabit that mystical zone where things connect.

Two other writers of whom I suspect that was true are the Swedish Nobel laureate Tomas Tranströmer (see my chapter, 'Dreaming') and his American translator Robert Bly. Their very first exchange in late 1964 involved a poetic synchronicity. Tranströmer had heard about Bly's poetry journal, *The Sixties*, and wrote a letter of enquiry. Bly reveals in the published correspondence* that he had actually just driven halfway across the state of Minnesota to get hold of Tranströmer's *Halvfärdiga himlen* (*The Half-Finished Heaven*) from the university library. When he returned, the note was waiting for him.

A better known and rather wonderful example is how the surrealist poet David Gascoyne attended therapy sessions for depression, where they would occasionally read poems. The group leader, Judy, later told the *Independent* that on this occasion she had chosen 'a more recent poem that had always intrigued me called 'September Sun' and announced to the group:

'This afternoon we're going to read a poem by David Gascoyne. It's quite complex so I'll read it slowly and then we'll see if we can understand what it means.' The tall, sad-looking man touched me on the arm and said quietly, 'I wrote that poem. I'm David Gascoyne.' I said, 'I'm sure you are, dear.' I didn't believe him for a moment. Some of them do have delusions of grandeur, you see. *

He insisted, and when she asked him during the tea break if he really was the author, he said, 'Of course I am,' and signed the poem. Reader, she married him.

There's really nothing much one can say to such a tale, except something about love finding a way. It's a diverting 'Convergence of the Twain' – and how Thomas Hardy loved coincidence! – like news of Wilfred Owen's death reaching his home on Armistice Day or George Mackay Brown's funeral falling on the feast day of his beloved St Magnus. 'And if you call that a coincidence,' the minister said, 'I wish you a very dull life'. Perhaps one needs a dull life in order to make room for noticing coincidence.

I have more personal examples of coincidence than I can possibly relate: the mosquito in my ear as I typed a poem about the death of Lord Carnarvon from a mosquito bite; reading Kipling's 'Boots' just before the song came on the radio; dreaming of R.S. Thomas's death and waking to hear it announced; showing my poem about the White Horse of Uffington to Penelope Shuttle who revealed she was wearing a necklace with a design featuring the same horse; finding a feature on Achill in the newspaper the day I received my book of Achill Island sonnets; writing a poem about the railway line at Helpston, then turning on Channel 4 News to see Michael Crick standing... you can guess. And just this week, to divert myself from a noisy fireworks display, opening at random a back issue of *Agenda* and seeing a haiku by Masaoka Shiki, translated by that fine, neglected poet Harry Guest. Of course the poem was about fireworks.

Most striking of all was at a Royal Literary Fund dinner a year or two ago, when a latecomer took the only empty seat, which happened to be next to me. We had little to say, but I vaguely recognised the name: not only a celebrated playwright, it turned out, but someone I had long regretted being unable to meet twenty years ago, who knew my wife's family well and was closely involved in their tragic history. Then, very recently I was editing a new collection of poems and decided to insert one about coincidence and synchronicity which alludes at the end to that occasion ('To C.G. Jung, Probably', which precedes this chapter). Having pasted this poem into the book, I decided to check my emails. There was one from the RLF (their weekly newsletter) and right at the end they had included a mention of my forthcoming pamphlet. But immediately beneath that – the only other announcement – was the name Louise Page, and the news that she had died. It was Louise who came and filled that empty seat at the RLF dinner.

Most people, I suggest, do 'notice such things', as Hardy put it, but laugh them off or shrug them away. For poets they can be a kind of reassurance that the magic is working, as when Sylvia Plath happened to find a flat in Primrose Hill in a building where Yeats had lived. In Ted Hughes's case, he would try and tap into that magic, whether it was that dream I have

Blue plaque commemorating Sylvia Plath in Primrose Hill.

already mentioned of a fox-headed creature telling him to switch from studying English at Cambridge or the occasion he discovered a small model fox while burying a dead one – his 'first thought-fox' Jonathan Bate calls it. But it's worth remembering too that he consulted astrological charts to find the most propitious dates for his books to appear.

Nowadays authors are more likely to check who's on the judging panel of any likely award. What they probably should also check is that the gods of synchronicity haven't led them to write the same book as someone else. Coincidence is often raised as a defence for plagiarism, but sometimes it just feels like the right moment for, say, a novel about Henry James. Three came out at the same time a few years ago, though it was Colm Tóibín's that received all the attention.

The sceptic will suggest that people like me have become so bewitched by coincidence that we see it everywhere. I would agree, and it's what makes writing poetry so exhilarating. For example, a few years ago, as Covid continued to sweep through the country and face masks became compulsory in shops, Jane and I were in Swaffham, Norfolk, tracking down the cottage where Howard Carter grew up, visiting the Tutankhamun Emporium run by his great-niece. I suddenly saw the irony of visiting such a place on the day all the living had to be masked – not in gold, but in plastic or cloth. So a poem began. You have to appreciate – as Les Murray advised – the doubleness.

Tutankhamun by Rosie Greening.

Egypt has always invited 'the intersection of the timeless moment', and one incident I cannot forget from during the years Jane and I were living in Aswan. A terrific storm hit the region. We saw and heard it approaching as we were sitting down to a meal of Nile perch with some Egyptian friends, as I described in my memoir *Threading a Dream*:[*]

Jane was the first to point out the distant flashes of light beyond the railway lines, over towards the eastern desert – a rockier, and much darker reddish landscape than across the river, rich in iron, a source of those vibrant brown colours in the tomb paintings. At first we thought it must be something to do with shunting trains or wheels making sparks in the heat. But eventually we decided that it was lightning, although there was no thunder. No sooner had we agreed on this than there was a clattering and banging and shouting from somewhere outside. The long, broad main street of Atlas was, like all Egyptian thoroughfares, extremely dusty, but the dust usually stayed where it was, stirred by the odd gust from the Nile, or kicked up by donkey carts, perhaps a *wallad* playing football. What we saw now was an enormous cloud of dust advancing down the street, bringing that same clattering and banging and shouting towards us.

We flew indoors as the building was engulfed. Dust was everywhere. The noise was terrific. Our hosts set to nailing up the shutters while the rest of us cowered in the flat. We had been planning to leave for the new university quarter out at 'Sahari City' that evening – one of many invitations we had not yet learnt how to refuse – but even the jeep that was ready to take us would not have coped with such conditions, so the driver was invited in and there we all sat. The storm raged – wind, rain, dust, great forks of lightning over to the east, though still no thunder. Next thing, the lights went out.

We learnt later that 20,000 people were made homeless between Aswan and the Red Sea, and over sixty were killed in a village in the desert we could see from our balcony. Surface mail was the only means of communicating with home, and letters took at least ten days each way. About a month after the storm, we received one from my mother, who has always had a psychic streak. She asked whether anything particularly momentous had happened on the 25th of October. It was, of course, the night that we had been stranded in our neighbours' flat, the night a village was washed away.

If Egypt has tended to breed such coincidences in my life, so has another 'waste land'. As I have explained earlier, one of my collections was the result of a pilgrimage to Iceland to track down my father's wartime 'Valhall Camp' – whose very name is inviting to the mythically minded. *Iceland Spar*, you may recall, takes its title from a kind of calcite which splits light so that everything seen through it appears double. One of the book's longest and weirdest poems is a version of the Old Norse poem, *Völuspá*, which I called 'Coming Soon' and reshaped into a 160-line disaster-movie vision of apocalypse:

> …The world-web shivers, the system
> hacked and trembling, the lone anarchist
> breaks loose and the viruses spread.
> How are the fatcats? How are the mice?
>
> The radio masts are trembling, the gods
> are talking, trapped workmen wail
> in the lift they repaired.
> Then what? Shall I go on?
>
> Garm howls his feedback at the opening
> to the final scene, in Gnipahelli – but he'll
> be cut. The title will be *Ragnarok*.
> The posters will slogan and blare its triumph.*

I was printing off the final draft of 'Coming Soon' as news came of 9/11. Iceland does seem to have haunted me since. At my mother's funeral, as we waited for the cortège in our suits of solemn black – just a few minutes after I had mustered a prayer asking for some kind of sign that all was well – a taxi sped up. Dazzlingly white, decorated with imagery of ice and snow, it was emblazoned 'ICELAND'. A door opened in the word and out stepped my best friend – looking for all the world like his beloved C.G. Jung. And I felt the grip of coincidence again in 2017 at Hawthornden Writers' Retreat, where one of the other five fellows proved to be the distinguished Icelandic poet Gerður Kristný, who has since become a very good friend.

A cairn for the elves in Iceland.

Odin allegedly had two ravens, Thought and Memory, one on each shoulder. I think there is a third that maybe he doesn't tell us about.

My literary coincidences are usually too convoluted to explain or too trivial to mention, mere puns along the way – like when I spotted a girl reading *The Tin Drum* as my train stopped at Tyndrum. Or they relate to some private preoccupation, as when I heard I'd had work accepted for the distinguished American journal, *The Hudson Review*, and strode happily into town, finding myself at a library sale. There on top of the pile were three copies of that very publication for 30p each. Not only is it a very unusual journal to see anywhere this side of the Atlantic – especially in Frome, which I was visiting – but I had never actually owned a copy. So, significant to me, but no one else really.

If you don't let it disconcert you, coincidence can be reassuring, even thrilling. You are part of a novel someone else is writing. Indeed, when I realised that an Indian gentleman sitting next to me at Little Gidding was the novelist Vikram Seth, or when some years later it proved to be the location for my unforgettable conversation with Seamus Heaney, these felt like plot moves. In the latter case, we talked almost entirely about Dennis O'Driscoll, who has been a force for synchronicity in my life for a good while. For example, I have already explained in the chapter 'Dreaming' how my visit to Achill Island coincided with an email from my old German teacher. He had in fact seen a sonnet of mine about Dennis in the *Spectator*, and since he too was Irish he thought he would get in touch after twenty-odd years. *Achill Island Tagebook* is dedicated to Dennis's memory, and was accepted for publication on what would have been his sixty-fifth birthday, New Year's Day 2019. Dennis died prematurely on Christmas Eve 2012, and his life too had been full of overlapping significances. Or maybe it was some deeper instinct that led him, having lost both his parents young, to spend his life working in the Death Duties department of the Irish Civil Service.

There is a divinity that shapes our ends, I suppose. And it assuredly felt that way during our 2017 family holiday in Crete. I was composing a crown of sonnets, which I'd begun on the flight out – to be titled *Europa* until Sean O'Brien got there first.* This is one of the most intricately connected of poetic forms, in which the last line of each of its fourteen sonnets is the first line of the next and the whole 'corona' ends with a fifteenth made up of those lines. I had wanted to

Plane tree by Rosie Greening.

visit the tree where Zeus is said to have brought Europa, but we decided it was too far north. On our last day, the family headed instead to the beach at Matala, not even knowing it had inspired Joni Mitchell's 'Carey', Jane's favourite – a song we often listened to together. That was coincidence enough, but on the way there our taxi driver suddenly pulled over at an archaeological site, Gortyna, and said he would take a smoke while we looked around. It wasn't anywhere we'd planned to come – but inside, beyond the odeon and the sixth-century engraved Laws of Gortyna, to my astonishment, I found the very thing I had most wanted to see, that I had mistakenly believed to be out of reach: the evergreen plane tree of Europa.

Lines

From near the well, beside that burnt-out barn,
a footpath re-emerges, only lightly worn,
across young sugar beet. But when I reach the turn
I'm staring down a barrel at the setting sun.

This must have happened here before, of course, except
it's not recorded – can this really have escaped
my notice, my own private solstice? The sun stopped,
is what they used to think; but I am blinded, rapt

and moved to thinking how, beneath the twists of life,
modernity's weird warp, the calculated weave
of industry, through ridge and furrow, lord and serf,
past Anglo-Saxon routes that plunge and wheel and curve

down far beneath the Romans' perfect paving crust,
where mystical remains of ley lines might be guessed
between a church, a fort, a tumulus (or traced
with Alfred Watkins' zeal from pub to mobile mast)

a force is running. Never moving, yet it guides
those who will give it time: its non-existence leads
where our desire paths couldn't go, because their gods
enjoy the maze we've made too much. The source explodes

in red and yellow flame across our little home
and suddenly I'm grey again. It was a dream
of absolute direction. Now I must assume
I know the way, that my familiar path will come

to light where it has always been. The moon gives weak
support, and if I weren't quite so much in the dark
of school-day trigonometry, I think I'd take
some other wisdom from this February walk

and measure out these lines, and aim them at the sun
as Druids' lines of solstice used to... though they're gone,
and what's on top is what we have. Which will go soon.
So don't forget to notice when you're off the phone.

Roots

Some poets are particularly attuned to location. Wordsworth, for instance, wrote instinctively about the place of his birth. Not being lucky enough to have been brought up in the Lake District, I find myself turning to somewhere equally magical in my imagination: the area around Heathrow Airport. I have written about it on and off since my teens, which was when our family moved north from Hounslow and its noise – though only north as far as the end of Betjeman's Metropolitan Line. As I have suggested already, living away from a place seems to make a writer feel it more intensely, but Eastcote didn't affect me that way (I hated it), and while we were living in Barnes, after we married, although I tried to produce suburban poems, it didn't work: 'the suburb is an awkward and unlikely theatre for a poem', according to Eavan Boland. If I had only known the poetry of Eavan Boland then, that might have helped.*

No, it wasn't until after our time in Egypt and after our spell in Scotland that I began to turn to the land of my childhood. When we were living in New Jersey, I wrote a longish poem called 'Under the Flight Path', which summoned versions of the various characters who lived in our cul-de-sac. There was also an attempt at a longer sequence, 'Crossing the Heath', which appeared in a much-reduced form in *The Home Key*. And single poems kept emerging such as 'Hounslow' in *To the War Poets*, which is a shape poem that could be a plane or a house, but it recalls my little bedroom with its steam-train wallpaper and its view of the incoming flights. Even now I remember particular distinctive sounds (not only the planes), such as the clink of the gate, as in the poem which precedes the chapter, 'Listening'.

It's not quite true to say that it all began in Hounslow, because one of my roots is still firmly in the old allotments where the Public Record Office is situated, by the River Thames in Kew. I spent the first few years of my life in Kew, because it was where my parents had both lived before they met and where my grandfather continued to live until his death in the 1960s. Those walks by

The pagoda in Kew Gardens.

the Thames have become part of my childhood 'capital' – to use Seamus Heaney's metaphor. And what poet could resist the idea of their very own Eden, even if you did have to pay one old penny to pass through the turnstile into the Botanical Gardens? Eden is an image that recurs in my books, though not quite to the extent that it does in Edwin Muir or Charles Tomlinson. And the pagoda continues to fascinate me. It was always closed when I was a boy, and I have yet to climb it, even though it has been restored. My last opportunity was stymied by Covid-19.

The culmination of my obsession with the place where I spent most of my childhood, the old Hounslow Heath, came – as I have suggested in earlier chapters – with the publication of a collaborative book. It all began in February 2014 when I read the poem 'Heath Row' from *To the War Poets* at a Falmouth event organised by Penelope Shuttle. It's a poem that works backwards, leading the reader's imagination through time to when there were Druids on Hounslow Heath – as the remains of a temple suggest, which emerged when the first runway was laid at Heathrow. After the reading, Penny and I were reminiscing about our childhoods on opposite sides of the old Heath. I laughingly said we should write something about it together... then I returned to Cambridgeshire and thought no more of it. I was still teaching at the time, though about to retire, and had plenty to occupy me. But I did write three poems, imagining two characters setting off across the Heath like Macbeth and Banquo, out of time, or into a timeless zone, and I emailed them to Penny in Cornwall. She quickly replied with poems of her own. Mine had Roman numerals, hers had titles. Mine were long-lined, hers shorter. I sent some again – and so it went on, the collaboration becoming more and more 'inward'. At first there wasn't much comment; we just sent poems back and forth by email. Gradually the synchronicities began to creep in, and we found ourselves both working on similar topics at the same time. Penny felt she was 'still hovering on the perimeter of the Heath both historically and geographically, viewing it through the prism of the airport, and from a Stainesish perspective', whereas I was uncharacteristically allowing myself to be more wide-ranging. But by April we were on a roll.

There was no agreed 'plot': we never discussed the how, why or where. We began gently criticising each other more and responding to formal elements – so my 'If as' is a response to Penny's 'As if', and her 'What the Heath knew' picks up on my 'XX' on the opposite page, which ends each couplet with 'what the Heath desired' or 'what the Heath feared', etc.* We echoed and alluded to each other. One or two poems were actually co-written – 'Rites'/'XVIII', for example; I reshaped one Penny had written about place names, and helped rejig the layout of her 'Wildlife Sightings', acting as a kind of editor; and I seem to remember us working on our different interpretations of Hounslow dialect. Penny was much less ruthless towards my work, however strongly I encouraged her not to spare my lesser lines, and she was always ready to give advice if I asked.

I had not collaborated like this before, but Penny often worked collaboratively with her late husband, Peter Redgrove, whose spirit I am maybe acknowledging stylistically in 'XLIX', which imagines all kinds of unlikely exotic creatures fleeing from Heathrow's quarantine building. We often stumbled on similar subjects – perhaps because we explored the same sources. We both ended up with a Harlington Yew poem, for instance. I sent mine first in this case, and Penny emailed back:

I have a particular fondness for yew trees, and so the Harlington yew poem delights me – I love the format and the sinister imagery (cats with their tongues cut out particularly) and the poison/antidote line, and the whole assemblage. And then the very different elegy mode of VII with its tenderness and regret, its owls and nightingales.

I can't say how much I'm enjoying the interchange and inter-relating of the poems, and also the way we're each jumping off to new places... from time to time, and engendering new energies. So much unexpected material bursting through... And yes, the unpredictability is very enthralling...

I'm attaching two poems, my V and VI, responding now to your V with a swerve away into criminality and the demotic (so I plan a more direct response to your lyric and music/silence theme of your V a little later), and responding to your VI with a like focus on the yew.

181

On we went into May, into June, exchanging and commenting and indeed submitting to magazines. Some of the Heath sequence began to make its way out into the world, those initial three of mine appearing in *PN Review* and a shared spread in *Manhattan Review*. There were weeks when nothing happened and hours when a lot seemed to. By mid-July I was on to my fifty-seventh poem, whose focus was the 1972 Staines air crash in which a Trident ended up in a cabbage field next to Penny's brother's house; and my collaborator was preoccupied with 'found poems'. She sent one of them to me and I set about 'savaging' it, aiming to make it – as I wrote in an email – 'a damaged Roman mosaic… with fragments of people's words coming and going'. Penny replied:

I *love* the savaging and the echoing nature of the suite as a mosaic – and isn't it good that we have one poem that is a collaboration in the other sense – both of us working on the one poem, as contrast to the collaborative ping-pong process of one poem by x inspiring a poem by y! I'm delighted with your jigsaw-ing of those voices. I wanted to have actual Hounslow voices, but I was aware of the copyright issues, and (in one bound) that has been solved. It is now truly Heath-worthy. Its evocative, mysterious, and has a music of history and life as it was lived, but freed from the heaviness of my original draft.*

As for human history – yes, the human stories thread the sequence, especially my story and Penny's. She tended to foreground the wider human narrative rather more; I was inclined to bury it or divert it to my own symbolic purposes. My family and friends come in quite a lot, often obliquely. There's one about my Uncle Ray, an insurance salesman, who loved music, and rode his moped over the old Heath. There are several about Penny's relatives and ancestors. But stories from our researches or recalled from the common myth-kitty are pretty crucial to the book.

There's something of Peter Ackroyd, possibly, in the way we use layers of history in the sequence, in both our contributions – that urban myth of the ghost with a briefcase at Heathrow, for instance, or Dick Turpin and co. Often it's a tale that appeals and the characters come with it, as with the story about Osterley Park, which Queen Elizabeth I visited. Apparently the Queen took issue with the design of the court in front of Sir Thomas Gresham's house, considering it too large. She suggested that it would look more handsome if there were a wall dividing it in the middle. That night the financier Gresham, founder of the Royal Exchange, arranged for his men very silently and swiftly to build just such a wall, prompting much mirth among the courtiers the

Penelope Shuttle on what remains of Hounslow Heath.

next morning: 'No wonder he could so soon *change a building* who could *build a change*… 'any house is more easily divided than united'.

By late summer of 2014 we both knew we were approaching completion – poems came more sporadically and it was already a hefty book – but even the title wasn't decided (*Heath* or *The Heath*?) and we needed to meet to organise everything and discuss publishers. We both live away from London, though Penny returns regularly from Cornwall. I have no relatives in Hounslow any more. But we felt we had to go there, so one day we met up in Hounslow High Street and had a drink at The Bell, where travellers used to strengthen their nerves before setting forth. In the days of footpads, the gibbets next to the inn would creak with corpses. But we only heard planes and traffic, then went for a perfectly unthreatening stroll on what remains of the unspoiled heathland, which there are inevitably plans to develop – just one of many ways present events impinged on our poem.

Heath was published at the time of headlines about a Third Runway, when no one had any idea that within a few years the airport would be struck dumb by the pandemic. Hounslow Heath these days is a smallish nature reserve, squeezed between high-rise flats and the Post Office depot: you do get some sense of what the old terrain must have been like. You certainly find yourself looking from any westward train from Paddington with a new understanding of what those flat, built-over reaches must have meant once, and how they might have been used for the first Ordnance Survey, as they were. But I don't think I ever actually went to the heathy bits of the Heath when I was growing up – it was considered to be slightly dodgy, and as Stephen Spender put it, 'my parents kept me from children who were rough'. Hounslow Heath is really as much an imaginary place as the 'Huntingdonshire' I now live in.

So what might have been a pamphlet grew over a period of weeks in 2014 into something much larger – the original version of *Heath* is almost two hundred pages. Its final structure was the result of two or three meetings and floors covered with printouts. The last editing session was under a tree in Osterley Park, appropriately, with the planes passing by in the distance, a day commemorated by Penny in a poem she included in her 2020 pamphlet *Father Lear*.* We reorganised the original order, and the Nine Arches editor, Jane Commane, suggested further changes and cuts. There were a few poems I was sorry to see go, but I have found room for these in subsequent collections, and I suspect Penny has been recycling too – in fact, tesserae from some of hers became the linking epigrams that thread the finished sequence. Jane had practical objections to some of the poems, mainly concerning the length of my lines. One I managed to save by, as it were, setting it in concrete. I like to think nobody would guess that my poem 'X' hadn't always resembled three scarecrows. In fact, it was originally in three exceptionally long-lined stanzas which simply wouldn't fit on the page without ugly breaks. The change helped the poem come to life. I was delighted too that a scarecrow poem should end up as the crossed sticks of number X. That was just one of several serendipitous aspects to our editing, such as my poem about planes ending up as number 'XLV' – as a boy in Hounslow, I used to love Gerry and Sylvia Anderson's puppet shows, particularly *Fireball XL5*.

In short, there was a great deal of shuffling and the kind of compromises you might expect in a play production rather than a book of poems. Quite how it all ended is as mysterious as how it began: we seemed to reach a natural conclusion in that summer of 2014, but it proved rather a Haydnesque false ending, and a few poems came after the apparent final chords. A little later, I looked back at the emails we exchanged during the writing and printed them out. They would make a book in themselves.

If Hounslow is one of my candidates for what Seamus Heaney called an 'omphalos', then Upper Egypt is sacred in a different way, but still a rich source to which I frequently return. I have referred to it several times already here, and have explored it in full in my memoir *Threading a Dream: A Poet on the Nile*. But I am not rooted in Aswan as I am in Hounslow, and in a sense it is easy to write about somewhere so exotic, somewhere to which you owe no allegiance.

What is more challenging is to write about the place where you eventually settle. In our case – after a brief spell among Vietnamese refugees in north-east Scotland – that place was Huntingdonshire, a county that doesn't officially exist any more. That is where we 'put down roots' in 1983. The idea of inhabiting my own version of a Wessex or Barchester appealed from the start, but even more enticing was the fact that in our particular corner of Huntingdonshire we would only be a cycle ride away from Little Gidding.

It took me a few years to find a satisfactory way of writing about our new home and, as I touched on in the chapter 'A Happy Medium', it occurred as a result of technology. In the late 1980s we acquired our first computer – or rather, a word processor. The effect of Alan Sugar's Amstrad on my writing was curious and liberating; I suddenly found I could use a long line in a way I had never tried before. Was it because I suddenly didn't have to worry about retyping? Carbon and correction fluid, at any rate, were history. What I found myself writing was a series of what I called 'Eclogues', all exactly the same length, just fitting on a page, and all in a kind of loose hexameter, halfway to prose – with what Ted Hughes would have called, as he did years ago in a letter to me, a 'holdall' quality.

My thirty-two *Huntingdonshire Eclogues* were begun in late 1988 and finished early the next year, and, although unfashionably bucolic, were one of the most radical things I have done. Suddenly I received a lot of acceptances from magazines who had never liked my work before, and the sequence eventually appeared in *Fotheringhay and Other Poems*. More than one reviewer raised an eyebrow at that title, suggesting that the *Eclogues* should have been more prominent.

Where did the long line come from? Maybe the American poet C.K. Williams, whose work I discovered when I was briefly on the Bloodaxe list. But I was simply writing about 'what happened' as Robert Lowell advised: everyday life in a shire which had been lured by the Pied Piper of progress into – not a mountainside, but a Silicon Fen. Since 1974 Huntingdonshire has been in the County of Cambridgeshire, though the name is retained for the district council, and our neighbours continue to speak with a distinctive Huntingdonshire accent. The place, after all, has its own very specific history and legends. I suppose these poems from the late 1980s were part of my determination to write about my own back yard, to come to terms with a landscape which sometimes bored me, yet at the same time attracted me.

Ten years later came *Huntingdonshire Nocturnes*,* a more summery sequence, lit by moon and stars. Now there were forty-two poems, still in unrhymed tercets, but this time of different lengths and more strictly controlled, six beats to a line. With the publication of *Hunts: Poems 1979–2009*, I wanted to bring the sequences together and experiment with rhyme, while indulging in a little twenty-first-century melancholy. So the *Huntingdonshire Elegies* were born – a shorter sequence, but I felt a fitting conclusion to three sequences representing three decades. Like the couple in Robert Frost's 'Two Look at Two', I thought – '*This*, then, is all'. But just as the sudden entry of that 'antlered buck of lusty nostril' shakes any preconceived notions ('This *must* be all'), so it was 2018's 'Beast from the East' that brought with it a Huntingdonshire Quartet. I began the sixty-four *Codices*, in fact, during a walk on Boxing Day 2017, and they continued as that unwonted chill descended – a wintriness that is evident throughout. They are all of fifteen lines, in tercets, and that long six-beat line remains, but now I was using a very noticeable *aaa* rhyme. The final poem was composed on my sixty-fourth birthday in March.*

Although I sometimes wish that there could be hills and forests, or cliffs and dunes, I have come to appreciate the landscape of what the maps insist on calling Cambridgeshire. The very absence of those obvious delights which make other counties tourist destinations keeps our footpaths generally deserted – although that changed during lockdown – and there are patches among these wolds and copses and rivery pieces of fen-edge that have managed to hold on to something precious from the past. The patches may not be attractive in themselves, but they connect points of profound interest. Here is the cross-country route along which the body of Queen Catherine was carried from Kimbolton Castle to Peterborough Cathedral. And there is where John Clare rested on his walk home from the asylum in Essex. Down this quiet lane John Donne must have trotted when he came to inspect the church he was to take over in Keyston. Here's an oak beneath which Bunyan is said to have preached. And that's the way Wordsworth travelled en route to St John's College, one 'dreary morning when the Chaise/ Rolled over the flat plains of

Milestone at Kimbolton.

Huntingdon'. Passing such spots, it's easy to see how Eliot felt that 'History is now and England'. Possibly because of this, or maybe simply that – as our ancient village stone engraved '63 miles from London' would suggest – the metropolis is near enough to reach within a day by coach or on horseback, the area has attracted many distinguished poets. But a good few were born or lived nearby – Clare, of course, but Dryden and Cowper too.

Little Gidding features in all four of my Huntingdonshire sequences. Long before it became associated with a much more famous poem than any of mine, it was already a place name with considerable resonance. In 1626, Nicholas Ferrar, MP, fresh from his heroic work with the doomed Virginia Company and some uncomfortable associations with the slave trade, had settled here with his family. Ferrar was a widely travelled and popular man, exceedingly well read, a successful high-flier, but determinedly and quietly devoted to his faith. He took over the manor house, restored the tiny church, which was being used as a hay-barn, and founded a religious community, whose reputation quickly spread. It would be visited by, among others, Charles I and his nephew Prince Rupert. When T.S. Eliot 'came this way' just before the Second World War, some 310 years later, the story was already well known, and he was by no means the first literary pilgrim. Nicholas Ferrar had been very friendly with both Richard Crashaw and George Herbert, and Herbert held the living of the church at Leighton

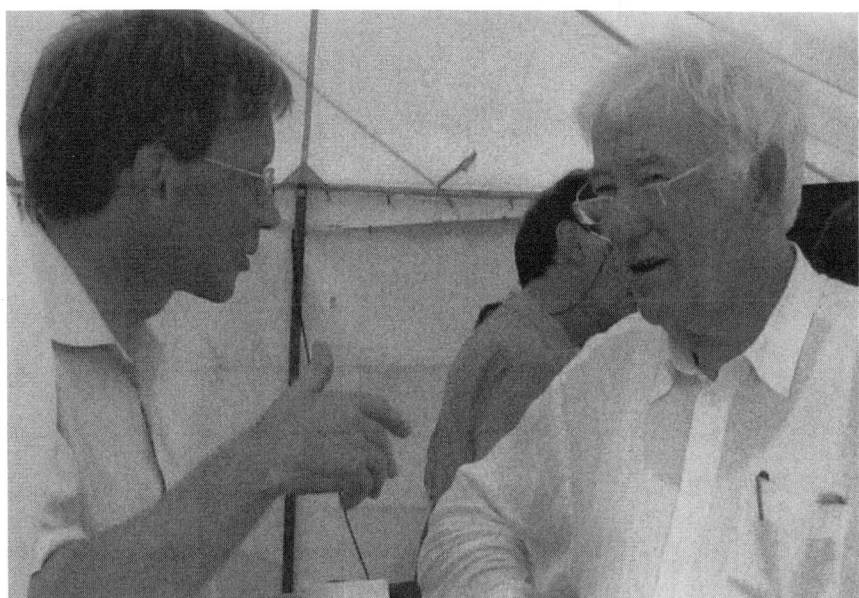

With Seamus Heaney at Little Gidding.

Bromswold, within walking distance – at least, in the days when no one thought anything of going five miles on foot.

Little Gidding has become a very important place to me. I have walked there, but more often cycle, passing the old cruise-missile base and the zoo with its eerie jungle cries, towards the converted windmill at Great Gidding. Beyond Steeple Gidding I turn off the lane and follow a track for a few hundred yards to where the community once lived. It has gone, but the footpath where in 1642 they saw the King approaching still runs away south-west beyond the farmhouse. Charles came on three occasions, the last when he was on the run after the Battle of Naseby. It was here that in 2009 I met and had my only proper conversation with Seamus Heaney, who for many at the time – including me – was undisputed sovereign of contemporary poetry. It was one of those encounters that make such a deep impression they begin to take on the power of personal myth. The occasion was the annual T.S. Eliot festival, and the Nobel Laureate was speaking along with other distinguished writers and critics such as the Scottish poet Robert Crawford, the biographer Lyndall Gordon and the critic Denis Donoghue. But it was Heaney whose presence filled the marquee in the garden behind Ferrar House.

It was a glorious late June day, he was in shirtsleeves, and after hearing a superb Hiberno-Caledonian rendition of Eliot's poem – what a privileged handful we were – I knew I had to speak to him. We had a friend in common, after all, Dennis O'Driscoll, who had recently published *Stepping Stones*, his Faber book of interviews with Heaney, a kind of aural biography. In fact, Dennis had dropped hints to me over a snatched lunch in Dublin that the interviews were happening, that the book was on its way, long before the rest of the world knew anything about it.

When Heaney heard me mention his friend's name he was all smiles, peering over his little glasses (tilted at a jaunty angle) saying how much the man had done for Irish poetry... and astonishingly, seeming to know who I was, even complimenting me on my work. I muttered about the personal significance of the occasion, that this part of Huntingdonshire was in many ways my own 'omphalos', as the boglands of Mossbawn had famously been for him – though in all honesty, mine should be Heathrow Airport. Then the conversation moved on to the recent controversy about the Oxford Professor of Poetry, the etymology of the word 'ambition', and how Derek Walcott would have made a good job of the lectures had he been appointed. Chatting with one Nobel Prize-winner about another, I somehow kept up my side of the conversation. The ideas welled out of him, and there was no hint at all that he was recovering from a recent stroke.

Then suddenly he was approached to read at a service in Little Gidding Church, some lines from St John, and it was about to start. Unprotestingly, still full of bonhomie, he left.

I wish I'd had a copy of my *Selected Poems* to give him. That book, *Hunts*, which had only just come out, has at its heart the place where we stood talking poetry: the very spot where Richard Crashaw may have done the same

The church at Little Gidding.

with Nicholas Ferrar; where Ferrar was handed a package containing George Herbert's complete poems, sent from his deathbed, and decided to have them copied for publication; where T.S. Eliot lingered in 1936, on just such a glorious day, a few lines taking shape in his mind about the may blossom and the pigsty. I did phone Dennis O'Driscoll to ask whether I should maybe send my book to Dublin, but on hearing the size of the great man's daily mailbag, I felt it was better not to. Shortly after, first Dennis (who was my age) and then Heaney himself died unexpectedly. I'm glad that he spent what little time he had left reading more important things than my poetry, not least Book VI of Virgil's *Aeneid*, which he finished translating in those final months.

In the decade that followed, and before I embarked on the *Huntingdonshire Codices*, I began to feel that I had not fully explored the extraordinary story of Ferrar's life, deterred understandably by the fact that T.S. Eliot had all but claimed the name for himself and posterity. 'If you came this way', through old Huntingdonshire, you would notice signs to 'The Giddings', and this is really the starting point for my 'cantefable', a mixture of verse and prose, which I didn't know I wanted to write until I found myself many hundred miles from home for my second visit to Hawthornden Castle Writers' Retreat in 2017.

A month without Internet but with many hours of silence seemed to invite something more than the usual page-length poem. My previous stay in 2010 had led to the verse and prose sequence, *Knot* (which I discuss in the chapter 'Reading'), and initially I resisted anything too similar, planning only to write about trees. As I began to write, however, finding myself pulled once again to the seventeenth century, I also felt again that delight in artifice. I imagined an unnamed man from our own day who leaves his car in a service station on the A1 and sets out on a walk in search of the famous spiritual community, travelling back 'through time', addressed as he walks by the trees. Against my instinct and every piece of advice I give to other writers, I found I needed to sketch out a detailed plan, which I still have among my papers. So, for example, the man firstly hears an ash, the Norse *askr* or spear, speak to him of war, before he heads on past the old cruise-missile base at Molesworth, which was the focus of much protest during the 1980s – the suspiciously wide country lanes are there to make room for the missile convoys. An elm speaks to the man of extinction and Hamerton Zoo's tigers join in the chorus. A poplar's ever-active leaves discourse on energy before the traveller reaches wind turbines and the old Gidding windmill. A hawthorn summons magic; an Eliotic elder mentions faith. At Little Gidding itself the protagonist finally encounters Nicholas Ferrar in the process of burning his books, and there is a grand formal centrepiece, an elaborate verse monologue, during which the two men seem to merge. On the return journey, the trees continue to sing, but the prose promenades are a reverse biography of Ferrar.

A frosty Huntingdonshire lane: used for the cover of The Giddings.

Apart from the obvious debt to Mussorgsky's *Pictures at an Exhibition*, there is also something of Heaney's *Station Island*, and much more of Ted Hughes's underrated book *Gaudete* – but little, I felt, of T.S. Eliot. Yet I think my poem engages as much as Eliot's with the spirit of Little Gidding. I should add that Hawthornden is very near the extraordinary Rosslyn Chapel, well known to fans of Dan Brown, and allegedly on a convergence of ley lines. Rosslyn's ornate splendours could not be more different from the plain simplicity of Little Gidding church or chapel, and I think the style of my poem owes more to the former. *The Giddings* incorporates all kinds of intricate formal challenges. That central encounter with Nicholas Ferrar, for instance, is a 'canzone', an even more dastardly form than the crown of sonnets. I often remember that remark of Archibald MacLeish's about loading himself with chains,* and Frost's response about not having many readers.

As to whether *The Giddings* will have many readers, Mica Press will tell me, I'm sure, but I don't think Dan Brown need worry.

Beyond the Silence (I)

All his life he has been walking away from the heath towards the forest.
The first tree he found he could make his own he hacked down
and hollowed into a canoe. But this was not what he wanted, so on
to where there were spinneys, copses, groves. These he felled, forced

into wondrous shapes to sell, which made him richly dissatisfied.
So he tried at the next tree, shaping it where it stood, a weird
topiary, ungainly, unsightly, yet inside it an invisible songbird
whistled something that might have been his own and seemed to lead

to where there was a mustering of the forest itself. Approaching the edge,
this time he only trimmed a twig here, and there
a branch and carved his initials on the bark. He wasn't far
from what he'd come looking for, and as his shadow merged

with the true dark, no need to cut or throw a tree:
sensing, instead, and feeling at one with these forces so that if
they would at last make clear what they wanted him to have
he could write it down on paper, the forest's poetry.

Clearing the Way

After completing my long poem about Sibelius's three-decade silence, I became rather preoccupied with the creative process itself and with what happens when there's a fallow patch – a difficult 'middle stretch', as Louis MacNeice put it. It's nowadays agreed that the composer wasn't really silent at all, but kept working on small commissions and tinkering with an eighth symphony. It's almost certain that he eventually destroyed this, burning it in the green-tiled stove at his house, Ainola, as his wife watched, out of sight. She said he was a much calmer person thereafter. He could not have borne the idea of an inferior work being left to posterity. He didn't really have any difficulty writing music, it's just that he wanted it to be good music, even if it was one of his numerous crowd-pleasers.

Such determination and rigour can unquestionably help the artist focus on what matters and move forward, but sometimes it needs a more practical 'spur'. Yeats, for example, born the same year as Sibelius, confessed to suffering from many 'long desert periods', but he found that a procedure to help his sexual potency, the Steinach operation, somehow improved his performance with the pen as well. Whether this effect was imagined or not, it gave a wild old wicked man the confidence to approach his final period and to produce the masterpieces of *Last Poems*. Virility, 'lust and rage', the quest for a theme – these became his leitmotifs.

A more recent case of late creative rejuvenation is that of Geoffrey Hill, whose medication for depression had a surprising side effect. Hill had not published a new collection for over a decade following the modest 1985 *Collected*, which was dominated by earlier poems, but once lithium kicked in there was no stopping him. *Broken Hierarchies: Poems 1952–2012* covers much the same ground as the Penguin volume – except that it carries on for another 800 pages. Hill certainly made up for lost time, although it's hard to think of a poet who hasn't been stuck at some point. The objectivist George Oppen stopped for twenty-five years, having 'ground on at his minor craft until the dry rot set in', according to William Logan: 'His poems wanted to be a poem, which wanted to be a line, which wanted to be a word, which at last wanted to be just a single letter, perhaps "I" or "O!"'.* A few, like Philip Larkin, Laura Riding, Hope Mirrlees or Rosemary Tonks, never quite started up again, sometimes because they had other priorities – Judith Wright's ecological concerns, for instance; what interests me is the sheer variety of methods poets have used to clear the way and get moving.

As I have suggested in earlier chapters, it can often be a particular location that prompts the change or sets the juices flowing. I remember Roger Garfitt telling me how *The Kilpeck Anthology* was induced by taking visiting poets Anne Stevenson, D.M. Thomas, Fleur Adcock and Seamus Heaney to see the sheela-na-gig at Kilpeck Church. Whether any of those particular poems opened some new direction is not clear, but I suspect that most poets can point to one poem they value because it marked the breaking of a blockage or a break-through to something new or more fully achieved.

At Villa d'Este, Tivoli.

For me it was Egypt. For Elizabeth Jennings the spur was Rome, looking at a fountain and finding 'a sense of ease and delight', although the fact that she was a Roman Catholic is surely significant. Eavan Boland, when she was a student, met an old woman carrying water on Achill Island and 'sensed a power in the encounter', recognising it as a key moment, duly commemorated in verse much later. Basil Bunting's career seemed to be over by 1966 – he was largely forgotten in the UK except as a minor Poundian – when the Northumbrian poet found his voice again in a memory of the humble Quaker Meeting House, Brigflatts. His autobiographical poem of that title (but a different spelling) became, as much as any poem can, a cult phenomenon.

Sometimes the *genius loci* might lead to a change in style, as when in 1986 Michael Longley, self-confessedly 'depressed and drinking too much', had barely written any poetry for seven years, and took himself off to Carrigskeewaun in County Mayo, which immediately yielded thirty new poems. His rough contemporary Derek Mahon had an equivalent experience when he went to the writers' colony at Yaddo in the midst of a prolonged creative drought, yet drinking 'uncontrollably', according to his biographer Stephen Enniss, and was suddenly able to write a very personal verse letter, marking a new, more easy-going, conversational epistolary phase.

In the case of the Welsh poet Vernon Watkins he was shaken into the change of style by a traumatic event. In 1927, as he was sitting in his lodgings reading Blake, he heard a terrific noise. A motorbike had crashed right outside, the rider killed instantly, the bleeding pillion passenger staggering up the path towards him. Watkins became convinced that he was in some way responsible, and this prompted not only a nervous collapse but 'a complete revolution of sensibility', so that he discarded or destroyed virtually everything he had written – about a thousand poems. From then on, he was convinced his poetry needed in some way to conquer time. Instead of being a pale shadow of Shelley or Blake, he became a modern Metaphysical.

There are plenty of examples of writers being pushed into a new kind of poetry by some trauma. Robert Lowell's early spell in hospital had a profound effect on the way he wrote: the astonishing free verse of *Life Studies* is a world away from the dense formality of his earlier collections. This kind of radical transformation is especially true among war poets, who were often obliged to mature quickly. In the case of Edmund Blunden, the changes were all beneath the surface: he persevered with his pastoral pentameters, but a poem such as 'Third Ypres' shows the traditional forms cracking under the strain. Wilfred Owen would surely have gone on writing sub-standard Keats had he not experienced the trenches. Lyrically inclined Siegfried Sassoon would not have become a master of the satirical put-down. Many of the women gathered in Catherine Reilly's ground-breaking anthology *Scars Upon My Heart* would probably not have been heard at all without the experience of war – and, of course, an editor as good as Reilly.

Less dramatically, but with equal intensity, Adrienne Rich, radicalised by the experience of motherhood, chose to abandon her early much-praised formalism, to escape its patriarchal associations. Thom Gunn's adoption of syllabics too was involved with his own coming out. Naturally, a formal reinvention is in itself refreshing: the challenge of a complex form can be the necessary red rag to the sleepy bull of inspiration. The author of short poems turns to the long poem, and vice versa. Or there is a late realisation that it's time to drop the masks, as Yeats did when he emerged from the Celtic twilight and reinvented himself (even then there were moments when he 'sought a theme and sought for it in vain') and as Wallace Stevens did in his final collection, when he came to appreciate 'the plain sense of things'. Ted Hughes's decision to tell the story of his relationship with Sylvia Plath right at the end of his life prompted a completely new, much more direct and prose-like verse in the bestseller *Birthday Letters.*

Then there is the encouragement of friends. It was the arrival of young Tom Pickard that prompted Basil Bunting to turn his visit to the Quaker Meeting House into *Briggflatts* ('to show the boy how it was done'), which is in a different league from any of his earlier poems. Robert Frost looked at his best friend Edward Thomas's prose writings and pointed out that it wouldn't take much to change them to verse and it could even be argued that this was a change of style, rather than a change of genre, so 'poetic' is Thomas's prose – although the liberating trauma of volunteering for the trenches played its paradoxical part.

For the troubled William Cowper (1731–1800), his innocent friendship with Lady Austen at Olney provided the necessary spark. Cowper's whimsical Muse happened to be sitting on a sofa (pictured here), so she challenged him to write a poem in blank verse on that comfortable subject. It became his masterpiece in six books, *The Task.* There was something equally playful going on two centuries earlier when George Gascoigne, about to enter Gray's Inn, was asked by five friends 'to write in verse somewhat worthy to be remembered' on themes that

they provided – something I tried myself in a poem during the Covid lockdown, 'Greening's Request', following Gascoigne's formal structure.* But such an undertaking draws closer to the commission, a useful set of jump leads for any poet. At one time it was the aristocracy who put in the request; nowadays it's radio or

William Cowper's sofa, Olney.

the press. Sometimes the lines have staying power – for instance, Carol Ann Duffy's popular school anthology piece, 'Valentine'.

There are also ways of commissioning yourself, as we have seen – that roll of adding-machine paper A.R. Ammons put into his typewriter, those Ouija board transcripts collected by James Merrill. Two unique and distinguished long poems emerged. Neither Ammons nor Merrill knew what they would end up writing, but poets are invariably happy when they stumble on the right subject, the right form. It's hard to imagine what George Mackay Brown's poems would look like if he'd never read the story of St Magnus or Kathleen Raine's if she hadn't discovered Blake. Or had James Lasdun and Michael Hofmann abandoned the idea of inviting all those poets in the early 1990s to rework Ovid's *Metamorphoses*. There would have been no *Tales from Ovid* – Ted Hughes's crowning opus – and many other millennial collections would have been the poorer. *After Ovid* shaped a decade's poetry; its influence is still felt.

A sad truth of literary history is that death is the most dependable and effective patron. Chidiock Tichbourne wouldn't even be remembered if it weren't for 'My prime of youth is but a frost of cares', the elegy he wrote before having his head chopped off. And Anne Sexton was just one of many mid-twentieth-century American poets indebted to 'the ruffian on the stair'. Writers are often, to paraphrase Auden, 'hurt' into poetry: by war, loss, self-destructive tendencies, by the death of a partner, or a personal battle with illness, as in the case of Clive James, whose late output was phenomenal.

At the same time, the desire to get a poem right can be a strong incentive to live, as Robert Graves believed when he claimed that working on the thirty-five drafts of 'The Troll's Nosegay' saved him from being carried off by Spanish influenza, a useful fact which I disseminated on Twitter/X during our own pandemic. Graves is perhaps the most famous of those modern poets who have found the spur to poetry in the inspiration of a new love: 'Stirring suddenly from long hibernation,/I knew myself once more a poet…'. And such poets are still writing.

As I've already pointed out, Stephen Romer is content to call himself a 'Muse poet', while recognising the label is controversial. The love affair need not be anything particularly Byronic. The Hebridean poet Iain Crichton Smith was hardly the kind of chap to be consorting with the White Goddess, yet his late commitment to his partner Donalda clearly affected him profoundly as his long poem *The Leaf and the Marble* proves. However, the idea of a Muse has been a problem for women poets. Eavan Boland felt she could not escape the shade of Yeats – or indeed Maud Gonne – knowing that 'the project of the woman poet, connected as it is by dark bonds to the object she once was, cannot make a continuum with the sexualised erotic of the male poem.'* It could be that the recent relaxation in gender boundaries has freed things up – consider Alyson Hallett's *Toots*, for example. Whatever the inspiration, or lack of it, however, a poet must remain alert, ready to be 'surprised by joy' as Wordsworth was... on a bridge in central London, by the words of a leech-gatherer, or remembering someone called Lucy.

But this is all well and good. What if you start writing and can't stop and end up producing far too much? That can be just as crippling. Staring at a vast amount of work that needs cutting is in fact a good deal more painful than staring at a blank page.

I often quote Basil Bunting's advice to young poets that you should 'cut out every word you dare'. Bunting practised what he preached in his own wonderfully economical work and even applied it to others quite fearlessly – to Shakespeare, for instance, whose sonnets he 'improved' (as a pastime while living on a boat) by deleting lines and phrases he considered inessential.

But when I was myself a 'young poet', I don't think Bunting's remarks on the craft quite registered. I would probably have said I'd learnt from his work, because I regularly listened to him reading *Briggflatts* in those distinctive Northumbrian tones. But in the 1970s I wasn't yet ready to take advice from anyone – not Bunting and definitely not George Bernard Shaw, who declared that if you find a line you like, you should cut it out. For many years I found this apparently

simple editing process one of the most difficult things to manage. Although I would write twenty or thirty drafts of a poem, revise and revise, reshaping, rejigging, I was far too attached to what I had written to allow it to undergo major surgery.

As with many things in my creative life, it was Egypt that brought about a change. In late 1979 or early 1980 I had written a poem of some fifty lines

JG with parents at the Aswan granite quarry.

which I regarded as something of a new departure. I have already explained how most of my Egyptian poems were imagistic sketches, composed under the influence of William Carlos Williams and Ezra Pound. But I had also been reading – goodness knows where I got hold of it so many hundred miles up the Nile – Louis MacNeice's 'Autumn Sequel', not usually regarded as a very successful long poem, but a tour de force nevertheless and composed in exemplary *terza rima*.

I had wanted to write something about the cracked obelisk which lay abandoned in the ancient granite quarry just outside Aswan, the town where Jane and I had been posted by Voluntary Service Overseas. Imagining how the Pharaoh must have reacted when he heard the news, I told the story in rolling *aba bcb cdc* pentameter rhymes: how he arrived in Aswan, confronted the workmen and was informed about the fatal crack which had appeared in what would have been the biggest obelisk ever made. Read today it might be seen as a Trumpian allegory…

> But that day it was as if the earth's core
> had pumped a deep black vein of evil up
> out through the granite slab, and the men saw
>
> the crack, as if they were watching a heart stop.

That is how the poem now ends, but originally there were three or more additional stanzas. Nothing beside remains. I had the sense to cut them out, and I am still rather pleased with that half-rhymed final line.

I suppose we have no choice but to learn to part with things we love as we grow older, as that brilliant and intensely self-critical poet Elizabeth Bishop knew, and expressed so memorably in 'One Art'. Her poem is an object lesson in how to achieve the same tricksy tumbling of *terza rima* I attempted in 'The Crack', although hers is a villanelle, so incorporates the complication of added repetitions. Not many poets are as tough on themselves as Bishop, and few have critical

The cracked obelisk by Rosie Greening.

201

readers as helpful and keen-eyed as her beloved Robert Lowell. He, of course, was a poet who should have been encouraged to cut entire books – how many versions of *Notebook* are there?

For those of us less likely to appear on the cover of *TIME* magazine, simply putting together a collection, especially a *Selected*, is a painful lesson in 'one art'.* A poem you cannot imagine parting with suddenly sounds far too similar in tone to another or hinges on an image you are already using elsewhere. How different this poem now looks in its new context! It has to go. The good thing about computers (though it can also be the bad thing) is how clinical they have made this editing process – all the writer has to do is decide whether to use 'cut' or 'delete'. There's something less irrevocable about this than the screwed-up sheet of paper in the basket, which all too quickly gets into the outside bin and has been removed for ever to the recycling centre. And troubling memories of that little wheel-of-fate-shaped eraser or the embalming power of correction fluid are safely contained beyond the bright screen. There is an 'undo' button. An archive. Limbo files. Backup. History. What also helps is the fact that the page glowing before our eyes is somehow impersonal, more like the work of A.N. Author.

That was, I suppose, true of the typed foolscap I was correcting in Upper Egypt forty years ago. When J.D. Greening (as he was then) cut out those lines from 'The Crack' it may have been a typescript he wrote on, but more likely it involved putting a line of pencil through his own handwriting: and terrible though J.D.G.'s handwriting was and is, it has always been his own. Those squiggly *m*s and *s*s are begging their maker to spare them. Times New Roman does help keep it all a bit less emotional, though admittedly when working at the computer I will sometimes edit out a passage or a whole poem, but – because I'm secretly fond of it – paste it at the bottom of the document as if I might come back to it. More often than not the words are quickly forgotten, like all those old gadgets and heirlooms and souvenirs and toys we thrilled over for a while then put in the garage, never to be retrieved, enduring what Robert Frost called the 'slow smokeless burning of decay'.

I come back to Sibelius, whose Seventh Symphony (1924) had consisted of a single movement, a masterly compression of the essence of symphonic thought into just over twenty minutes. By contrast, his very first symphonic work, the *Kullervo* symphony from 1892, which he suppressed (it's now a repertoire piece), had lasted almost three times as long. Here was an artist who learnt how to cut. It's hardly surprising that an eighth symphony eluded Sibelius in the end. In writing my long poem about this struggle, I failed to notice the irony

– subsequently a *TLS* reviewer did – that 'The Silence' would not stop talking. It had reached some 1,200 lines, far too long to be part of my next collection. I realised soon after completing it that I would have to take a leaf or many leaves out of my subject's book, and this proved more difficult than I expected. There were some obviously weaker passages I wasn't sorry to see go; and I found I could extract a couple of hundred lines without too much pain. But I simply couldn't find any way of reducing the poem further. I was happy with the way it all worked, and that was that. Yet I knew it couldn't work – not at such a length. Almost every day it seemed I would sit in my 'word-house' – the writing shed at the back of our terraced cottage – and go through the pages, sometimes reading the quatrains aloud, looking for ways of cutting. Where were Bunting and Shaw when I needed them? In the end, just as I had decided that 'The Silence' must stay as it was, that I would have to try and publish it as a separate chapbook, muttering in self-justification about 'heavenly length' and how we all wish Bruckner hadn't made those cuts his friends insisted on, something unexpected happened.

One afternoon I was sitting staring at the printout, when I felt a kind of conviction come over me, the kind of surge of self-belief you hear Olympic athletes talking about. I was suddenly capable, although this was a negative capability, of moving back from my own words, hovering above them, almost, and seeing what needed to be done. I found myself coolly cutting a clear way through the stanzas like a topi-wearing colonialist with his machete. What had

Ainola, Sibelius's house.

The entrance to Sibelius's house near Järvenpää

happened? I had lost, I think, for an hour or two that passion we are told is so essential to creativity and had found the necessary disinterest – such a useful word, so often misused. Slash, slash. Sibelius himself might have made something of the sound of creative destruction, as he did in *Tapiola*, when the wind stirs the forest to a fury of whirling semiquavers, and again before 'the Silence' in his incidental music for *The Tempest*. I worked the magic with the satisfaction of one breaking his staff and drowning his book. The art of losing isn't hard to master, it turns out.

Beyond the Silence (II)

Reading Swedenborg. Inner breathing. Mystical states
of peak experience, which he recognises. The notion that science
and art are not distinct, which he believes. Divine Providence,
wonderful logic. The readiness to answer to whims and dictates

of a higher power. As metallurgy tells us how to smelt copper
and iron, philosophy forges finite to infinite.
Visions that overthrow dreams… Everything seems to fit,
although he hasn't met a man at the pub who offers super-

natural worlds to him, only the usual *diabolus*.
Escape the mines and come to me, sings Emanuel,
devote yourself to never-ceasing union with the spiritual,
all doors left unlocked in readiness.

Genius

When the death of Peter Maxwell Davies was announced, I tracked down a handful of recordings and began to listen. 'Max', as he was generally known, is often a dauntingly difficult composer to grasp, and I have struggled to keep up with his output, which included ten symphonies and ten string quartets. On this occasion I felt I really should tackle the gritty, dissonant First Symphony once again as recorded by a very young Simon Rattle in 1978, but at the same time my instinct was to put on one of his many delightful occasional or descriptive pieces. Not *Farewell to Stromness* – the news bulletins had already found it made a perfect musical soundbite – but rather the audacious *Orkney Wedding with Sunrise*, which culminates in a *coup de théâtre* involving a bagpiper; or *Mavis in Las Vegas*, a riotous pastiche of American popular genres sparked by a misunderstanding in a Las Vegas hotel where the composer was signed in as 'Mavis'. Or perhaps one of the less well-known showpieces: *Cross Lane Fair* for Northumbrian pipes and orchestra complete with evocations of a ghost train, a bearded lady and a five-legged sheep; or *Maxwell's Reel, with Northern Lights* – swelling brass, glockenspiel and 'crotales' – tiny tuned cymbals.

I did grapple with the symphony, but once that duty was over I indulged in a personal Maxfest, lay back and relished the Northern Lights, the various species

CDs of Maxwell Davies.

of bagpipe and Mavis's raunchy glitter-ball. As I basked in these lighter pieces, what Graham Greene might have called 'entertainments', they confirmed a suspicion that I have had for some time: that the truest genius can sing both high and low.

Poets are my theme, of course, and I shall be coming to them. But it is something that seems to apply to composers in particular, as can be seen by observing any concert audience: rapt attention for the serious passages, nods and smiles for the lighter ones, but something deeper still, that inimitable silence when light suddenly merges with dark and we feel 'the complete consort dancing together'. Haydn or Mozart might seem in every sense classic examples of artists who mix soaring seriousness with earthy jokes – the composer of the *Seven Last Words of Our Saviour from the Cross* also added a loud fart to his 93rd Symphony – since the very form they pioneered provides a showcase for the sublime slow movement and the jokey minuet and trio (later the scherzo).

But let us rather look at Ludwig van Beethoven, who by the time he reached his last symphony or the late quartets was stretching the possibilities of earthiness and heavenliness further than Haydn or Mozart could have imagined. Beethoven appeals at both ends of the spectrum; he had a rumbustious and wicked sense of humour that enlivens even his most troubled passages, sometimes turning on them, toying with them, mocking them, deconstructing them, before returning to them in all seriousness with redoubled intensity. He composed the barely playable *Grosse Fuge*, which still sounds as though it were by a disciple of Arnold Schoenberg. But he also served up bagatelles fit for a chocolate ad. He could storm the heavens in the *Missa Solemnis*. Or rage over a lost penny. He would have special fun with other people's trivia – as he did with Antonio Diabelli's banal little theme for his phenomenal *Diabelli Variations*. He is never monotonous. But most importantly, and what makes him the greatest master, my 'truest genius': he was doing all this *within individual works*.

Only the very greatest composers can shift successfully from the Grand to the Populist within the same piece, and if Beethoven showed one way of doing it, Gustav Mahler offered another, even more difficult to emulate. The best of the rest tend to specialise in producing either the substantial main course or a fluffy dessert, although a select few are skilled at both – think of Hector Berlioz's *Requiem*, then of what he did with Carl Maria von Weber's *Invitation to the Dance*. And there are many who, brilliant though they be in their way, remain merely fluffy (Camille Saint-Saëns, Gioacchino Rossini) or relentlessly weighty (Anton Bruckner, Max Reger). Brahms could serve up some delightful Hungarian dances and *Liebeslieder* waltzes, but he meant it sincerely when he jotted down a theme from Johann Strauss's *The Blue Danube* on a lady's autograph fan and added 'Unfortunately not by Johannes Brahms'. Fortunately for Johannes Brahms, however, he was one of those who could blend high and low seamlessly within his masterworks, risking that tinkling twenty-second variation in his Op.24, for example, or a student drinking song at the end of his *Academic Festival Overture*. Some composers do this more than others, but it seems to me that the most interesting ones do it a great deal. It's why Schubert's song cycles are his finest achievements. It's what we love about Georg Frideric Handel. A personal favourite of mine is Carl Nielsen, forever juxtaposing a growling dissonance with a jaunty folk song. He was a Dane, but one who understands a smorgasbord.

It might not be so easy to find something light and refreshing among the meaty offerings of Richard Wagner – unless his *Siegfried Idyll*, which was designed as a birthday breakfast piece for his wife Cosima – although who would deny greatness to the author and composer and producer of the *Ring* cycle? In fact, some years ago in a festive Radio 3 'balloon debate' about composers it was Wagner who came out as the sole surviving genius. Nevertheless, there is something even more impressive about a composer who can do all the operatic manoeuvres and orchestral flamboyance, but can also construct a convincing sonata form, turn out a touching ballade, a perfect string quartet, or a simple song of longing. Some towering creative artists just cannot offer simple gifts even when presented with the perfect opportunity.

Commissioned to write what could have been a roof-raising populist number for the Last Night of the Proms in 1995, Harrison Birtwistle chose instead to test the crowd's patience with his nightmarish *Panic* for saxophone, drum kit and orchestra. It assuredly raised the roof, and a few eyebrows. Birtwistle was a genius, but didn't compose anything that could be popularly associated with his name as 'Farewell to Stromness' was with 'Max', his fellow Manchester School enfant terrible. Ralph Vaughan Williams, by contrast, was always able to write for 'the people' – he collected folk songs, edited and composed hymns, produced film scores – as well as shocking them with his cacophonous and angry Fourth Symphony. Moreover, he conforms to my definition of the truest genius, frequently merging memorably accessible moments with uncompromisingly bleak passages, as in the Sixth. Benjamin Britten and Michael Tippett fit the definition too. Not only did they both write some of their best work for amateur forces – for children, even – but listen to what Britten achieves as he leaps between parody and elegy in his early Frank Bridge *Variations*, or to the effect of the Spirituals in Tippett's *A Child of Our Time*. All this is in a direct line from Johann Sebastian Bach, the composer as practical man, a figure within the community, producing what he's asked to, inviting the people to sing along, throwing in a *Coffee Cantata* for fun.

There is a darker aspect to this subject, however: under the Nazis, 'difficult' equalled 'decadent', and in Soviet Russia compositions were required to be relentlessly upbeat and heroic. Whereas an English composer could introduce folk songs for purely aesthetic reasons or just because they wanted to (try everything once, said Arnold Bax, except incest and folk dancing) there was pressure on Stalin's artists to make a literal song and dance about the joys of communism. They were expected to provide a service – much as Bach was, only for distinctly ungodly reasons. Dmitry Shostakovich's gift was such that he could write entertainments and at his best make no concessions to the demands of propaganda. But anyone who has whistled a waltz from his First Jazz Suite then turned to his Eighth Symphony or his late quartets will not be in any doubt of the sheer scope and essential truthfulness of his genius. He went further than any other twentieth-century composer, combining both aspects into an ironic style which could subvert the cheerful heroics it was spouting.

Already these sweeping generalisations about music are threatening to divert me from a broader application of my nascent theory. I am not competent to say whether it might be relevant to the visual arts, although we could consider whether the genius of *Guernica* lies in the way it combines Pablo Picasso's skill as a quickfire caricaturist with his anger, grief and appreciation of the grand tradition; and no doubt every *Mona Lisa* needs a smile to offset its sober folds and fields. Similarly, I have always felt that it is film-makers like the Coen Brothers who achieve most, because they run the gamut of human experience. As for the art form I know best: can it really be said that the best poets sing both high and low? Surely the theory doesn't work for literature…

Yet consider Milton and Shakespeare, who were for a long time treated as equals, both mainstays at A-Level. If we were in the final moments of a poetic balloon debate and I had to give one reason why it should be my beloved Milton we throw out of our basket it would be that he only knew how to be lofty – the Fall would do him good. Yes, there are lighter passages in *Comus*. There is the joke of the '*Tetrachordon*' rhyme in one of his sonnets – 'A Book was writ of late called *Tetrachordon*[…] now seldom por'd on.' But even *L'Allegro* is hardly lightweight. And *Paradise Lost* is unrelieved solemnity – glorious, mellifluous, quotable solemnity, but solely that. Shakespeare, by contrast, was at his greatest when high and low began to fuse as they do in the characters of King Lear and the Fool. The grand blank-verse set pieces are there; but he relishes a snatch of bawdy, a mad song, a stand-up routine, or some sly couplets to cover a costume change. Dramatists tend to be pragmatists.

The poets of the Augustan age would follow suit, ready with an epigram when required, not afraid to amuse us with something slight or lowbrow or ephemeral, but always stylishly turned, brilliantly timed. If only Wordsworth

– whose work is extremely important to me – could have taken himself rather less seriously, could have recognised when he was risible ('I've measured it from side to side/'Tis three feet long, and two feet wide'), glanced down from the sublime, made the odd quip. Was it this that alienated Coleridge, who could certainly do a comic turn, chiefly as conversationalist? Both of the Lyrical Balladeers believed they were deploying language 'really used by men', but Jane Austen does that rather better, and includes women too. Of the Romantics, Blake is the genuine all-rounder, whose genius makes no distinction between high and low, whether he is illustrating or printing or writing. His 'Tyger' is loved by children; his 'Lamb' has become one of the most popular Christmas Carols; 'Jerusalem' is England's unofficial National Anthem. It's obvious too that Keats could drop the Romantic death-mask, laugh and poke fun at himself as 'a Naughty Boy'; Shelley couldn't, though he was a good deal naughtier. If Keats had lived he would have kept touching the earth as well as reaching for heaven. Shelley wouldn't. Nor were the Victorians much inclined to cater for non-sophisticates, which is why they are so easy to parody. But then we recall Christina Rossetti's 'Goblin Market' – and Alfred, Lord Tennyson at least did let his hair down even further for his dialect poems.

In our own time, it is somehow reassuring that a poet as 'highbrow' as T.S. Eliot could descend to cat-level, even if his other light verse descends to dark and offensive depths; but he had already achieved the century's most significant interweaving of high and low in *The Waste Land*. I think it is W.H. Auden who really reminds us of the scope available to a genius. Auden would try anything, could write at the drop of a hat on a given topic and in any given form; and he showed the same broad mind when it came to publishing – he had no objection to appearing in *Playboy*, for instance. If he felt

Yeats's tower, Thoor Ballylee.

like composing a book of clerihews he did so, and no one thought the less of him. They might have done had he only written such verse (*Academic Graffiti* is dedicated to a man who did – Ogden Nash), but this was the author of big serious poems like 'The Sea and the Mirror'.

If the suspicion that prompted this chapter ever becomes anything like a proper theory, there may have to be something in the formula that explains why it doesn't apply so reliably to Irish writers. Despite his remarks about stepping down into the 'rag-and-bone shop of the heart', Yeats stays in his isolated tower or on his high horse most of the time. It is something to do with the paradox of folk material that the fairy stories he draws on and actually interwove with early poems in a 1925 reprinting are ostensibly 'of the people' but at the same time quite sophisticated affairs, rich in diction and haughty in tone. Yeats doesn't really have the common touch, except in his lyric voice. There is no angry vernacular. If there is a rag-and-bone shop, Steptoe and Son are well out of the picture.

Some of this rubs off on Yeats's heirs. Seamus Heaney found an enormous readership, but he didn't capture the rude, raw-edged, rough-tongued life of the land the way Patrick Kavanagh did, nor could he so confidently introduce Homer into a local boundary squabble as in the older poet's sonnet, 'Epic'.

Farmer's boy though he was, native of the boglands, Heaney was happiest on the poetic heights, keeping his eyes sharp, his hands and shoes clean, only digging metaphorically. He admitted he felt uncomfortable when his friend Ted Hughes tried to drag him off to fish in muddy backwaters. Like Yeats, Heaney tends to mythologise people, as he does in *Station Island* or even in simple poems to his wife: in that collection's opening poem, 'The Underground', she is both Gretel and Eurydice. Similarly, Eavan Boland is a brilliant and widely admired poet who stormed the men's round tower,

Patrick Kavanagh bench, Dublin.

challenged the notion of status of the muse, and reclaimed women's experience as a subject fit for Irish poetry. But for all that preoccupation with 'the oral tradition', her natural voice remains one of elevated concern. There are no laughs. No one swears. In her celebrated sequences, there are shifts of tone, but not from very high to very low. Perhaps that isn't necessary; the work is potently musical already. The point may be that there is something about the way the Irish distil their poetry that imbues their work with a unique blend of light and shade. They don't need to step down. They find popularity without that. Besides, there is a tradition of Irish entertainers who are virtually poets; and a good number of Irish poets – Brendan Kennelly, Micheal O'Siadhail, Paul Durcan, Rita Ann Higgins – who are highly professional entertainers.

It would be hard to say where the high ends and the low begins in a poet such as Paul Muldoon. But Muldoon (like the very different Greg Delanty) has become thoroughly Americanised, and that brings a different perspective on this theory, because their writers from Whitman onwards have made a point of shifting gears dramatically: it's become as much a convention for American poets as the car chase has for American film makers. Indeed, it arrived with Modernism, which was largely learnt from film. It is in the very DNA of Dr William Carlos Williams's *Paterson* and endures into the later, long-lined Williams, (C.K). The Beat Poets thrived on it. Those Americans who only choose to lift their eyes to the abstract heavens with Wallace Stevens's angels are, I would argue, the weaker for it. W.S. Merwin, John Ashbery, even Louise Glück, do lack an earthy component that we find in, say, Denise Levertov, A.R. Ammons, Marie Ponsot, Greg Delanty, A.E. Stallings or the miniatures of Kay Ryan and the blues of Kevin Young. Further back, we may wonder why the ever-various Edna St Vincent Millay was sidelined, and – more radically – ask ourselves whether Marianne Moore's sheer range gives her more staying power than either Elizabeth Bishop or Robert Lowell. Moore's might be thought the most obscure and elitist of voices, but she it was who appeared on television throwing the first pitch in a baseball game. Lowell's dramatic fall in fortunes is surely connected to his humourlessness, his unrelenting density of texture. His work makes this reader think of packed rooms, crowded seas, a noisy dinner table, allusion jostling with irony. Bishop is more likely to bring to mind those fragile fire balloons in 'The Armadillo' – possibly floating past Moore's immortal steeplejack.

Is any of this more than just an ignis fatuus glimpsed from Max's ghost train at Cross Lane Fair? The theory certainly works best for modern British composers, and generally applies more convincingly to home-grown artists.

Take Ted Hughes. If you only knew his *Collected Poems*, you would have no idea of the light touch he reveals in his *Collected Poems for Children*. Hughes's problem was that he seldom managed to merge the two voices effectively; when he did, in *Season Songs*, he produced some of his most authentic work. In the past seventy years, British poetry has lurched from high to low and back again, with only a handful of writers managing to maintain their equilibrium. There sit Kathleen Raine and Vernon Watkins on a steadily eroding Parnassus, still 'defending ancient springs', glorious but unsmiling. Watkins, it's true, did try his hand at what he regarded as comic verse. But reading these neglected poets can be – much as I love them – like listening to too much plainchant. It's easier to play with the circus animals in the lowlands, which is what most of us do these days, though we versifiers know that to aim low in poetry is an even faster track to obscurity than the Parnassian Line.

It is probably – and surprisingly – Philip Larkin who shows how to strike the right balance. He was a poet whose life was devoted to finding the ideal blend of high and low, under the influence of Yeats and Hardy respectively; the title poem of *High Windows* is a demonstration of this aesthetic. Since his death, British poets who seem to get it right and don't lapse into stand-up routines, playing for laughs and exit-lines (or become Larkin clones) are not always those winning the prizes.

But there are a few who have shown they are willing to attempt a lively reeling earthdance like Maxwell Davies's *A Spell for Green Corn*, as well as to conjure the slow, dark immensities of his *Worldes Blis*. I think of particular works by Patience Agbabi, Robert Crawford, Philip Gross, Zaffar Kunial, Gregory Leadbetter, David Morley, Carol Rumens, Penelope Shuttle and of Max's friend and inspiration, George Mackay Brown. Our own High Hill (Geoffrey), unashamedly lofty, but amusing, light-hearted, sardonic, makes the strongest case for a specifically English genius. Yet I wonder whether even he properly sounds the depths of human experience, which includes the dart of human insight as well as the spark from heaven, the belly laugh as much as the Damascene vision. In truth, there is 'nothing of the circus' about him... any more than there is in C.H. Sisson, whose troubled, shadowy, unrelievedly serious music continually draws me in. Perhaps we should be listening instead to the extraordinary and unexpected late poems of R.F. Langley, where high and low share a Modernist dance floor.

That phrase about the circus was Jean Sibelius's, a way of preparing audiences for his bleak Fourth Symphony, the so-called 'Barkbröd', written after an operation for cancer of the throat. His symphonies may not 'contain the world'

Hawthornden Castle, where Ben Jonson and William Drummond discussed Shakespeare.

as Mahler famously insisted to Sibelius himself a symphony should, but he is a composer who was happy to produce popular miniatures alongside those intense masterpieces. He learnt early on that tea rooms would pay good money for a sad waltz – though foolishly he opted for a lump sum rather than royalties, and thereafter his worldwide hit, *Valse Triste*, would taunt him whenever he heard it played.

It is easy to forget that much of what we are discussing comes down to the need for a creative artist – genius or not – to make a living. Shakespeare understood that, and knew there was no better way to please a paying audience than to briefly loosen the tightening knot of his dramas with a song:

> O mistress mine, where are you roaming?
> O stay and hear your true love's coming
> That can sing both high and low…

To the Muse

after Horace: *Odes*, Book IV, iii

The one whom you blessed from her birth
with your own luminous vision, Muse, is
  never going to be famous for
waving her arms at the Albert Hall, or
  achieving pole position at
formula anything, nor will she be
  decorated for her beating
back of all those assaults by male hubris.
  But the sally gardens bending
to her flow, its hidden tributaries,
  will whisper of what she has done
with words. This most Nobel city at last
  deigns to invite her up on its
high horse, letting envy slither down. Muse
  of the holy well, polishing
your symbols, testing their gold standard, who
  if you were moved to could compose
a song as simple as the dawn, your gift
  is that she's out there when we search,
this place's poet. Thanks to you, she writes
  and (to my ear, at least) delights.

Some Contemporaries

The poetry world is a kind of community, though as much 'through time' as within any given period. I feel I count among my friends many writers I have never met except in dreams, and I have had encounters with a good few of them in the night, as my 'Dreams' chapter explains. But I'd like now to revisit some of those contemporaries from the waking world who have been important to me.

Every poet needs someone they can show their drafts to, someone with whom they can talk the curious cryptic language of contemporary poetry. In my early days it was the poet and printer Colin Honnor – we went to the same school and the same university – then at Exeter the poet and playwright Shaun McCarthy, whose brother Roland John brought out my first collection with Hippopotamus Press. In Egypt and Scotland I didn't really have a kindred spirit to consult, other than Jane, who was (and still is) unfailingly nice about my work. I got to know Douglas Dunn well, but not well enough to ask him what he thought of this or that line. Then when we came to Kimbolton, I struck an instant rapport with a fellow teacher who was born in the same year as me, and who was just anticipating his first Peterloo collection, *The Impossible Jigsaw*.

Stuart Henson

Stuart Henson had had work published in magazines I admire, such as *Argo*, and won a coveted Eric Gregory Award. What's more, he was very successful as an adaptor of plays for schools, and some were published by Heinemann, including his superb versions of Ian Serraillier's *The Silver Sword* and John Steinbeck's *The Pearl*, both of which are still being produced today – most recently in Trinidad and Tobago. For the next few decades, my daily conversation about poetry would be with Stuart in the 'Coote Room' of Kimbolton Castle, where we each had a desk. Every morning I would come in and share some minor success or major setback;

Stuart Henson at ease amid the Huntingdonshire stubble.

he would do the same, though unlike me he would never brag. Sometimes it would be a chance to berate whichever editor had returned our work, or to compare notes on the latest Heaney or Hughes volume. Another day we might discuss the merits of Bob Dylan as a poet (Stuart is a major Dylan fan). Or we would plan our next visitor in the Poetry at Kimbolton series.* Occasionally typescripts would be surreptitiously left on one of our desks – mine chaotic, his immaculate. While all those about us were marking, preparing, discussing students, checking watches, we could be found comparing the virtues of a particular line break or the aptness of a certain metaphor. The Coote Room windows looked out on a folly – a permanent reminder not to get above ourselves.

Stuart is what Hans Keller might have called 'a major master of minor forms' (Hans was thinking of Gershwin). Not quite a miniaturist,* nevertheless he is very much at home with the attentive still life. He also has a particular gift for children's writing, and when Hutchinson brought out his picture book *Who Can Tell?* in 1996, it looked as though his literary career was shifting in that direction. But although it was a charming tale in verse about badgers, and it was beautifully produced, the book was rather overlooked and then slipped out of circulation, largely because of the publishers' indifference. That affection for the natural world is typical, and I never fail to learn something about the local landscape and its wildlife when we go walking. Although he doesn't make a big deal of it, Stuart is a true Huntingdonshire poet, and feels very close to neighbouring Northamptonshire's John Clare – not only as a fellow nature poet but as one who has sympathy for the neglected and marginalised. I was not surprised, for instance, when John Gohorry's sudden death in 2021 prompted him to edit a fine selection of that poet's much undervalued work with commemorative essays.*

Stuart has not produced a vast amount himself, but what he writes somehow touches a nerve, strikes a chord with the 'the common reader'. I have already remarked on this with regard to his poems about his grandfather's Chinese bridge and the dead heron (see p. 82 and p. 168), the last of which featured in Bloodaxe's hit volume, *Staying Alive*. He has another genuine anthology piece, 'The Price', which turned up on Forward Prize posters and in major anthologies. It neatly expresses 'what oft was thought but ne'er so well express'd' about modern life, how 'the colour supplements have lied/and some have pleasure and some pay the price'. Moreover, it's a perfect example of how an unrhymed sonnet can be made to resonate. As is often the case, I sense that it's not necessarily the poem Stuart would want to be remembered by, but I recall Douglas Dunn feeling the same way about the poems he had in the *Penguin Book of Contemporary British Poetry*, and indeed Yeats got very tired of reciting 'Innisfree'.

The Impossible Jigsaw was followed in 1994 by *Ember Music*. This collection includes a sequence about St Guthlac of Croyland Abbey out in the Fens. One of our 8.30 a.m. conversations in the late 1980s involved a possible collaboration about the Fens, but it came to little more than a few verses of mine. I suppose it's possible that the talk unconsciously prompted those Guthlac poems. 'Croyland' is one of several extended pieces excluded from Stuart's *Selected*, and I wish a wider readership could be found for them – especially the Nicholas Ferrar and Catherine of Aragon sequences in *The Impossible Jigsaw*. Nevertheless, that second Peterloo collection is one of his strongest, including a series of 'Brickyard Poems' to mark the arrival of the Henson family in their new home on the remotest imaginable road in the Huntingdonshire wolds. I've often cycled out to that house – which used to be a place where bricks rather than poems were made – and I somehow associate it with the emergence of my own Huntingdonshire eclogues, which I regularly shared with Stuart. I also like to think that John Donne may have trotted along there on his way to the nearby village of Keyston, where he held the living.

After the last Peterloo book and the closure of Harry Chambers's list, Stuart had many competition successes and high-profile appearances, such as his reading for *The Hudson Review* at the US Embassy in London. The collections kept on coming, but as pamphlets from John Lucas's Shoestring Press: for example, the illustrated nocturnal sequence, *Clair de Lune* in 1998, and five years later *A Place Apart*. Stuart calls this 'a love story without a happy ending', and it's the result of a trip he made to Canada on a sabbatical to explore the mysterious circumstances of his great-grandfather's disappearance to Canada. Stuart is good at love poems, which I envy.

The Odin Stone came out in 2011, with its 'lost god's eye' – the source of poetry in Norse myth – peering from between ink bottles and sharpened pencils on the cover. It seems to be warning us not to be lulled by the apparently tranquil fin-de-siècle settings. A stony gaze pierces the sepia casements of his verse: a missile will turn up in 'the heartwood's depth' of a childhood tree; along a country lane there may be 'cyanide in the backs of... four-by-fours'; and there is always the 'wasps' nest, swaying in the hawthorn'. The collection still has the nature studies, spiritual probings, snapshots of domestic tenderness and everyday fragility of those earlier books, but I felt when I reviewed it for the *TLS** that there was now a more cosmopolitan, literary voice: Woolf at Rodmell, Verlaine in Camden, a sequence of sultry Rilke pieces – nine 'Hours' imagined as women in Florence – and a section of 'Pushkin Variations'.

The unspoken presence, however, is D.H. Lawrence, even if Stuart's formal virtuosity has outgrown his master. I'm not sure he has quite forgiven me for a teasing comment about use of the word 'loins' in that review, but even he would admit there are certain difficulties with Lawrence in the 2020s. I particularly enjoyed those poems where he leaves the twilight and sets his masks aside – in 'After Pushkin', for example, 'Caught in the clatter of a city street,/or stepping through the still hush of a church,/or at a gig, maybe, crushed in the mosh-pit,/my mind plays God, reminding me that each//of us must pass into the world of darkness'; or in the masterly 'Bridge' (which Kevin Gardner and I were very pleased to feature in our *Contraflow* anthology). That stone eye glints. But it can wink, too, as when he tosses us a riddle or one of his Martian similes: youngsters sharing an iPod are 'Like roped climbers,/a yoked team,/like Castor & Pollux floating in space'. Or in his fridge-magnet parody of plums in the icebox, which ends with a flourish worthy of Charles Ives.

The Odin Stone was followed in 2015 by *Feast of Fools*, another sequence – about misericords – most entertainingly illustrated by Bill Sanderson. This was launched in Stuart's local church, with folk music to accompany, though the event was nearly derailed when an audience member stepped into a ditch on the way through the Huntingdonshire night. In 2019, Stuart drew on all these books to create a Selected, *The Way You Know It*, which I was honoured to find jointly dedicated to Kathy Henson and to me as his 'first readers'. Bill Sanderson went on to win a Michael Marks award for his contribution to a later pamphlet of Stuart's, *Twelve Days*, which came out in 2021. His next full collection was *Beautiful Monsters* (my thoughts on which can be read online at the High Window website),* to be followed in 2025 by *A Handful of Wasps*. And, of course, there was the postcard collaboration, discussed in the chapter, 'Waiting'.

We like to think of poets as solitary creatures: the idea of them sharing inspiration with each other or co-writing something as personal as a poem is hard to take in. But then we remember Wordsworth and Coleridge, Eliot and Pound – *The Waste Land* is demonstrably a work of more than one hand – and soon the examples begin to multiply. Sylvia Townsend Warner and Valentine Ackland come to mind. Or Robert Graves and Laura Riding. And of course Auden and MacNeice, who in 1937 produced their verse and prose *Letters from Iceland* for Faber (in 1996, the same publisher brought out Simon Armitage and Glyn Maxwell's *Moon Country: Further Reports from Iceland*). Sylvia Plath and Ted Hughes didn't publish anything together, yet they drew on each other's drafts, and Plath's posthumous collections after *Ariel* were compiled by her husband. Less well known are Philip Gross and Sylvia Kantaris, whose *The Air Mines of Mistila* feels as magical now as it did in 1988. Suddenly such collaborations don't seem strange at all. No stranger, certainly, than when one poet translates another – and in fact some translation processes involve very close personal contact between author and translator, as with Robin Fulton Macpherson's work on Tranströmer or Clare Cavanagh's on Wisława Szymborska.

Penelope Shuttle

A Post Card to had been building, delivery by delivery, for thirty years; but the project with Penelope Shuttle came as a surprise. Penny and her husband Peter Redgrove collaborated all the time, particularly in their groundbreaking prose study of menstruation, *The Wise Wound*. I have written at length about Penny's elegies for Peter in my book of essays, *Vapour Trails*, and I have already elaborated on the background to our 2016 book, *Heath*, in the 'Roots' chapter. But Penny's work was important to me long before we became friends. I remember hearing her read at the ICA in London in the 1970s, and I bought many of the Oxford

Penelope Shuttle's Falmouth.

collections, whose free-verse intensities were close to the kind of thing I aspired to. We even appeared in a few magazines together, but it was only when I got to review one of her later books that we met. *A Leaf Out of His Book* appeared from Carcanet in 1999 after OUP had shamefully disbanded its poetry list, and although it is a substantial volume it rather fell under the radar. Penny once told me that she regards it as the most Cornish of her books, although that must surely have been displaced now by *LZRD* and *Lyonesse*. It remains one of my favourites. In many ways she is exploring Eavan Boland's mystical/feminist territory, but whereas we accept dreams and wells and dowsers from Irish poets, that particular area of English sensitivity is being steadily tarmacked over.

In my review for the *TLS*, I remarked that she seems to get the balance right, tempering her innate sense of myth with considerable humour and common sense. In 'Penelope' she plays with her own name: 'I bend over my loom/and throw my shuttle, weaving/the world, its weathers…' Weather is a subject she writes about with flair, much as Peter Redgrove did. I recall a quirky (and long-lost) television programme in which they both talked about the importance of weather in their work – Redgrove, characteristically, sought out storms, plunged into them. Like Boland, Shuttle is attentive to the sensitivities of the language; her poetry blossoms from the words' assonantal interiors, their rootballs of sound. Her generally short lines highlight particular images and allow spaces for silence. Their sparse gleam reminded me twenty years ago of a line from an even earlier poem – 'crescent moons of gold/from the sunken district/of the dark'. Those 'lunulae' were in Truro; but this collection seems now to anticipate what we produced together in *Heath* fifteen years later. Penny kindly sent me a postcard thanking me for the review (it was only an 'In Brief') and although our paths may have crossed in Cornwall I think we didn't meet properly until we were both at Ledbury Festival in 2005, where she attended my talk on the First World War poets. That date stays in the mind because it coincided with the London bombings. A decade later we would be back in Ledbury, launching *Heath*.

Anne Stevenson wrote a very nice blurb for our 'piece of double-imagination', as she called it, adding that readers would 'never tread the proliferating wasteland of Heathrow Airport without being grateful for this warm, sprightly, thoroughly entertaining introduction to its rural past.'

Anne Stevenson

I have known Anne's work for decades, probably since she, like Penelope, was one of the featured poets in the Blake Morrison and Andrew Motion Penguin anthology.* She reviewed my 1984 pamphlet *Winter Journeys* for *Poetry Review* – not desperately enthusiastically, it has to be said. We shared a lot of interests, music especially, though she was always a far more skilled practitioner than I am. There are other odd things too, such as a mutual fondness for George Gascoigne. She told me once that she kept his 'Green Knight's Farewell to Fancy' sellotaped above her desk to remind herself 'what poets be'.

Anne herself we have known since she was living in Grantchester, which is next to Cambridge and only a short drive from where we live. Sadly, the pressures of teaching and 'parenting' – a verb I usually resist – meant we didn't see as much of her as we should have before her death in 2020. She had been raised in the US, but was actually born in Cambridge during a period when her father was in England studying philosophy. For years, however, Oxford University Press was her publisher; she was another of the poets unceremoniously dumped when they closed their list. Bloodaxe were quick to snap her up – a perfect fit, especially with her attachment to the north. In fact, she was the first recipient of the very generous Northern Rock Award, not long before Northern Rock became a notorious casualty of the 2008 financial crisis. Anne Stevenson is a poet of international significance. You have to be of considerable importance to have a volume in the Library of America series. Nor are there many contemporary poets who have corresponded at length with

Elizabeth Bishop. That's not to mention her widely acclaimed and frequently criticised biography of Sylvia Plath, *Bitter Fame* – although there was always a deep sigh whenever I mentioned to her anything about 'the Hugheses'.

Anne came to read for the Poetry at Kimbolton series and attended the launch of my 1995 collection, *Fotheringhay*. We met up once or twice thereafter – on one occasion at a village pub near us known for its fish and chips, when she and her husband, Peter, were on their way to their second home in Wales. I remember on that occasion Anne pointed out that I was wearing a new shirt, noticing it had come straight from the packaging, unironed. That was typical of Anne. She will bring the same directness to commentary on one's poems. For example, I once sent her a villanelle which mentioned a seagull's nest, and she was convinced that gulls don't build nests. Gerry Cambridge, who published the poem, sent her a photo to prove they did, but she insisted that for her a nest meant 'something basket-like in a tree'. As one for whom such details matter, I have often left a meeting with Anne wanting to go back and revise a text. Her letters are full of textual commentary – one, for example, on a poem of mine about Jane's spiritualist interests,* in which she gives very specific technical advice, as well as expressing some anxiety about the very idea of consulting mediums. Anne could be quite firm about such things, which is perhaps what moved me to compose a 'Fugue' to her 'Arioso Dolente', in which I play with the possibility of 'something out there'.*

The view from Anne Stevenson's cottage in Wales.

Responding to this some years later, Anne wrote to me shortly before her death (she was 87) that she did indeed think 'the best, the highest art, is personal' and believed that, regardless of time or century, through some 'universal expressions of feeling we communicate as "souls"'; although she went on to express fears for the disappearance of our entire culture through war or cultural upheaval or simply 'loss of taste for a certain grace and beauty that has disappeared for ever, it seems to me, from most of the creative arts in the West today.'

In the late summer of 2001, we spent a memorable family weekend at Anne's Welsh cottage, Pwllymarch in Cwm Nantcol, which is just as magical as it looks on the cover of her first Bloodaxe Collected, *Poems 1955–2005*.* She and Peter weren't in residence, but we took my mother there, whom I hadn't seen since my pilgrimage to the Arctic Circle to revisit Dad's old haunts. I remember showing Mum my new sequence of Iceland poems for the first time as we sat in the garden, a remote and glorious spot, in a pre-9/11 stillness. I associate Anne with various specific places like that: the Poetry Bookshop in Hay-on-Wye, for instance, which she founded; Michigan where she studied; Dundee, where she was writer in residence previous to Douglas Dunn, just before we moved to the area; and Durham, where she established the magazine *Other Poetry*, where I had some of my earliest poems published and some rejected – I still have the kindly slips of apology. But it was at her house in Grantchester I spent one of the most memorable literary evenings with Stuart Henson and Dana Gioia, the conversation and the drink flowing joyfully into the small hours.

It is to the north that Anne returned, and she suggested in one letter that 'the combination of Durham and Wales' had been good for her poetry. Certainly *Granny Scarecrow*, which emerged soon after the move, is one of her most appealing collections. The majority of her many postcards and letters are from Durham. Not only marvellous long letters – some on the backs of proofs – but poems too, and especially signed Christmas poems such as 'Carol of the Birds' or 'Christmas Comfort and the Green Man'.* Anne also liked to send recently completed poems, sometimes in holograph, usually typed. I have, for example, a typescript of 'Arioso Dolente', one of her very best* and her self-confessed favourite. Most of Anne's letters refer to her ambivalence towards poetry, how she goes 'on and off' it. In 2007 she emailed me to say that after her next book, *Stone Milk*, she was going to stop writing poems entirely. In fact, for the past couple of decades Anne's letters almost always announced she had written her last poem or published her last collection. I even have a typed copy of 'Anne Stevenson's Farewell to Poetry', though it's more of a farewell to other people's bad poetry, lamenting as she gazes over 'miles and miles of cut-up prose,/

Plausible troubles and lives./How they smother in sand the fire that was the rose./A plastic Ozymandias survives.'

We were very sorry when she and Peter moved away, but she was such a good correspondent that we never lost touch. Anne was severely deaf – one of her abiding themes – so conversation was not always easy, but that's not an issue with letters. And it sometimes feels as though poets have a way of remaining in contact even after they have left this earth. Only a few weeks ago I found myself in Barmouth on the Welsh coast browsing a second-hand bookshop. The poetry section was well stocked and had a certain *je ne sais quoi* to it. The collections weren't the obvious ones. I picked out a selection from an American poet I'd never read: William Matthews. It seemed rather overpriced, so I asked the woman at the till whether they could knock something off. 'Ah, but that book has an interesting provenance...' To which I replied: 'Did it by any chance belong to Anne Stevenson?' It had. And at that moment my eyes fell on a postcard showing her valley, her house, the very photograph that's on her Bloodaxe *Collected*. The card had only just come in that morning.

William Scammell

I met William Scammell for the first time at the Sotheby's prize-giving for the 1987 Arvon International Poetry Competition judged by Hughes and Heaney where we were both receiving awards, he for a poem called 'Dunmail Raise'. I took at once to this stocky, bearded chain-smoker, to his energy, cheerful demeanour and lightning grasp of the literary world. I never heard the full story of his life from him personally, but I have learnt since that he had anything but a privileged background (his father was a plumber, his mother a chambermaid), working in a series of largely unrewarding jobs from the age of fifteen. There was a spell as a copy boy on the *Southampton Evening Echo*, then menial work in various factories, before he became a photographer on cruise ships. Later there were posts as a copywriter for the Potato Marketing Board, as a house-cleaner, and much more besides, but all the time he knew he wanted to write. As a teenager he had produced a novel and short stories, meeting resistance when he tried to get them published, he felt, because of his humble background and lack of education. In fact, he had a brother who wrote. Michael Scammell, a professor at Cornell, had produced the standard biography of Solzhenitsyn, and was highly regarded. Bill went to university in his twenties as a mature student, and teaching jobs followed, mainly in adult education. That's when the poetry began, which he had for many years resisted, again fearing that to succeed in such elite company you had to have passed the eleven-plus.

We met again at a launch party, where I found myself caught in a quarrel between Bill and an eminent poet whom he had recently reviewed. The argument was over whether he should have called said poet a 'lefty' in a review (probably for the *Independent*) and fisticuffs were threatened. I came to realise that Bill was quite easily moved to anger, and occasionally he apologised in his letters for the bile, usually blaming the chaos of his life. My first letter from him was after that occasion in the late eighties, when he lamented the perils of reviewing. But being the generous soul he was, he was quick to forgive, and subsequently awarded the above-mentioned poet a Poetry Book Society Recommendation. We discovered that we had interests in common, particularly the obscurer corners of classical music, about which he knew an extraordinary amount. Our letters are full of CDs, which were then at their height of popularity. He enthuses about Roy Harris's Third Symphony and Arthur Grumiaux's Bach. He loved Claudio Monteverdi, Heinrich Schütz, Dietrich Buxtehude – but also Indian music, following a trip to Goa. We disagreed about Bruckner's 'slow boat to China' and Arnold Bax ('life's too short'), and about a good number of poets. But we shared enthusiasms too – A.R. Ammons, for instance – and both had doubts about others such as John Ashbery, though Bill was more outspoken than me, calling his work 'tiresome rubbish'.

I have looked out our extensive correspondence and am reminded that Bill wrote some of the best letters I have ever received. They are typed in the pre-computer manner with occasional corrected misprints, some of which he enjoyed leaving: 'I think academic critics are hopeless, by and marge'. Some of the later letters are on fax paper because he discovered he could avoid paying for cartridge ribbons that way.

In the early 1990s, when we began corresponding properly, his first marriage had just broken up – 'complicated but amicable', he told an interviewer. He had moved to 'the middle of nowhere' in Cumbria and was now a freelancer, exceptionally busy, editing a Bloodaxe anthology of 'New Lake Poets' and the selection of Ted Hughes's prose, *Winter Pollen*, for Faber. He had already written for them the standard guide to Keith Douglas in John Lucas's incomparable critical series. Bill was very supportive of Hughes, while recognising that his output was uneven. The letters are full of names: poets admired or despised. I must have sent him similar lists. He refers in one of the letters to the Cumbrian poet Norman Nicholson and the lack of a *Collected*, which I had evidently mentioned, and he says he'll see if he can talk Faber into it, before typically

throwing in the titbit that Nicholson left over a quarter of a million at his death
– 'we were all flabbergasted, thinking that he lived on tuppence a week'. The
volume did appear in 1994, but I think it didn't sell well. Somebody from Faber
once remarked to me with a sigh that if only all those who had asked them to
do a Nicholson *Collected* had bought a copy…

Apart from an unfortunate experience with the short-lived Sinclair-Stevenson
poetry venture and a few other small presses, Bill (like Stuart) was for many
years published by Harry Chambers's smallish but prestigious house, Peterloo.
The first from them was *Yes & No*, in 1979, and the last, thirteen years later,
Bleeding Heart Yard. Harry was a character in his own right and a constant source
of exasperation to Bill, though he along with U.A. Fanthorpe must have been
one of their most successful names: 'Scammell is the luck any small publisher
deserves', as John Lucas once remarked. His most entertaining book from
Peterloo is *The Game*, a series of brilliant parodies about tennis. Bill played
tennis for Cumbria and was one of that small clan of enthusiastic poet-players
such as Randall Jarrell and Vernon Watkins (who died playing in Seattle). 'The
Golden Dawn' is Bill's take on Yeats:

> A backhand slice is but a paltry shot,
> no backbone in it, *sauve qui peut*, unless
> hit to the corner, baseline, asymptote
> plus foxy coda, underspun duress
> allowing one to charge in, tête-a-tête,
> and do a hotshot number at the net…

He continues with meditations on the days 'when I was young and skinny', and
addresses the sages ('Kenny, Fred') who will be 'the singing-masters of my game'.
Elsewhere there is a Henry Reed ('Today we have eye on the ball'), MacNeice ('It's
gone to rack and ruin, chaps'), Graves ('There is one dress and one dress only'),
Betjeman ('Dave, I think your tracksuit's smashing./Yes, I like your headband
too./You've got the gear, you've got the passion,/Just like teenage McEnroe'),
Wordsworth ('Three sets long by two sets wide'), Donne, Raleigh, etc.

Bill knew the only way to play tennis is with the net up. He loved using metre
and having fun with it; and he regarded it as perfectly natural, pointing out that
people speak iambic pentameter all the time, and that 'a lot of Dickens is in
metre'. Bill and his partner, Jan, came to stay with us when he gave a reading
in Kimbolton. It was a lovely visit, and he seemed to appreciate life in our tiny,
crowded cottage, though I was too taken up with schoolwork to spend much

William Scammell visiting the Greenings.

time chatting. Thus it has been with all my poetry friends, except the one with whom I actually taught.

In the early 1990s 'William Scammell' was about as well-known a name as it would ever be, even earning a double-spread feature by Hunter Davies in the *Independent*, something inconceivable for such a poet today. He was fearless, and would have given Geoffrey Grigson a run for his money, although in one of his letters he calls Grigson 'pompous and snide' for some comment about poets like Ted Hughes shortening their names. As often as one journal invited him to contribute, another would drop him because he had said something they found politically incorrect. 'I am persona non grata at the *TLS* and *LRB*,' he wrote. Goodness knows how he would survive in an age when, as James Campbell put it in a recent column in the *TLS*, 'there is no longer any critically authorised tradition of merit in poetry. The contemporary scene is run to a large extent on identity approval, not critical judgement.'*

Bill's last letters to me have all the same unselfish enthusiasm for the work of others and an inextinguishable delight in living, although there was a sense of being left behind too – readings drying up, fewer reviews offered. He had lost his publisher at Sinclair-Stevenson, Harry Chambers was on the verge of closing, and he could not persuade Enitharmon or Flambard to do the *New and Selected* he wanted, although there were some late individual volumes. He writes how much of the hoped-for *Selected* was set around his Cumbrian cottage 'gazing at sheep and trees and red sandstone barns or gravestones.

Under-the-feet stuff,' but included things from his 'rumbustious' Barnacle Bill sequence from Dedalus Press, along with some 'flighty and cerebral and bran-tubby' poems.*

In a letter from January 1998 he tells me about marrying Jan, and laments the death of Jon Silkin, whom he knew to be bloody-minded, yet was admiring of 'his energy and his wiles... above all, his forty years at the wordface'. He also mentions tantalisingly a long autobiographical piece he had composed about his days at sea which *Granta* commissioned but couldn't use (remarkably, they still paid him £800). In one letter from June of the same year he refers to Hughes's *Birthday Letters*, about which it appears he had a hint from the poet, 'mentioned casually in a letter', adding that he thought the Poet Laureate had 'enormously mixed feelings' about publishing it and what sort of reception it might get, but 'Now he feels glad, not just because of its success but because it's taken a great muddle off his shoulders, and "changed my environment", as he says, i.e. as a writer'. Whether Bill knew about his friend's own illness, I'm not sure. Of himself, he mutters darkly that his brain doesn't seem to be functioning very well, and puts it down to the 'unaccustomed sunshine', but he was still playing tennis well into his final year, despite a foot injury.

I heard from him again a couple of times – his usual buoyant self. 'Fancy having to write 2000!' he begins one letter from January posted a few days after his sixty-first birthday, not knowing that 2000 would for ever be beside his name; and he goes on to describe how he and Jan spent New Year's Eve 'under the stars and round a big bonfire, watching other people's fireworks go off far down the valley, and listening to the echoes from the rocks.'

But then the news came of his death. I can't recall how I found out. He had been begging us to come and visit the cottage in the Lake District for years, but I had put it off too long, taken up with family commitments and teaching duties. I learnt later that he'd gone downhill, rapidly following an enjoyable trip to the USA in July to visit his brother, which I'd known was happening from his final letter. What had begun as back pain proved to be lung cancer, and he died in November 2000. His widow, Jan, wrote movingly to me just after Christmas: 'at dawn the angels came without warning. They touched Bill, then they touched me to tell me'.

I dedicated my next collection *The Home Key* to Bill's memory, and I wrote a sonnet for the memorial, which I was unable to attend. Poetry has its uses, and offering some new lines in commemoration is in the end all another poet can do. Indeed, it's what we do best:

Too late. Let this go 'surface', be delayed –
it's all an email now into thin air
without those adders' tongues we used to stir
around our cauldron. Look, Bill, here, I've made
a start… now won't you tell me how you play
doubles, smoke, laugh, listen to Monteverdi,
unwrap angelic jiffy bags? Not fair
to pull the covers over before the day
has finished. Was it at that Bloodaxe reading
we first met, you in mid-dogfight, me confused
by how you read the game? A cut, a pass
from the low left, volleyed back into Bleeding
Heart Yard. Killed in action. Keith Douglas, Ted Hughes,
and you. On clay, on paper, under grass.

Dennis O'Driscoll

Bill was born in the same year as Seamus Heaney, whose name will for ever be associated with that of my good friend, Dennis O'Driscoll. When *Stepping Stones* appeared, I was not alone in being bowled over by it, and I may have been one of the few who knew it was coming, rather as Bill had that tip-off about *Birthday Letters*.

I used to meet Dennis for lunch in Dublin whenever my colleague Steve Pollard and I took students there for a study trip. On one of those brief escapes from his nine to five in Dublin Castle he let slip the fact that he was undertaking a major book about his friend, that the interviews had been going for some time. I can't think of any living poet who can plumb such depths in his talk as Heaney did, and every stone we are invited to step on in Dennis's interviews feels like a fresh one, yet the direction he is taking us is always clear. That's in no small part due to shrewd questioning – following up in interesting, unpredictable ways, asking for a little more about details of decor or personality, making some playful links. The reader learns so much about the origins and shaping of Heaney's poetry: the effect of those first French vowel sounds, for instance; the way he later purged some of the poems of local usages, even if I still regret the change from 'shod' to 'curve' in the second line of 'North'. What is especially impressive is the way Heaney always returns to real words from actual poems hoarded in his memory, whether by Czesław Miłosz, John Montague, George Seferis or

Dennis O'Driscoll in more informal mood, courtesy of Julie O'Callaghan.

William Wordsworth. He knows there is no substitute for close reading, even for intensive 'study' as mocked by Larkin. Indeed, when I first read *Stepping Stones*, the intensity of focus on the art kept sending me back to my own work, wondering about the shape of my *Poems 1979–2009*, being forced to ask myself again and again: is that something I could say about what I've produced?

In an era when poets tend to settle in universities or schools, Dennis was an exception. From the age of sixteen he was a civil servant (dealing at first with Death Duties), and he remained one for almost forty years. 'In the civil service you are assigned a grade. You know your status,' he told the *Irish Times*. 'Whereas with poetry, you never retire and you never really know your grade – it will be assigned posthumously.' I was always conscious when we met that he needed to get back to work, but we shared another bond apart from both being born in 1954: we both had day jobs, increasingly rare for any poet. So we'd gossip. We'd name-drop. We'd take a quick look at a nearby bookstall. Then before I knew it, he would be gone. Before any of us knew it he was gone, and I was writing his obituary for the *Guardian* and a tribute for *Poetry Review*.

Dennis had always known he wanted to be a poet, even before he heard a school recitation of Shakespeare's 'When icicles hang by the wall' and nearly fainted. He had lost both parents by the time he was twenty and was left in charge of his five siblings. Unsurprisingly, mortality and work would become

234

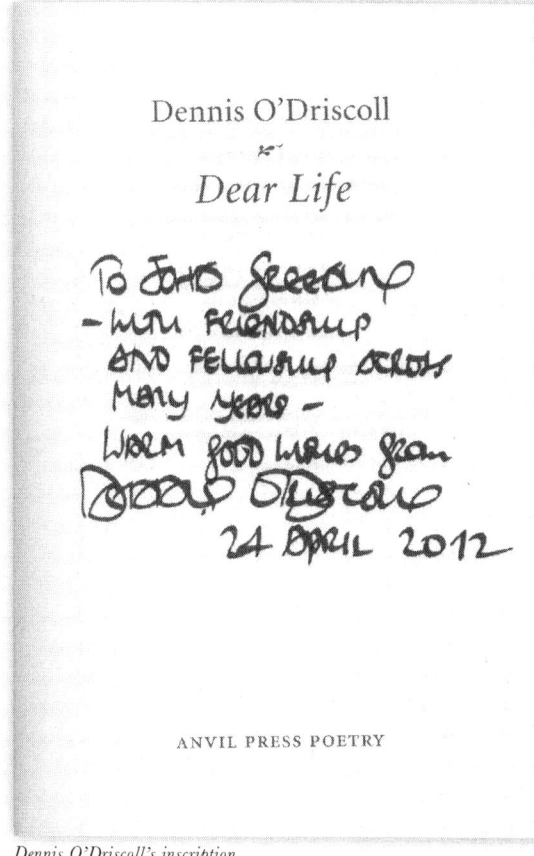

Dennis O'Driscoll

Dear Life

To John Greening
— with friendship
and fellowship across
many years —
Warm good wishes from
Dennis O'Driscoll
24 April 2012

ANVIL PRESS POETRY

Dennis O'Driscoll's inscription.

two of his preoccupations. He regularly drew on the jargon of business and bureaucracy, even in the titles of his slim volumes such as *Hidden Extras* or his pamphlet *The Bottom Line*, a ruthless dissection of office life, its 'hidden pain', which stirred interest well beyond the poetry bubble. In a field especially crowded with Irish poets, O'Driscoll's voice could be heard distinctly and at ever increasing distances. In 1999 he received one of the biggest international prizes, a Lannan Literary Award, which was the incentive for a move with his wife, the poet Julie O'Callaghan, out to Naas, County Kildare.

The books from this period* reveal a stylistic clarity learnt from Brecht and from O'Driscoll's beloved Eastern European poets; and an arresting directness – often using droll repetition – which catch perfectly a certain contemporary speech idiom which Larkin would have recognised, although he is much more courteous towards his own Warlock-Williamses:

> No, I don't want to drop over for a meal
> on my way home from work.
> No, I'd much prefer if you didn't feel obliged
> to honour me by crashing overnight.
> No, I haven't the slightest curiosity about seeing
> how your attic conversion finally turned out [...]

> (from 'No, Thanks')*

In person, Dennis was charm itself, a quiet man but immensely sociable, and his generosity to fellow writers was legendary.

Even as he scaled back the day job, the literary tasks multiplied – editing, broadcasting, judging (at one point he had to read 500 poetry collections for the Griffin Prize) and travelling to perform or promote books. No workshops, however; no creative-writing classes. His selfless nature and companionable manner, which would have made him a fine teacher, helped towards the success of the Heaney interviews, which appeared from Faber in 2008 to considerable acclaim. This engrossing volume, along with two further Anvil Press collections, *Reality Check* (2007) and *Dear Life* (2012), published a few months before he died, can be seen now as his 'final blazon'. Or perhaps he would have regarded that, smiling impishly, as the moment in 2008 when he was for the first time invited by his employers at Dublin Castle to write a poem – to mark the opening of their Revenue Museum.

A Mass of Life

after Horace, *Odes*, Book II, iii

Whether things go badly or unexpectedly well,
don't overreact. Remember, everything will

end in the end – despairingly, or sprawled on the grass
in a paradise garden with the local wine and an anti-mass.

Why do you think these orange trees and pines have joined
their hands to welcome us? Why that summery sound

from the river, if it's not for you and me, Delius?
Wine, perfume, roses… Bring them all to us

before they turn syphilitic, and while the weaving
path still leads to Bradford. Soon you'll be waving

goodbye to both your home town and that foreign retreat,
its pleasures and treasures will be scattered to the air's estate.

Rich or poor, a trump or the meanest card in the pack,
the cuckoo sweeps down on us all and takes the trick,

invading our nest. Sooner or later it will happen,
the famous ferry arrives, its bow-doors open.

Perfection of the Life
or of the Work

A new biography of Wallace Stevens set me thinking about a paradoxical truth captured in Yeats's phrase above: that apparently dull lives can lead to rich, sophisticated poetry. Although he worshipped European culture, and was very much a man of the world, Stevens famously stuck to his nine-to-five insurance job in Hartford, Connecticut until he was over seventy. He didn't go to war, hardly even left the USA, and was married unhappily for many decades to the woman who modelled Liberty on the dime. As we have seen, his chief passion beyond the arts was walking – like the Lake Poets, he thought nothing of a thirty-mile hike. Although he couldn't bear the idea of, for example, a cruise, he had an extraordinarily well-travelled imagination, relishing foreign news and friends' picture postcards, conjuring the rest of the planet on to his own highly polished table. In 1953, he wrote how, when he went home at night from the office, he would spend a long time 'dawdling over the fascinating phrases [in *Figaro*] which refresh me as nothing else could.'* He describes living 'in a Paris that has never existed'. He kept the poetry and the work entirely separate.

After the 1960s, with the Beats and the 'confessional' movement, it became almost de rigueur for a poet to offer the reader exciting slices of life – this was authenticity, like not wearing make-up or playing Mozart on the natural horn – in breakdowns and break-ups, affairs, violent controversies, preferably involving celebrities and exotic locations. Nor was it any longer acceptable to be a war poet; dying for your country was no kind of perfection. You were more likely to be heard if you could shout about peace like Allen Ginsberg or the more subtle and significant Denise Levertov, or tell the world of your most intimate acts along with Anne Sexton. Reputation and disintegration, revelation and revolution, danced in a circle holding hands. Sylvia Plath and Ted Hughes thus became poetry's spirits of the age, as the Shelleys had a century and a half before. While their precise biographical details remained buried under layers of mythology, veiled by allegory, it was always clear how their lives were driving their work. This was confirmed by *Birthday Letters* in 1998, perhaps also confirming that Hughes wrote best when the life remained buried. The same has been true of many poets who tried removing veils in order to sound more authentic: Thom Gunn on the gay scene in *The Passages of Joy*, for instance, or Robert Lowell's endless parade of Notebooks. 'Yet why not say what happened?' he wrote in his final collection. The answer is: because it's hard.

Meanwhile, there were contemporaries simply getting on with their undramatic lives, shunning 'sincere' verses because they suspected 'all bad poetry is sincere' (as Oscar Wilde didn't quite say), but trying to produce something authentic. Many of these are poets who have remained in the shadows, names we have already begun to forget.

The late Charles Tomlinson is one reported to have felt overlooked because he would not conform to the fashion for psychodrama. The drama in his writing is in the very sound and tensions of meaning, in the line breaks and the syntax – precisely where it should be, in fact. He dismissed the confessional trend in his poem 'Against Extremity', his targets obvious ('That girl who took/Her life almost, then wrote a book'), his observation salutary: 'The time is in love with endings'. Tomlinson was a devoted family man, a professor of English. Philip Larkin was neither, but while he liked to play up the drabness of his days ('What are days for?'), they were rather more interesting than Mr Bleaney's in his 'hired box', 'plugging at the four aways' (once mistranslated into German as 'taking four holidays a year'). My thoroughly unmarketable *Dull Lives of the Modern Poets* would include this university librarian, along with a good few professors and teachers, but also several civil servants, some secretaries, at least two Anglican priests, a building-society executive, and a certain Orcadian. George Mackay Brown, according to his biographer Maggie Fergusson, 'barely left the islands. He had never taken part in a book signing or a public performance of his work; he had only once been in London'.*

A candidate for English poetry's dullest ever life may be found in Olney, at the home of William Cowper, a poet who surrounded himself with churchy types and whose subject for an epic was, as we have seen, his own sofa. Yet he was considered almost dangerously racy at the time – 'if he is not to be animated by Cowper!' says Jane Austen's Marianne Dashwood, trailing off into audible italics. In truth, the concealed passions and his series of nervous collapses would have equipped him well for Alvarez's influential *New Poets* anthology – 'The Cast-Away' would not look out of place. The same might be said of John

The Cowper and Newton Museum in Olney.

Clare, whose fifteen minutes of fame make his subsequent neglect all the more poignant. Although celebrated now for his nature poetry, he puts his own life right at the centre of his greatest poem, 'I Am'.

In the case of both Cowper and Clare, what constituted a drama could be something as apparently minor as a move across the county border. Both would concur with Wordsworth, who kept his own French affairs well concealed, when he picks on the skylark as 'Type of the wise, who soar, but never roam;/ True to the kindred points of Heaven and Home!' It's no surprise that Byron despised and mocked 'Wordy' for his parochialism. Lord Byron, of course, had rock-star celebrity, swimming the Hellespont and dying in or near foreign action, but it could be argued that his poetry suffered. High though his reputation is in Europe, at home – for all the satirical ingenuity of *Don Juan* – he is not generally considered among the very greatest poets, and certainly not in the same category as Alexander Pope, whom he admired. Pope spent much of his own satirical energy attacking another kind of Dullness: the boring poems of his contemporaries. He portrayed 'her' in *The Dunciad* as a flashy Goddess, forever influencing modern writing. Pope's life was not exactly full of incident, although that didn't prevent Maynard Mack publishing a biography of almost 1,000 pages. But there is undoubtedly perfection of an epigrammatical kind in his work.

In the US, meanwhile, where there has long been a revivalist pressure for poets to bare their souls, the Oscar nominees for Dullest Life would naturally feature Emily Dickinson, although the critic Lyndall Gordon in *Lives Like Loaded Guns* has found considerable internecine excitement even in her retired existence in Amherst, and it would be hard to find more explosively dramatic lyrics. Until recently in literary history, women were all but obliged to opt for perfection of the work – assuming they could find time – and to accept obscurity with it. But anthologies such as Roger Lonsdale's *Oxford Book of Eighteenth-Century Women Poets* began bringing them to light.

In our own time, women have inevitably come late to the party, U.A. Fanthorpe or Amy Clampitt fully enjoying their eventual success, noticed for their work rather than for their apparently unexceptional personal lives.

Elizabeth Bishop is an interesting case, however, since she is so often set beside her friend whom she might well have married, Robert Lowell, whose imperfect life was more often than not the subject of his increasingly imperfect verse. There have been more books on the hyperactive Lowell than on almost any other modern American poet – the religious zealot, the conscientious objector, his set-to with the White House, his face on the cover of *TIME*, the assault on his father, the spells in hospital, affairs, crazy lectures, destructive rampages – but ironically it is Bishop, quietly hidden away in Brazil while he bestrode the literary world, who is now considered more important. She was always wary of Lowell's determination to exploit details of his and other people's lives in his poems.

Entanglement of the life and the work can indeed cause problems, as shown by the furore over Jonathan Bate's excellent biography of Ted Hughes.* When I was young and wondering how to survive as a poet, Hughes wrote advising me at all costs to avoid teaching or 'enclosedly safe' jobs. In order to keep the creative pressure high, he said, I should stoke my survival energies through the poetry itself and be prepared to live a bit uncomfortably, with a final reliance on my writing. This was advice which I spectacularly ignored, but haven't often regretted, only too conscious of the pain it is possible to cause others just for the sake of 'getting something right in language', as Howard Nemerov had it. As Elizabeth Bishop said to Robert Lowell after he had shamelessly included extracts from his ex-wife's letters in his poems: 'Art just isn't worth that much.' Most of us, I think, would be more than happy to find ourselves remembered as what John Ashbery called Bishop: 'a writer's writer's writer' – perhaps in the company of that splendid and largely forgotten Elizabethan, Samuel Daniel, or his 'Musophilus':

> Be it that my unseasonable song
> Come out of time, that fault is in the time,
> And I must not do virtue so much wrong
> As love her ought the worse for others' crime;
> And yet I find some blessed spirits among,
> That cherish me, and like and grace my rhyme.
> A gain that I do more in soul esteem
> Than all the gain of dust, the world doth crave…

'A Wand'ring Minstrel'

Whose idea was it
to kit me out like that
for the Sunday School
fancy-dress event?

Ridiculous, with my
plastic Skiffle guitar
(a ukulele really)
in a shirt of 'shreds

and patches'... no one
would have had a clue,
even in the sixties,
especially the sixties,

when minstrels were Rolling
Stones or Beatles.
Yet now I wonder
what it started, given

how I love to stitch
snatches into lines
and sizzle them out
for anyone who's listening:

lullaby, shanty, song
of war or love song...
like Nanki-poo,
I'm quite adaptable.

A High Calling?

For Edmund Blunden, the poet's calling was without doubt something lofty,* and Blunden himself kept that truth in mind as he wrote, always within earshot of John Clare, Edward Young, William Collins and another distant Edmund – Spenser. It's hard to imagine a more appropriate poet to be commemorated at Hiroshima, where a bronze, book-shaped sculpture bears his distinctive profile and his poem 'A Song for August 6, 1949'. Although Blunden wrote lighter poems – there is actually one about Gilbert and Sullivan's *Mikado* – and he never forgot that poetry is close to song, even his early pastoral work is richly scored. When he arrived in the trenches straight from school and just as his first full collection was being published, he seemed more than usually equipped to find the right tone for his troubled times.

Blunden represents a high watermark of poetry as a vocation. But the notion of loftiness had already begun to crumble. Yeats himself, as we have seen, lamented the riderless 'high horse', and in the end knew he must 'lie down where all the ladders start/In the foul rag-and-bone shop of the heart'. Of course, poets have been saying as much since Philip Sidney's Muse told him to look in his own heart and write, but Sidney's was a lofty pedigree, if not an exceptionally lofty voice: his sonnets can be read today without much difficulty. Yet at the same time as poets were apparently shucking pretensions, they were acquiring new ones: it came to be assumed, largely because of some remarks of Eliot's, that you had to be Difficult if you wanted to be taken seriously. The actual language could be as simple as you liked, and in fact should be – no more Poetic Diction, no more inversion of sentences the rhyme to assist. No more of anything, really, that made Blunden the poet he was. Ezra Pound's *Don'ts* led the way. The notion of a high calling, then, adopted Modernism's cloak – or more accurately its 'gown': after all, it is in the universities that the Big Serious Voices have sounded.

But there have been other voices away from the campus reminding us of poetry's popular roots, poets who achieve a seriousness and find a readership without 'dumbing down'.

Dana Gioia is one of these, a Californian poet and critic who began his career in the business world, and who has argued for decades that poets don't talk enough to anyone else, and that this insularity has been damaging – to American poetry in particular. The creative-writing boom has, he tells us, made his nation's poetry 'a modestly upwardly mobile, middle-class profession', confined to places of higher learning, divorced from public life and increasingly even from the study of literature in which 'the energy… which was once directed outward, is now increasingly focused inward.'

Dana Gioia giving a reading in Kimbolton Castle.

Poets on campus in the US are expected to publish regularly in the same way that all university teachers do ('the slow maturation of genuine creativity looks like laziness to a committee'), and there are obvious advantages to cooperation, to teaching each other's poems and anthologies.

Gioia's 1991 article, 'Can Poetry Matter?' in the *Atlantic** – one of his so-called 'prosaic excursions' – caused an uproar among American poets just at the time when Jane and I were living in New Jersey. I remember finding the article by chance during a free period in the high school where I was teaching on a Fulbright exchange. Dana and I subsequently corresponded and we became friends. We didn't actually meet until he came and stayed with us for a reading in the Kimbolton series (he is pictured performing in the castle Saloon) when, as I have already related, he tried to get me to recite poems by heart. He was right to expect it: the poems that etch themselves on our memories are those that matter, although the question of verse in advertising is something I will touch on shortly.

Had Dana Gioia never written 'Can Poetry Matter?', people would still be reading and remarking on his own poetry and concluding that it *does* matter. *The Gods of Winter* (1991) received much favourable attention in the UK, and the Peterloo collection was made Poetry Book Society Choice. At that point Dana could probably have been published by Faber or another major house, but he stuck with Harry Chambers, who didn't really promote him as he deserved.

The poem that struck many readers, together with Dana's elegy for his young son, 'Planting a Redwood', was the narrative, 'Counting the Children'. It is a work which seems to have grown from the trauma of the loss described in the elegy. In four parts, composed in flexible pentameter tercets, it is spoken by a Chinese American accountant sent to take an inventory of a house where a reclusive woman had lived. In a scene Alfred Hitchcock would have appreciated, the neighbour lets him in only to find row upon row of dolls – at which the narrator is understandably disturbed. 'Where were the children who promised them love?/The small caressing hands, the lips which whispered/Secrets in the dark?'. That night he has an accountant's nightmare in which thousands of numbers won't tally and even '2+2+2/No longer equaled anything at all'. It's impossible not to think of Gioia the one-time businessman at this point. In a particularly Macbethian touch, the narrator dreams of his father asking him why he can't 'find the sum', and then 'All my family, living and dead' stretching out to the crack of doom.

After the dream, which ends with him 'working on the coffin of my daughter' and the dolls going up in flames, the narrator has to go and check on his sleeping seven-year-old, confessing that he used to do this many times a night when she was a baby, in terror for a life 'we treasured but could not protect'. The fourth 'movement' shows the narrator contemplating his daughter and having a waking vision, its mood faintly medieval like the visions in William Langland or *Pearl*, 'beyond my daughter to all children'. He wonders 'if completion comes only in beginnings?/The naked tree exploding into flower?' He feels he can only believe in immortality by thinking of 'the ancient face returning in the child' and the strict iambic pentameter reinforces the importance of this belief. The hard-headed accountant can not account for death, still less for survival of death, but he does feel the presence in this moment of vision of something like a soul, 'perfect and eternal in the way/That only numbers are, intangible but real,/Infinitely divisible yet whole' – ironically breaking out of the pentameter's 'numbers' here. But the poem lurches back to melodrama: his own daughter's dolls are lined up; 'their sharp glass eyes surveyed me with contempt'. The dolls have been abandoned too often; they know their owners have gone. The narrator tries to cling to his vision, but 'they would trust no promises of mine.//I feared that if I touched one, it would scream.'

While it may be true that there's no exact equivalent to A.E. Housman, John Betjeman or Wendy Cope in the USA, there are genuinely popular poets, even some whose words don't require music to make them memorable. Dana has championed several such, along with others – often rather politically incorrect figures, including Archibald MacLeish, Robinson Jeffers and Robert Frost, who hardly needs a champion, but who knew a great deal about poetry as a high calling. It was Frost, don't forget, who was invited to read a celebratory poem at the inauguration of J.F. Kennedy – although it all threatened to go horribly wrong when he was dazzled by the sun at the ceremony and ended up ditching the commissioned piece and relying on his memory (this must have impressed Dana, who is a great performer) to recite 'The Gift Outright'.*

One cannot imagine a British poet being invited to read at the State Opening of Parliament, despite the existence of an official Laureate. Only Ted Hughes has really made any effective claim to loftiness in that role since Tennyson. It's true that Boris Johnson did read part of a newly discovered Blunden poem outside 10 Downing Street for the seventy-fifth anniversary of VE Day. But Tony Blair's one sniggering concession to poetry was some doggerel for his Party Conference, although he did allow his name to be associated with Brooke's 'The Soldier' in an anthology of celebrities' – or their spin doctors' – favourite poems. I suspect Dana would deny it, but I feel that there is a much stronger appreciation of poetry as a 'gift outright' in the USA, where they don't instinctively cut big thinkers down to size as the Brits like to. The lofty vein, which Hopkins would have called 'Parnassian', is to contemporary American poets the default style. Some do it well, some are dreadful bores.

British readers – and especially British composers, for some reason – have long had a taste for Whitman and a guarded enthusiasm for the Beats. But few are the British poets who can sustain such an elevated tone without self-consciousness. We respect prophetic Blake and his angels, but we are happier with John Clare in the hedgerows. We tolerate a Matthew Arnold, but really we prefer an Arthur Hugh Clough, a droll, ironic voice lobbing squibs. We love a Yeats, but we love it still more when he turns into Philip Larkin, noting a greenhouse flashing among the allotments, and an uncle shouting smut, with just a glimmer of Celtic or Humber Twilight in *The Whitsun Weddings*'s final arrow shower. Great claims were made for Geoffrey Hill during his lifetime, and few poets seemed to take more seriously the notion of poetry's noble concerns, but there are many who feel he belongs to the history of the crossword puzzle rather than the history of poetry. We'd really rather hear U.A. Fanthorpe or Simon Armitage.

It's always salutary to ask how many poets from another century anyone remembers. An English Literature graduate might know a few from the nineteenth, even the eighteenth. But – as I've said here before – take a look at the names in Dr Johnson's *Lives of the English Poets*. Or those in Anne Finch's 1709 poem, 'A Tale of the Miser and the Poet', listed as if they would be familiar to every reader. Or indeed the roll call of Anthony Thwaite's 'On Consulting 'Contemporary Poets of the English Language" from two and a half centuries later. For that matter, look at the poets listed on the back of any volume of poetry acquired when you were younger. Faber holds up pretty well, it's true, because they have so many big names most will recognise; but those advertised on the back of, for example, Hill's *Mercian Hymns* published by André Deutsch in 1971 are likely to draw a blank look today. Nevertheless, it could be that Eric Barker, Judith Earnshaw, Philip Oakes, Diana Witherby are the poets we should be reading. Only a tiny fraction of the poetry published in any era is going to survive, and it may not be the best. How can we know? And whose guidance can we trust?

Indeed, we may wonder whether twenty-first-century Britain regards the poet's voice as something worth listening to at all – or any more worth listening to than the voice on an advert or a voice note? There have been poets who attracted wider popular attention because of their passion for some cause, but these are not necessarily the same poets who are valued by anthologists. They tend to make one think of loud voices rather than a high calling. This is true of many celebrities of the sixties in the UK: the Liverpool Poets, highly politicised protest poets such as Adrian Mitchell or Michael Horovitz. A little after their heyday, Heathcote Williams brought out a series of large-format books protesting against and preaching about, amongst other things, the threat to whales and the dominance of the car. These are all but forgotten, though they were much talked about at the time.

The same may well prove to be true of the books by American poet Claudia Rankine, currently of immense popularity on both sides of the Atlantic since their concerns coincide with current preoccupations. Like *Whale Nation* and *Autogeddon*, Rankine's *Citizen: An American Lyric* is a very satisfying book as physical object. It uses the space of the page, has striking illustrations and is a thoroughly compelling read. A series of recurring prose anecdotes about Black experience, the treatment of Black people in America, with special attention to Serena Williams, is set beside commentaries that seem designed to accompany videos, along with mini-essays and dialogues. The anecdotes are told coolly, matter-of-factly, forensically even, with no direct speech, metaphors only subtly introduced – 'the space next to the man is the pause in the conversation you are suddenly rushing to fill' or 'Where he goes the space follows him'. Line breaks don't come into it; paragraphs act more like stanzas. The writer is always holding up our own treacherous language to inspect ('in proximity to, adjacent to, alongside, within'). And we are obliged to think about namelessness, invisibility, erasure, darkness, unvoiced hostility.

But the question is: can more than an impressive handful of the individual sections truly be called a *poem*? Didn't Eliot or Pound say that poetry should have the qualities of good prose? Yes, the writing in *Citizen* is excellent prose: lucid, sharp as you like. But poetry? Perhaps we should be considering the whole book as a poem, a kind of concrete poetry, in which case, other things start becoming poems too (Marshall McLuhan, Rachel Carson, Cal Flyn) and short-story writers, essayists suddenly seem eligible for a poetry prize. *Citizen*, which was indeed shortlisted for the T.S. Eliot Prize, is a book that seems to be calling to us from an intellectual pulpit, is undoubtedly a book that has 'a palpable design upon us' and – by Keats's standards, anyway – that may be a limitation in terms of its enduring power as poetry. Although its subject matter is naturally far more important than any question of genre.

If the idea of poetry as a high calling means anything at all today, it can only be because we appreciate how language has been debased. The poet can at least be relied on to appreciate the power and potency of the words they use. There has been something of an online debate in recent years about poets who allow their work to be performed for advertising, following a BBC radio programme, *Poetry for Sale*, which was broadcast when the first lockdown was in its third month and people had time to tune in to such things. It is a pity its makers hadn't read Bunting's advice on cutting, but there were some interesting observations. Will Harris made the point that poetry can hardly be called marginal if you take into account its use in advertising, adding shrewdly that the relationship between poetry and commerce is an uncomfortable area for most poets. He saw a direct line from Lord Byron to Charles Saatchi. Meanwhile, Jo Bell, who has performed poems on TV to advertise Nationwide, was able to bring first-hand experience to the discussion. She felt that the client paying for the ad wants the 'emotional investment' of poetry, but found they often thought rather too literally and so missed the point (which is doubtless true of clients' responses to non-poetic copy too).* *Poetry for Sale*'s presenter, Rishi Dastidar, suggested that poetry might be 'the branch of the entertainment industry closest to a vocation, a calling rather than a regular office-hours way of making a living'. Bell evidently believes her promotional verses are loyal to that calling (she has a distinguished publishing record), although there were questions raised subsequently by other writers on social media and by poet Clare Pollard on the programme itself. Pollard made no distinction between the craft involved in writing poems or writing copy, but was clear that the words of a copywriter can never be a poem because 'as soon as the intent is to sell you something, then it's an advertising jingle'. If Pollard and Keats are to be believed, that rules out not only some minor masterpieces such as Auden's 'Night Mail' and Kipling's 'If', but a great deal of the literary canon which has designs on us in one way or another. We no longer read much of the poetry popularly acclaimed in Victorian times because it was trying to sell us Christian morality. Earlier ages had preoccupations of their own. Who cares any more about the various cultural disputes that fired up Alexander Pope?

It might be worth noting, incidentally, that verse in the eighteenth century was regarded as the most truthful form of communication, a suitable genre in which to pen a scientific treatise (as Erasmus Darwin did), rather than to try and sell you snake oil. And according to an advertising professional interviewed on *Poetry for Sale*, this same authenticity made poetry appropriate for promoting a bank, and proved highly successful. Interestingly enough, during the sixteenth and seventeenth centuries (which can offer the highest number of familiar poets' names before our own era) there was no hesitation about using verse for even more practical purposes. Thus it was the natural medium for the popular drama, the equivalent of today's soap opera. It was, as Jo Bell says her poems aspired to be, something 'that people come into contact with… not as a luxury or a specialist activity, but a part of the fabric of daily life'. During his programme, Rishi Dastidar mentions the long-running series, Poems on the Underground, and the surprise of finding poems where ads would normally be, above the seats in London Tube trains. He also discusses Jeremy Deller's mural 'More Poetry is Needed', which

Swansea.

was painted beside a car park in Swansea to mark the Dylan Thomas centenary, and has now been removed to make way for a new commercial development. I remember visiting the city, which is where my first serious poems were written, to give a reading at the Dylan Thomas Centre in 2014. Jane and I had a meal at *The Grape and Olive*, on top of a new tower above the marina, and spotted the sign, pictured here. Whether I quite agree with it is another matter; I'm more inclined to side with Yeats as quoted at the end of Anthony Thwaite's poem, that 'we are too many'. Dylan Thomas is an interesting case, however, since he wrote in a high, bardic style, yet achieved incredible popularity. Partly this was through the sheer intensity and musicality of his own performances, and partly his turbulent lifestyle, so inviting to the popular press.

There is quite a tradition of poets who have actually worked in advertising, Rishi Dastidar among them. Lola Ridge must have been one of the first, but other respected writers come to mind: Fay Weldon, Salman Rushdie, Edward Lucie-Smith, A.S.J. Tessimond. Norman Cameron, best remembered for 'Green, Green is El Aghir', came up with the imaginary condition 'night starvation' in order to sell Horlicks. Edwin Brock – who wrote the 'Song of the Battery Hen' – was a copywriter too, although he is also one of the few poets other than Susan Hill's fictitious Adam Dalgleish to have been a policeman. Clive James swore he would never sell his soul by going into advertising, but soon, he reveals in one of his essays, 'Faust was ready to negotiate'.

Then there are James Dickey, Carol Rumens, Matthew Dickman... Even Mayakovsky turned out slogans for Mosselprom, the Russian state wholesaler. There doesn't seem to have been any negative impact on their work, though one suspects that many others have been paid for copywriting and kept quiet about it. It's hard to imagine certain poets entering an advertising agency. Robert Graves? Yet he had no qualms about turning out potboilers. Rudyard Kipling? He might have enjoyed seeing 'If' quoted or parodied in TV ads, whether for mobile phones or deodorant. T.S. Eliot? A bank suited him well. Kathleen Raine? Edwin Muir? C.H. Sisson? These are not poets much concerned with their public image, but it's simply not conceivable they would have written anything to help sell something. Kathleen Raine's best known book of essays is called *Defending Ancient Springs*, which tells us all we need to know.

The myth of the poet as prophet is not so easily dispelled. If I haven't discussed this directly in these pages, nevertheless some of my thoughts on coincidence and magic might bring us close. Poet as keeper of the flame. Poet as Prospero.

I think there is something of this in the poetry of a recent winner of the Nobel Prize for Literature, Louise Glück, and also in that of Les Murray.

Murray's achievement rises from the surrounding literary landscape, like Uluru in the bush of his native Australia. There really is nothing like it. Reading his 2015 collection, *Waiting for the Past*,* I was struck by the ground he covered, even wittily taking us to the mouth of the Murray. Yet he is not a poet we travel with for a smooth-running engine and easy gear changes, although he is always alert to the sound of what he writes, as he proved in his glorious *Translations from the Natural World*, poems which set out to imagine how animals might express themselves.

There are passages in *Waiting for the Past* where we seem to have been abandoned somewhere in his prodigious hinterland. What keeps us going is the excitement in the language, the unpredictability (has there ever been a poet so unwilling to give us what we expect in the next line?) and the entertaining variety of subject matter. It is unlikely anyone else has written an elegy on an octopus or a poem about in-flight racehorses. Since he composed those early essays on 'interest', Murray made a point of remembering, but never pandering to his audience. He loves to describe interesting processes with their particular lexical fields, such as 'scorched hook-steerers/down in the spatter' of steel-making or interesting incidents, as when a 'big neck, muzzle and horns, calmly gazing/at the play of speed on counter-speed', steps into moving traffic – a fit metaphor for Les Murray's poetic. Whether it's an urban myth or anecdote or statistic or news item, he will claim it: everything is a potential part of the poem he is writing.

The greatest pleasures in reading Les Murray are when he turns to the rural community he knows so well, poems about rain tanks and chickens and flood shelters, and to the Australian landscape. Sometimes he approaches from an obscure angle, as in 'Persistence of the Reformation', but more successful are the simple anecdotes. 'Clan-sized Night Chanting', for instance, is a direct and atmospheric piece about hearing distant music in the bush, although the meaning of its typically terse, ambiguous first line ('Best sleeps hitching through') is only clarified when we reach the main verb: 'desert country were always/just out beyond dust-throw/of the road'. His own peculiarly enigmatic music catches the ear here, particularly in the final cadence, those *d*s tapped in like fence posts:

> And you felt no fear
> only shyness at the notion,
> as the long lines rose
> parading diminuendo down.

Murray's scope is enormous, and in *Fredy Neptune* he even managed to write a successful and readable verse novel – one of two he published. Reading Murray we are constantly reminded of the poet's conviction that poetry matters, and his refusal to 'write down'. He dedicated his books to 'the glory of God' and he meant it; yet he was not patronising. He wrote about the most ordinary things in the most extraordinary way, much as Beethoven could take a banal tune and transfigure it, in full conviction his audience would stay with him through whatever virtuoso variations he dreamt up. For readers who don't know the work, my only advice would be to allow time to visualise what he is writing about in each line. Murray is a persistently metaphorical poet, using similar devices to those so-called 'Martian' British poets of the late twentieth century, but he is constantly finding ways of making us see imaginatively. Take 'Machine Portraits with Pendant Spaceman' from the early 1980s, which opens by describing a bulldozer as 'short as a boot on its heel-high ripple soles' and ends with a river ferry 'boiling cauliflower under her keel'. His many sequences are ambitious and sometimes difficult, but he was unapologetic about his love of 'sprawl', on which he wrote so entertainingly.

Postcards from Australia.

Yet he also grew into a master of the short poem, as he was master of the picture postcard. I have quite a collection of Murray's cards from Bunyah, the last one franked in 2018 in Krambach, New South Wales, and his biographer Peter Alexander has confirmed just how prolific a miniaturist correspondent he was. Les and I first corresponded after meeting in north Cornwall, where he was reading for Helen Wood's Indian King Arts Centre in Camelford. I was tutoring there, and all I recall of our first encounter is that he said he thought I had a great name for a poet. He agreed to come and read for us in Kimbolton – though he was, I felt, a bit annoyed with his agent for accepting our derisory fee – and he stayed over in our absent elder daughter's room. Even today I wonder how he fitted in that narrow bed, let alone the shower cubicle. I look at the sofa where he sat chatting to us in our living room, perhaps as William Cowper looked at his own sofa, remembering the occasion. But for all Les's somewhat intimidating breadth of reference in his poems and conversation, a less pretentious guest you cannot imagine. He grew up on a farm, ran a farm; he was a man of the people. That he was regularly tipped for the Nobel Prize would have made not one bit of difference to Les. If he wanted to write a poem about eating a curry in Merthyr Tydfil, then he would do so, and he reserved the right to do it in his loftiest vein.

One cannot imagine Louise Glück doing any such thing, yet she is a fitting representative for another kind of poetry which is popular, yet makes no concessions to popularity. As we were emerging from one lockdown and preparing for another, early in October 2020, I was involved in a WhatsApp discussion with a friend who was looking for poems about flowers for an online course he was running. I recommended some names – Norman Nicholson, Katherine Towers, Andrew Young – then remembered Glück. My friend's response, rather bafflingly, was to say that he had rarely heard of the foreign-language winners but wasn't even vaguely familiar this time. I was briefly confused, but then – 'What? Has she won the Nobel?' (I think I used four question marks.) A more deserving recipient than Louise Glück I cannot imagine.

The American hardback edition of her *Poems 1962–2012* takes up a good two inches on my American poetry shelves, and if others have to go to Oxfam to make way for her, then so be it. She is a poet who has earned her place and who knows that the art she has chosen may cost no less than everything. Her poems are object lessons in poetic judgement: how much to leave in, just what to excise – what she calls the 'telling omission'. Glück's voice is seldom a cry; she lets her poems speak quietly to us. They are watercolours or etchings, not tapestries or stage monologues or symposia or hymns, although there is a spiritual yearning at the heart of them, particularly in the sad, pale lyrics of her best-known collection, *Wild Iris* (1992), the book I was thinking of recommending to my friend.

I first discovered Glück's poetry in Helen Vendler's *Harvard Book of Contemporary American Poetry*, which I used to read during my free period when on a teaching exchange in Bridgewater High School, New Jersey. The early poems anthologised by Vendler did not always hit home and Glück has been dismissive of her debut collection, *Firstborn*, which I possess in the 1969 Anvil Press edition – bought second-hand for 75p. But one or two had that unmistakable effect produced by genuine poetry, that dark ripple of emotional recognition whose source runs obscure and deep.

One of those included, appropriately enough as I sat reading it in the school library, was 'The School Children',* less elusive than her later work, but with many of its hallmarks: the emblematic details from nature, the slightly glacial tone, the understatement. A simple sentence begins it: 'The children go forward with their little satchels.' They do not 'go to school' or 'leave' or even 'walk', they 'go forward', inviting us to see this as an allegory. The rhythm slows for the second line: 'all morning' is almost a yawn, and 'labored' speaks of more than just apple-picking. These 'late apples, red and gold' are fruits of motherhood, the leftovers. This is, in a way, a female angle on Frost's 'After Apple-Picking'. Frost's apples were all he had done or not done; the mothers' are all they had shared with the children, which is now done with, 'like words of another language' – literally, as you cannot use the old baby-talk to your schoolchild or they will never forgive you. Glück knows this is a momentous passage. The teachers are 'on the other shore', and are seen as gods, waiting to 'receive these offerings'. There is a faintly sinister feeling to all this, just a whisper of the concentration camp: 'How orderly they are – the nails/on which the children hang/their overcoats of blue or yellow wool.' Are those nails supposed to stick out like that? Are we meant to think of crucifixion? And should we really read that line 'on which the children hang' in so shocking a way with echoes of *Jude the Obscure*? The poem ends a little unsettlingly, too, with the disciplinarians at work and the mothers left bewildered in an orchard full of 'gray limbs' but little remaining fruit – or 'ammunition', as Glück puts it.

In the collections since 1992, *Meadowlands*, *Vita Nova*, *The Seven Ages*, *Averno*, *A Village Life*, *Faithful and Virtuous Night* and *Winter Recipes from the Collective*, she continued to draw her growing number of readers ever closer to something essential. Nothing artificially or sentimentally done, giving us just enough clues to her meaning – and she has always had plenty to say. Her essays on poetry – *Proofs and Theories* and *American Originality* – are some of the most cogent and probing of recent years, exploring demanding themes such as 'Ersatz Thought', 'Invitation and Exclusion', 'Against Sincerity', 'Disruption, Hesitation, Silence' and 'The Culture of Healing'. She writes like a philosopher, little escaping her gimlet eye. After the loss of Anne Stevenson, Derek Mahon and Eavan Boland during the pandemic, to hear the news of Louise Glück's award that October Thursday among the virtual flowers felt like a gift. And briefly, the news turned from the pandemic and Brexit and presidential elections and acknowledged the existence of poetry and poets. But then in 2023 she too died.

Until a poet's death is reported or they win a prize big enough to be known about, most people are unaware of these strange creatures that live among them. In so far as they figure at all in everyday life, they are generally associated with the classroom, thought of as dead or at best as another kind of entertainer. When Bob Dylan was awarded the Nobel Prize, it only added to the confusion, since he didn't seem to be a poet at all once you took away the music – but why would you? Thinking of Pam Ayres or John Hegley or Hollie McNish or Brian Bilston or Kae Tempest, few would understand why Plato might have wanted to banish them from his Republic for their dangerous lies. Fewer still would turn to them or to any other poets for truth. And nobody in their right mind would think to consult a poet for glimpses of the future. That all died out with the Romantics, when visions of the end of the world were only to be expected from such an unstable crew as Blake and Coleridge and Byron.

Yet retrospectively it is remarkable how prescient some more recent poems can be, even those by level-headed writers such as Louis MacNeice. His 1938 *Autumn Journal* seems to anticipate and sum up what was about to break out in Europe, as if he were writing it at least a year later. Similarly, some decades earlier, Georg Heym's 'Der Krieg' – 'War' – envisioned the First World War:

> He's risen now, who slept so long,
> He's risen from deep vaults among
> The day's remains. Huge and unknown
> He stands. His black hands crush the moon...*

Georg Heym died in a skating accident in 1911, the year 'Der Krieg' was written, and he cannot really have foreseen the First World War, but it became for many Germans its representative poem.

Poets often feel as if they are 'tuning in' to the zeitgeist and can find they are saying much more than they expected – that they have been given, to use a phrase of Wallace Stevens's, 'extended wings'. I suspect even those who only tinker with verses have some sense of this prophetic power, and it would appear from the number of people who want to be remembered as poets – the obituary pages are full of such surprises – that there is still some glory associated with the term. But it's not what you call yourself, it's whether you're called. And then you have to write the actual poems, which is the most unglamorous process imaginable, and the point at which the difficulties begin to become clear.

A poet is nothing, really, a hollow shell, the dullest person at the party, until the writing starts, as Keats pointed out centuries ago – and even then to the rest of the world you still look like nothing, shucking off draft after draft, bent over a notebook or a keyboard, digging like Seamus Heaney's turf-cutter or pushing through to the air like Louise Glück's wild iris or placing the paw in the snow like Ted Hughes's thought-fox. Only when the writing reaches that special pitch of intensity will you begin to know the cost of this high calling, the things you must put off or miss or avoid, the things you must confront, unearth, and even suffer in order to 'get something right in the language'. If you're lucky, the poem will arrive, may even survive.

Whether anybody will then care about it is quite another matter.

John Keats waiting outside Guy's Hospital.

Postscript

A short while ago I was invited by the Royal Literary Fund* to write a letter to my readers, which – even if you have treated this like a whodunnit and gone straight to the end – must include you. It seems as good a way as any to finish:

Dear Readers,

The first thing I want to say is that I do hope you exist. The statistics for the number of people who actually buy a book of poetry are fairly depressing, and buying isn't reading. You will have done some poetry at school, I'm sure, though many of the English teachers I've met are terrified of it – they'd rather do anything else. Then, even if you are confident enough to tackle a single poem, you might be less sure when it comes to an entire volume of them, even a slim one. Of course, it could be a narrative, a story in verse, with a clear beginning, middle and end (I've written a few of those), but more likely it will be the usual chocolate-box selection.

So, how to approach that collection of mine you found in a charity shop – and who got rid of it, I wonder? Is there an inscription in it? I suggest you begin with the soft centre: poems about family or travel… Egypt, Iceland, America. Try one of the liqueurs – that Elgar piece, or the Cézanne miniature. Some of the tree poems, walnut whips. Then the hard centres. War, mythology, ageing.

If you're really not used to reading poetry, then think of yourself as a baby dropped in a swimming pool. You won't drown, you'll instinctively know what to do, and fairly quickly, once you get over the shock of the medium, may even find you're enjoying the experience.

What you might not think to do is read aloud – yet that's the key. Listening to someone else read a poem isn't always helpful, even if it's the author, and actors can miss the *music in their efforts to be expressive; but reading it to yourself, catching the music, the play of sound against sound, is fundamental. It was Hugo Williams who made the point that when reading lines on the page you're aware of different parts of the poem simultaneously: you can see the opening even as you read the ending.* That isn't the case when you're only a listener, so you're likely to miss that crucial interlacing of sound and meaning.*

As to why you should do any of this, when you are perfectly happy with novels...?

Well, I too enjoy novels, but – and this is going to sound perverse – in the end they are a form of escapism, they leave you in the dream, without analysing it. Even the most ingenious prose can't do as effectively what real poetry does, which is keep you pleasurably conscious of the language in which it is written, your language, and make you hear its overtones and etymologies, its echoes and allusions – above all, the silences implied by its line breaks, the gaps and 'cliffs of fall' opened up between words, the looming blank white spaces prose can only ignore in its relentless urge to entertain.

After all of which, dear readers, I trust that you remain my readers and that the time you spend with my poetry is time in some way illuminated.

With very warmest wishes,

John Greening

Cinna the Poet

'tear him for his bad verses'

Cinna returns from the play,
remembering little more
than *et tu*, and the need to stop for
cat food on the way.

Cinna enjoys the applause
that comes as he opens the tin,
a perfectly metrical musical invocation of the Muse.

Cinna inspects the *Review*
and finds illiterate scrawl
by his dumbest former poetry pupil
hailed as brave and true.

Cinna puts on the news
and notes how the latest Caesar
has found that rhyming tends to appease
opposing political views.

Cinna walks in the park,
where strewn about the grass
are empty cans of light verse,
hurled by the world at the dark.

Cinna discovers his lunch
uneaten, and from it the head
of a famous bard now safely dead
glares as he comes to the crunch.

Cinna tries not to rhyme,
but sometimes he feels the urge,
to rush and release a creative blockage,
and just gets there in time.

Cinna opens a book
whose very title repels,
whose list of contents quickly reveals
a plagiarist and a crook.

Cinna crouches and sweats,
imagining all the new
collections he's going to be asked to review,
unscrolling as he sits.

Cinna looks at the words
on the back of the book, and sees
they're all Cinna's: *this poet displays*
a remarkable talent for...

JG on the Appian Way.

Notes

11   Basil Bunting, *Collected Poems* (Fulcrum Press, 1968), p. 130.

11   Les Murray, *New Collected Poems* (Carcanet, 2003), p. 457.

12   'An Epistle to Dr Arbuthnot', lines 125–132.

12   Richard Wilbur, *New and Collected Poems* (Harcourt Brace Jovanovich, 1988), p. 55.

13   The vexed question of Englishness is explored in some depth in *Contraflow: Lines of Englishness 1922–2022* (Renard Press, 2023). I am simplifying the problem by avoiding the word 'British', whose complexities are highlighted by the fact that I have recently edited Iain Crichton Smith, who isn't just a British or Scottish poet either, but a proudly European Gaelic-speaking and writing Lewis man.

14   Simon Armitage, *Zoom!* (Bloodaxe, 1989).

14   Eavan Boland, *Object Lessons* (Carcanet, 2006).

14   Lucy McDiarmid, *Poets and the Peacock Dinner: The Literary History of a Meal* (OUP, 2014). See also John Greening, 'Peacock Fans', *TLS* (April 2015).
      https://www.the-tls.co.uk/culture/food-drink/peacock-fans

15   I shall return to Nemerov in a later chapter. The phrase is from his essay 'Poetry and Meaning' in *A Howard Nemerov Reader* (University of Missouri, 1991).

15   *Letters on Poetry from W.B. Yeats to Dorothy Wellesley* (Oxford University Press, 1939), p. 24.

15   George Herbert, 'The Flower', *The Temple, Sacred Poems and Private Ejaculations* (Cambridge, 1633).

20   As discussed with Aled Jones on *Songs of Praise* in September 2024.
      https://www.bbc.co.uk/iplayer/episode/m0023j60/songs-of-praise-faith-in-poetry

20   John Greening, *Threading a Dream: A Poet on the Nile* (Gatehouse Press, 2017).

21   See *The Interpretation of Owls: Selected Poems 1977–2022*, ed. Kevin J. Gardner (Baylor UP, 2023).

22   *The Selected Poems of Howard Nemerov* (Swallow Press, 2003).

23   John Montague, *A Chosen Light* (MacGibbon & Key, 1967). According to Montague, the only one of his books to have been 'a complete flop'.

23   John Montague, *New Collected Poems* (Gallery Press, 2012), source of the other poems mentioned here too.

23   'Under the Flight Path' is reprinted in *The Interpretation of Owls* (Baylor, 2023).

23   John Greening, *The Bocase Stone* (Dedalus Press, 1996).

23   John Greening, 'John Montague Obituary', *Guardian* (27 December 2016). https://www.theguardian.com/books/2016/dec/27/john-montague-obituary

25   Christopher Reid included one of Hughes's letters to me in *Letters of Ted Hughes* (Faber, 2007), p. 385.

26   John Greening, *Westerners* (Hippopotamus Press, 1982).

28   Joan Forman, *The Mask of Time: The Mystery Factor in Timeslips, Precognition and Hindsight* (Macdonald & Jane's, 1978).

29   Geoffrey Grigson, *The Private Art* (Allison & Busby, 1982).

29   In *Winter Journeys* (Rivelin Press, 1984), *The Tutankhamun Variations* (Bloodaxe, 1991), *Hunts: Poems 1979–2009* (Greenwich Exchange, 2009).

31   Paul Newman, *Gods and Graven Images* (Robert Hale Ltd, 1987).

31   It did appear: my sequence 'Chalk' in *The Silence*.

32   According to an essay by August Kleinzahler in *Sallies, Romps, Portraits and Send-offs* (FSG, 2017).

35   Anthony Stevens, *Private Myths* (Hamish Hamilton, 1995).

35   Stevens takes this for his epigraph, although in *The Power of Myth* (Doubleday, 1988, p. 40) Campbell's wording is slightly different: 'The myth is the public dream and the dream is the private myth'.

35   Les Murray, 'Poetry and Religion', *New Collected Poems* (Carcanet, 2003), p. 265.

35   Tomas Tranströmer, *New Collected Poems* tr. Robin Fulton (Bloodaxe, 1997, rev. 2002).

36   See in particular Glück's 'Disruption, Hesitation, Silence' in *Proofs and Theories* (Carcanet, 1999).

37   It appears in Anne Stevenson's *A Report from the Border* (Bloodaxe, 2003), p. 45.

37   Charles Tomlinson, *New Collected Poems* (Carcanet, 2009), p. 162.

37   *The Bloodaxe Book of Poetry Quotations*, ed. O'Driscoll (Bloodaxe, 2006), p. 30.

39   Lindsay Clark, *Green Man Dreaming* (Awen Publications, 2018), p. 160.

40   Hunter Davies, 'He knows his words' worth', *The Independent* (16 November 1993). https://www.independent.co.uk/life-style/interview-he-knows-his-words-worth-william-scammell-has-given-up-his-day-job-to-try-to-wring-a-livelihood-from-his-verse-he-d-be-better-off-taking-photos-on-the-qe2-1504653.html

41   *Achill Island Tagebuch* (Redfoxpress, 2019), reprinted in the forthcoming collection, *Crowning* (Baylor University Press, 2026).

46   A.R. Ammons, *Tape for the Turn of the Year* (Norton Library, 1972).

46   *How Poets Work*, ed. Tony Curtis (Seren, 1996), p. 137.

46   Derek Mahon, *New Collected Poems* (The Gallery Press, 2011), p. 116.

47   Op. cit., p. 159.

48   ibid., p. 84.

48   For more about this collaboration, see the chapter 'Roots'.

53   Our time is described in my memoir *Threading a Dream* (Gatehouse, 2027) from which this map is taken, drawn by Rosie Greening.

54   My 2024 essay on the late Helen Vendler and her importance to me appears on the *Poetry Birmingham Literary Journal* website: https://poetrybirmingham.com/digital-features/john-greening-on-vendler-2024.

55   Some have been rescued from oblivion by my editor Kevin Gardner for *The Interpretation of Owls* (Baylor, 2023).

55   Iain Crichton Smith, *Deer on the High Hills* (Carcanet, 2021).

58   *Contraflow: Lines of Englishness 1922–2022* (Renard Press, 2023).

59   *Nightwalker's Song* (Arc Publications, 2022).

59   The book is due to be published this year in the USA. Rilke, *New Poems* (Baylor University Press, 2025).

59   David Constantine, *Hölderlin* (The Clarendon Press, 1988).

60   Paavo Järvi conducting the Orchestre de Paris (RCA), 2019.

61   *The Silence* (Carcanet, 2019), p. 103.

63   This drawing by Allan King was used on the cover of *Iceland Spar* (Shoestring Press, 2008).

64   *European Union* is included in both *Hunts* (Greenwich Exchange, 2009) and *The Interpretation of Owls* (Baylor, 2023). Many of the poems from Iceland are reprinted in the latter.

64   New Walk Editions, 2019.

69   It is reprinted in full in *Hunts: Poems 1979–2009* (Greenwich Exchange, 2009).

69   From T.S. Eliot, *Little Gidding* (Faber, 1942).

70   *Fotheringhay and Other Poems* was published by Rockingham Press in 1995. The following year, *The Coastal Path* (taking its title from the poem Hughes and Heaney selected) appeared from the aptly named Headland Publications, with a spectacular cover painting by Christopher Baker.

70   'Circles' dates from 2020, was published in *Agenda*, Vol. 53, No. 4, and will be reprinted in *Crowning* (Baylor University Press, 2026).

73   Peter Kane Dufault, *Looking in All Directions: Selected Poems 1954–2000* (Worple Press, 2000).

74   A.R. Ammons, 'Love Song (2)' from *Collected Poems, 1951–1971* (Norton, New York, 1972), p. 209.

74   Ibid, pp. 147–151.

74   The Norton Library, 1972.

76   *Poets Don't Drive*, presented by Ian McMillan, was broadcast in February 2006.

77   See Kinsella's 'Nightwalker' or 'Phoenix Park' in *Collected Poems* (Carcanet, 2002).

77   Paul Farley and Michael Symmons Roberts, *Edgelands* (Jonathan Cape, 2011).

78   John Wedgwood Clarke, *Landfill* (Valley Press, 2017).

78   Angela France, *Terminarchy* (Nine Arches Press, 2021).

81   See *True to One Another: Poems by Matthew Arnold* (Renard Press, 2025).

82   *a Post Card to* (Red Squirrel Press, 2021).

83   'Bridge' is in Stuart Henson's *The Way You Know It: New & Selected Poems* (Shoestring Press, 2018).

87   Redfoxpress, 2018.

88   Dennis O'Driscoll, *The Outnumbered Poet* (The Gallery Press, 2013).

94   Kudryashov's work is now quite well known. See Lodder, Lucie-Smith, Golomstock and Reviakin, *Oleg Kudryashov: Bridge to the Future* (London Collectors Club, 2017).

94 Rosie's drawings illustrate my Egypt memoir, *Threading a Dream*, my pamphlets *Europa's Flight* and *The Giddings* and the country house anthology *Hollow Palaces* edited with Kevin Gardner.

97 If you must know: *Igam Returns, Eight o'clock in the Morning* and *The Man from S.P.A.M.S.*

99 The American poet James Merrill has written about this, and the experience seems to lead directly into his later Ouija board masterpiece, *The Changing Light at Sandover.*

101 *Housing the Image: English Poetic Drama.*

123 Daljit Nagra: 'In six hours I played the Jam's Sound Affects album six times', *Guardian* (5 May 2017).
https://www.theguardian.com/books/2017/may/05/daljit-nagra-my-writing-day

123 It was published as *Europa's Flight* (New Walk Editions, 2019).

125 Jamie James, *The Music of the Spheres* (Little, Brown, 1994).

126 See the chapter, 'Magic'.

128 The original broadcast may be heard at:
https://www.youtube.com/watch?v=6maWI85kSxU.

129 Cecilia McDowall, *Three Songs After Schubert* (Oxford University Press, 2019).

129 *Winter Trees*, an album that includes *Fallen* by Philip Lancaster and works by Sally Beamish, will appear from Resonus Classics in 2026.

131 Evelyn Glennie, *Good Vibrations* (Hutchinson, 1990).

134 28th March 1931.

134 A fragment of these remains in his poem, 'Barkbröd', alluding to the bleak Fourth Symphony. See *Beneath Tremendous Rain* (Enitharmon Press, 1990).

136 *Beyond the Notes* (The Boydell Press, 2004). Also highly recommendable is *A Musician's Alphabet* (Faber, 2006).

137 *Benjamin Britten's Poets*, ed. Boris Ford (Carcanet, 1996).

141 Clare Brown and Don Paterson, *Don't Ask Me What I Mean* (Picador, 2003).

143 Shoestring Press, 2003.

143 This is a different piece from the libretto quoted in the chapter, 'Magic'.

145 *Best American Poetry 1990*, ed. Jorie Graham (Scribner, 1990).

146 Jorie Graham, *The Dream of the Unified Field: Selected Poems* (Carcanet, 1996).

146 Billy Collins, *Taking Off Emily Dickinson's Clothes* (Picador, 2000).

147 Hugo Williams, *Strong Words, Modern Poets on Modern Poetry*, ed. Bill Herbert and Matthew Hollis (Bloodaxe, 2000), p. 229.

148 Edmund Blunden, *Undertones of War*, ed. John Greening (Oxford University Press, 2015).

148 'Dance of Death' – a composition by Franz Liszt.

154 Published in *Hans Keller 1919–1985*, ed. Alison Graham and Susi Woodhouse (Routledge, 2019), p. 275.

156 Brenda Maddox, *George's Ghosts* (Picador, 1999).

156 Jeremy Noel-Tod is more enthusiastic and has written about Browning's 'furiously brilliant poem' on his blog: 'Vomiting Truth', *Some Flowers Soon*.
https://someflowerssoon.substack.com/p/vomiting-truth

158 The full text is at:
https://www.agendapoetry.co.uk/oldsite/documents/EssaysandLibretti.pdf.

158 Cargo Press, 2000.

161 The drawing here is by Rosie Greening.

168 *Staying Alive*, ed. Neil Astley (Bloodaxe, 2002).

169 *Poets of the First World War* (Greenwich Exchange, 2004).

170 Robert Bly and Tomas Tranströmer, *Airmail* (Bloodaxe, 2013).

170 The *Independent*, 1994.

172 *Threading a Dream* (Gatehouse Press, 2017).

173 The whole poem appears in *The Interpretation of Owls* (Baylor, 2023).

175 The sonnets begun on the plane became *Europa's Flight* (New Walk, 2019).

179 Kevin Gardner included one poem from those years ('Suburbs') in *The Interpretation of Owls* and my distaste is evident.

181 All references are to the collaborative book which eventually emerged: *Heath* (Nine Arches, 2016).

182 Sadly, after all this collaborative work, the 'voices' poem was not in the final cut.

184 Poetry Salzburg, 2020.

185 They can be found in *The Home Key* (Shoestring Press, 2003).

186 They are collected in *From the East: 60 Huntingdonshire Codices* (Renard Press, 2024).

191 See p. 15.

196 William Logan, *Our Savage Art: Poetry and the Civil Tongue* (Columbia University Press, 2009).

198 To appear in the forthcoming collection, *Crowning* (Baylor University Press, 2026).

200 See Boland's *Object Lessons* (Carcanet, 2006).

202 This seems a good place to acknowledge my gratitude to Kevin Gardner for taking on the responsibility of editing my 2023 Selected, *The Interpretation of Owls*, and sparing me the pain. It includes 'The Crack' and many other poems mentioned in this book.

220 At the last count our guest readers included: Sebastian Barker, Anne Berkeley, Alan Brownjohn, Tessa Rose Chester, David Constantine, Kevin Crossley-Holland, Martyn Crucefix, Hilary Davies, Maura Dooley, Michael Donaghy, Douglas Dunn, Sasha Dugdale, Roger Garfitt, Dana Gioia, John Gohorry, Philip Gross, Emily Grosholz, Kathleen Jamie, Elizabeth Jennings, Lotte Kramer, Hugh MacMillan, Ian McMillan, David Morley, Les Murray, Bernard O'Donoghue, Rennie Parker, Lawrence Sail, Carole Satyamurti, William Scammell, David Scott, Jo Shapcott, Penelope Shuttle, Caroline Smith, Pauline Stainer, Jon Stallworthy, Anne Stevenson, George Szirtes, Adam Thorpe, Charles Tomlinson, Susan Wicks, Kit Wright. (We still can't decide whether Anthony Thwaite came or not.)

220 His newest pamphlet, however, is a sequence of haiku: *A Handful of Wasps* (Shoestring Press, 2025)

221 *Bold Heart*, ed. Stuart Henson (Shoestring Press, 2022).

222 The review may be accessed at https://www.stuarthenson.co.uk/poetry/the-odin-stone.

223 My thoughts on *Beautiful Monsters* (Shoestring Press, 2022) can be read in *The High Window* online at:
https://thehighwindowpress.com/2022/11/29/reviews-winter-2022/.

225 *The Penguin Book of Contemporary British Poetry*, ed. Blake Morrison and Andrew Motion (Penguin, 1982).

226 'Sludge, Sosostris and You', never published, perhaps because of Anne's misgivings.

226 The poem is in my *Moments Musicaux* (Poetry Salzburg, 2020).

227 In 2023 a new *Collected Poems* appeared from Bloodaxe, arranged chronologically rather than thematically this time.

227 I have a full seasonal collection of these not only from Anne, but from Stuart and Lawrence Sail too.

227 From *Granny Scarecrow* (Bloodaxe, 2000): See *Vapour Trails*; also anthologised in *Accompanied Voices: Poets on Composers from Thomas Tallis to Arvo Pärt*.

231 *TLS*, July 10, 2020.

232 An excellent but largely overlooked Selected, *Inside Story*, was produced after Bill's death by Arrowhead (2008, edited by Christopher Pilling), and is worth seeking out. The selected essays, *Nightwatch* (Shoestring Press, 2008), are also very fine. Renard Press hopes to issue a new selection of the poems, edited by John Greening.

235 *Quality Time* (1997), *Weather Permitting* (1999), *Exemplary Damages* (2002) and *New and Selected Poems* (2004), all from Anvil.

235 'No, Thanks', *Collected Poems* (Carcanet, 2017).

239 Letter to Paule Vidal, April 1953, *Letters of Wallace Stevens*, ed. Holly Stevens (Knopf, 1966).

240 Maggie Ferguson, *George Mackay Brown: The Life* (John Murray, 2006).

242 Jonathan Bate, *Ted Hughes: The Unauthorised Life* (William Collins, 2016).

245 See the epigraph to this book, taken from his introduction to Wilfred Owen's poems.

246 Dana Gioia's essay became the book *Can Poetry Matter? Essays on Poetry and American Culture* (Graywolf, 1992).

248 Dana Gioia himself, who had been an executive with Kraft foods, eventually became chairman of the National Endowment for the Arts under George W. Bush, thus stepping into the front line of another battle in the same war.

250 The poem of Bell's which has drawn most attention had its own emotion unnecessarily bolstered, I felt, and its authenticity undermined by Elgar's 'Nimrod', which suggested a certain lack of faith on the part of the investor. 'Nimrod' is only ever removed from its original enigmatic variations with an underlying motive, whether to draw tears at the cenotaph or to beef up a scene in a movie: it is made sentimental, and sentimentality is what sells. Although it must be admitted that Elgar himself didn't hesitate to recycle the tune in other works such as *The Music Makers*.

253 There has since been a posthumous collection by Les Murray, *Continuous Creation: Last Poems* (Carcanet, 2022).

255 From Louise Glück's *The House on Marshland* (Ecco Press, 1975).

257 JG's translation from *To the War Poets* (Carcanet, 2013).

259 This talk and many others written for the RLF can be found at: https://www.rlf.org.uk/writer/john-greening/.

260 Hugo Williams, *The Bloodaxe Book of Poetry Quotations*, ed. Dennis O'Driscoll (Bloodaxe, 2006), p. 127.

Index

Acknowledgements

Some of the chapters in this book are based on pieces originally written for the following journals, and thanks are due to their editors: *The Author* ('Perfection of the Life or of the Work'), *The Dark Horse* ('Some Contemporaries'), *European Literature Network* ('Flitting' from an original piece titled 'Sounding European'), the *Guardian* ('Some Contemporaries'), *The London Magazine* ('Genius', originally 'Fantasia on the Nature of Genius'), *The Poetry Review* ('Some Contemporaries'), *The Times Literary Supplement* (passages in 'Listening', 'Meaning' and 'A High Calling?'), *Wild Court* ('Making the Cut'). Other material grew out of a series of talks written for the Royal Literary Fund's *Vox* podcast (https://www.rlf.org.uk/writer/john-greening/) and articles for their online magazine, *Collected*. They are reproduced by kind permission of Steve Cook and the RLF.

Most of the poems are previously uncollected, but some first appeared in the following publications: *Acumen* ('Beyond the Silence, (II)'), *Iota* ('Missing a Trick'), *Poetry Salzburg Review* ('Pavement Artist'), *Raceme* ('Cinna the Poet'), *The Spectator* ('Arcadian', 'Next', which was also part of the 'Elegies' sequence in *Hunts* (Greenwich Exchange, 2009). The poem from *Huntingdonshire Codices* first published in *Long Poem Magazine* is also included in *From the East* (Renard Press, 2024). The short extracts from 'The Orchard' and 'Coming Soon' are from poems which appear in full in *The Interpretation of Owls* (Baylor University Press, 2023), ed. Kevin Gardner. I would also like to thank Kevin for helping with some of my Alexander Pope references and for supplying the photo of Little Gidding. I am grateful to Marie Heaney for agreeing to my inclusion of the photograph of Seamus Heaney at Little Gidding, and to John F. Deane for his assistance. Thanks to Ben Scammell and to Jan Scammell for permission to quote her remarks and to reproduce some of William Scammell's correspondence, as well as to Tom Chivers and Annie Fisher for allowing me to use their anecdotes; to Penelope Shuttle and Philip Gross for permission to include extracts from their emails; to Ian Colford, for helping me identify a photograph of the interior of

Hawthornden; and to Margi Blunden and the Blunden estate for reproduction of 'The Midnight Skaters' and the book's epigraph. I am grateful to Gatehouse Press for use of a small section from my memoir, *Threading a Dream: A Poet on the Nile* (2017). The sketch of the hut at Valhall Camp is by Allan King. Several of the drawings are by Rosie Greening (see RosalindArt on Etsy): thanks to her for images of the Cretan olive tree, the map of Egypt, Tutankhamun's mask, Sety I, the Aswan obelisk, Edmund Blunden, the Spirit of St Louis and Kimbolton Castle. Some of the photographs of the author and local landmarks are by Jane Greening, who also kindly read through the text. I am grateful to Dana Gioia, Stephen Hanvey, Penelope Shuttle and Stuart Henson (along with Kathy Henson, who took the portrait of her husband) for permission to reproduce photographs of them, and to Julie O'Callaghan for finding an unusually informal picture of Dennis O'Driscoll. The epigraph is taken from Edmund Blunden's introductory memoir to *The Poems of Wilfred Owen* (Chatto & Windus, 1933). Thanks to Cat Conway and Aaron Kent for their work on an earlier version of the text, to Imogen Allen for looking through my text with such care and above all to Will Dady for making it fit for Renard Press.

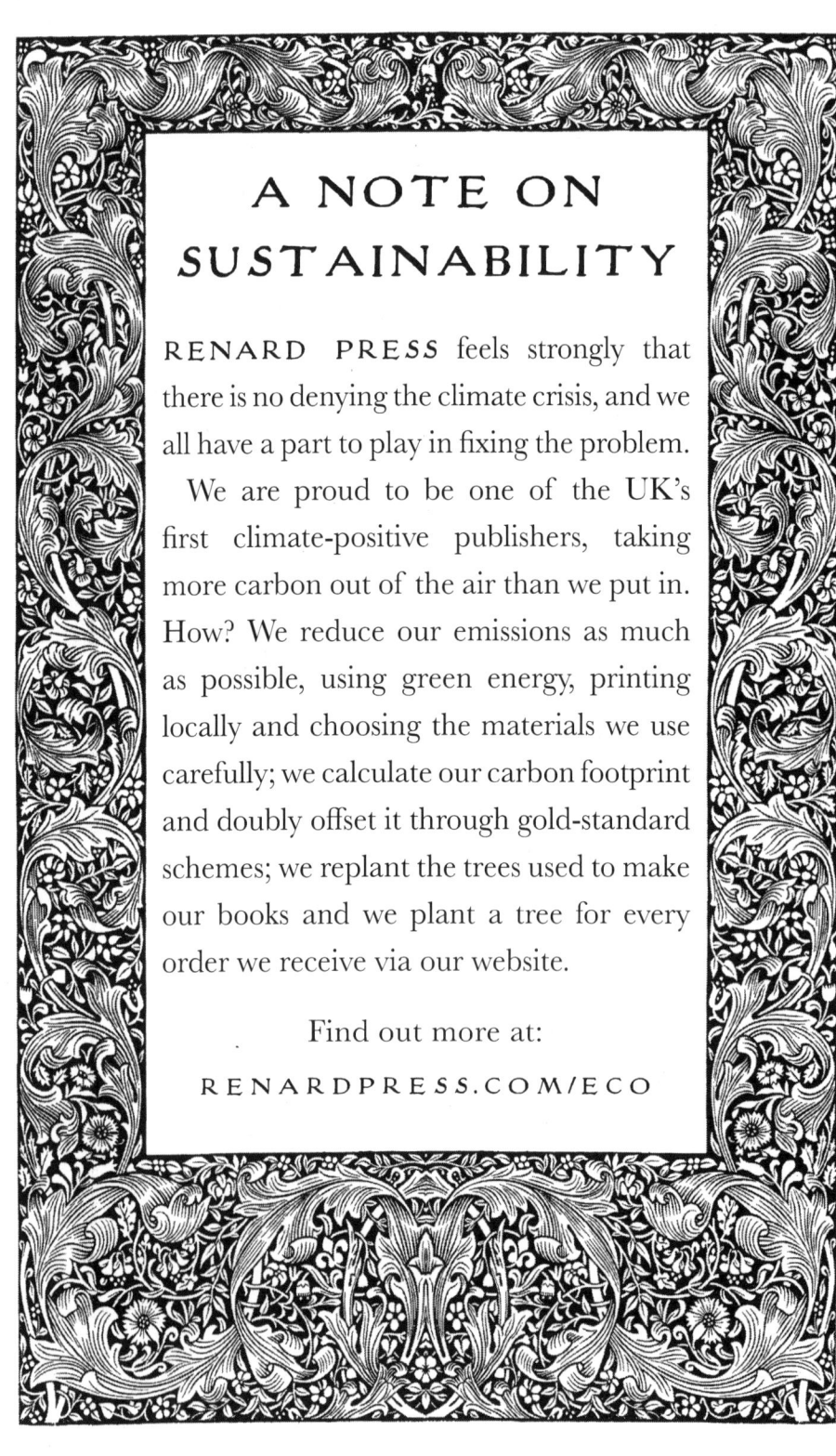

A NOTE ON SUSTAINABILITY

RENARD PRESS feels strongly that there is no denying the climate crisis, and we all have a part to play in fixing the problem.

We are proud to be one of the UK's first climate-positive publishers, taking more carbon out of the air than we put in. How? We reduce our emissions as much as possible, using green energy, printing locally and choosing the materials we use carefully; we calculate our carbon footprint and doubly offset it through gold-standard schemes; we replant the trees used to make our books and we plant a tree for every order we receive via our website.

Find out more at:

RENARDPRESS.COM/ECO